Learn Medical Spanish For Healthcare Professionals

Speak Medical Spanish in 30 Days!

7 Books in 1

Explore to Win

THIS COLLECTION INCLUDES THE FOLLOWING BOOKS:

Introduction to Medical Spanish and Basics

Spanish Medical Communication: Terminology, Anatomy, Procedures, Prescription, and Emergencies

Cultural Competence in Healthcare and Additional Practice

Advanced Medical Spanish:
Specialized Vocabulary for Healthcare Disciplines

Clinical Conversations:
Mastering Complex Medical Dialogues in Spanish

Patient Care in Spanish:
Focused Practice for High-Impact Scenarios

Comprehensive Medical Spanish Review:
Integrated Learning and Application

Table of contents

BOOK 5

Clinical Conversations: Mastering Complex Medical Dialogues in Spanish

BOOK 6

Patient Care in Spanish: Focused Practice for High-Impact Scenarios

BOOK 7

Comprehensive Medical Spanish Review: Integrated Learning and Application

$550+ FREE BONUSES

**Medical Spanish Video
Course Masterclass**

**100 Digital Flashcards
+ 30-Day Study Plan**

**100 Medical Spanish
Audio Pronunciations**

**Real-life
Medical Scenarios**

**Spanish Patient
Communication Cheatsheet**

**Bilingual Prescription
Glossary**

Scan QR code to claim
your bonuses

— OR —

visit bit.ly/4fyA9Kf

BOOK 1

Introduction to Medical Spanish and Basics

¡Complete guide to learn medical Spanish!

Explore to Win

Book 1 Description

Welcome to 'Introduction to Medical Spanish and Basics,' the first part of our groundbreaking series. As a healthcare professional, you hold the key to bridging the communication gap with your Spanish-speaking patients, and this book is your gateway to success!

In 'Introduction,' we emphasize the importance of medical Spanish for your career, breaking down barriers and fostering deeper connections with patients. Explore the benefits of bilingualism in healthcare, opening a world of opportunities in the healthcare landscape.

Join us on an empowering journey to:

- Understand the significance of medical Spanish for healthcare professionals
- Embrace the advantages of bilingualism in healthcare
- Explore the book's well-structured content and learning path
- Utilize a suggested study plan tailored to your busy schedule

Build Strong Foundations with 'Spanish Basics':

- Master the Spanish Alphabet, Sounds, Vowel Sounds, and Consonant Sounds
- Learn Medical Spanish for greetings, introductions, and essential phrases
- Acquire effective strategies to confidently retain and use Spanish
- Practice with exercises and measure progress with the answer key

Embark on a transformative journey today, unlocking the power of communication in healthcare! This experience will elevate your patient interactions, enrich your professional life, and make a lasting impact on those you serve. Together, let's build a bridge of compassion and inclusivity in healthcare.

Chapter I: Introduction

Las palabras abren puertas sobre el mar

- Rafael Alberti

The importance for healthcare professionals to learn medical Spanish

Did you know Spanish has become the second most spoken non-English language in the United States? If this pattern continues, it is anticipated that by the year 2050, the United States of America will have surpassed all other nations and will have become the largest Spanish-speaking nation. In addition, it is anticipated that the Hispanic population will reach 111 million by the year 2060 (Figure 1), and more than 25 million people in the United States have a limited ability to communicate in English. Learning Spanish is now necessary for people in many professions, including those who work in fields such as medicine and commerce, as well as those whose primary language is not Spanish. Join the millions of people who are already broadening their linguistic horizons and discover a whole new universe of opportunities by learning a new language.

The difficulty of expressing essential medical information with a patient who does not speak your language may become overpowering for you when you are engaged in hospital activities. Because of this, it has become more important for medical practitioners to be able to communicate successfully with the public they serve. Unfortunately, language problems can frequently get in the way of efficient communication, which can then result in misunderstandings, incorrect diagnoses, and insufficient treatment.

It is crucial for medical professionals to communicate clearly and effectively to guarantee that their patients receive the highest possible level of care. Medical personnel can give higher-quality care to patients, boost patient happiness, and advance their careers if they can communicate effectively in the patient's native tongue. However, learning a new language can take up a lot of time, and it is not possible to become fluent in every language that your patients speak. But imagine for a moment that there was a way to fix this issue. What if you could quickly and easily learn the Spanish words and phrases that are most commonly used in medical situations?

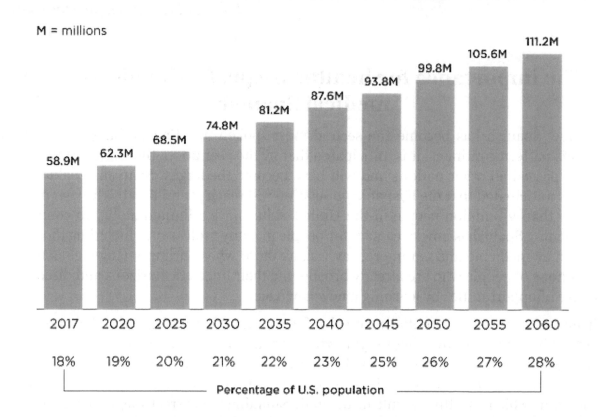

Hispanic Population to Reach 111 Million by 2060
Projected Hispanic Population 2020 to 2060

M = millions

									111.2M
								105.6M	
							99.8M		
						93.8M			
					87.6M				
				81.2M					
			74.8M						
		68.5M							
58.9M	62.3M								
2017	2020	2025	2030	2035	2040	2045	2050	2055	2060
18%	19%	20%	21%	22%	23%	25%	26%	27%	28%

Percentage of U.S. population

United States® Census Bureau

U.S. Department of Commerce
Economics and Statistics Administration
U.S. CENSUS BUREAU
census.gov

Source: 2017 National Population Projections and Vintage 2017 Population Estimates
www.census.gov/popest and
www.census.gov/programs-surveys/popproj.html

The benefits of being bilingual in healthcare

Bilingual healthcare professionals have the ability to serve as cultural intermediaries, facilitating communication between patients and their healthcare providers. Moreover, the acquisition of a novel language can expand an individual's personal and occupational outlooks, imparting a more profound comprehension of diverse cultures and viewpoints.

As previously mentioned, the escalating linguistic heterogeneity within the United States carries extensive ramifications for the healthcare sector. Various remedies have been suggested to tackle this predicament, such as interpreter amenities that may incur a substantial expense for medical facilities.

Some healthcare providers use translation aids, such as MediBabble or Google Translate, though these aids can occasionally produce inaccurate translations, highlighting the importance of bilingual proficiency in healthcare. Additionally, despite the substantial presence of Spanish-speaking individuals in the United States, only a modest percentage of physicians identify as Spanish speakers. This underscores the urgent need for bilingual nursing staff and healthcare interpreters who can facilitate clear and effective communication of health-related information.

Also, many healthcare facilities are actively seeking to hire bilingual healthcare professionals, particularly nurses, for many reasons, especially as first-line personnel.

Improving the Quality of Care: Communication fluency is essential to delivering high-quality care in healthcare settings. Speaking in a patient's first or native language can provide many benefits, including:

1. Increased comfort with the healthcare provider.
2. Reduced fears and anxieties related to navigating healthcare settings.
3. Receiving critical medical information in one's native language.
4. The ability to ask questions in one's native language.
5. The ability to advocate for one's needs in the full expression of one's native language.
6. Demonstrating Respect and Cultural Competency.

In addition, cultural competency is vital to respecting, understanding, and effectively interacting with individuals from diverse backgrounds and belief systems. Therefore, healthcare professionals must demonstrate cultural competency by communicating effectively with patients while respecting their cultural values.

In today's healthcare landscape, having bilingual healthcare professionals who speak their patients' native language is a sign of respect. When healthcare facilities prioritize the need for care providers to speak the same language as their patients, it shows that those patients are valued. For example, The Clínica Esperanza/Hope Clinic (CEHC) in Providence, Rhode Island, has developed the Advanced Navegante Training Program (ANTP) to address the growing demand for bilingual Community Health Workers (CHWs) in the healthcare sector. The ANTP, developed and taught by CEHC's own bilingual and bicultural CHWs, prepares community members to become certified CHWs who can provide patient navigation, lifestyle coaching, and professional medical interpretation services. Bilingual and bicultural CHWs are highly sought after to serve as healthcare navigators, patient advocates, and medical interpreters in settings with a substantial Spanish-speaking patient population.

Overview of the book's content and structure

The "Learn Medical Spanish for Doctors and Nurses Workbook" is a complete tool made to help medical professionals overcome language hurdles at work or in daily life. The workbook is a must-have for medical professionals since it gives them the most important Spanish vocabulary and phrases they need to communicate effectively with their Spanish-speaking patients,

This workbook was written by Elizabeth González Cueto, an accomplished infectious diseases medical doctor who is fluent in English and French and is a native Spanish speaker. Her large educational background includes attending prestigious institutions such as the National Polytechnic Institute in México, the University of Tours in France, the Hannover Medical School in Germany, and the Autonomous University of Barcelona in Spain. Additionally, she has done a research internship at the University of Oxford in the United Kingdom and at the Mount Sinai Hospital in New York. With various years of experience as a medical writer and editor for various global clients and companies, Elizabeth is an expert in the healthcare and scientific fields, and her passion for medical writing makes her an exceptionally reliable source for medical Spanish education.

In addition, this workbook is full of real-life examples and exercises that medical professionals can use to improve their Spanish language skills, enhance their confidence, and create trust with their Spanish-speaking patients. Also, they can learn the most important medical Spanish words and phrases, which will help them give better care to their patients.

One of the most important reasons to use this workbook is that it can help Spanish-speaking patients get better care, and it can also help patients and healthcare providers create trust, which can make patients more loyal.

The book is structured into several chapters. Each chapter is focused on a different aspect of medical Spanish, from basic vocabulary to cultural competence, with various activities, including grammar exercises and dialogues that simulate real-world medical situations.

The "Learn Medical Spanish for Healthcare Professionals" is an excellent resource for medical professionals who want to improve their communication with Spanish-speaking patients. With its practical exercises, user-friendly layout, and expert author, this workbook is a great way for medical professionals to acquire the key Spanish terms and phrases they need to know to give their patients high-quality treatment. By learning medical Spanish, doctors and nurses can ensure their Spanish-speaking patients receive the care they need to heal and continue with their lives.

Guidelines for Learning Medical Spanish

Purpose	The book aims to help healthcare professionals improve their Spanish language skills to communicate more effectively with Spanish-speaking patients.
Audience	The book is intended for doctors, nurses, and other healthcare professionals who want to communicate more effectively with Spanish-speaking patients.
Use	The book can be used as a self-study guide or as part of a classroom course. Each chapter includes exercises and an answer key for self-assessment. The appendices provide additional resources, including a

	glossary of medical terms, medical abbreviations, and a Spanish-English and English-Spanish medical dictionary.
Create a study plan	Break down the book's content by assigning specific chapters to each day. Ensure you dedicate enough time to complete the exercises and answer keys for each chapter.
Practice consistently	Consistency is key to learning Spanish quickly. Set aside a specific time each day to practice and stick to it.
Start with the basics	Begin with the first two chapters, which cover Spanish basics and medical terminology in Spanish. This will help you understand the fundamental concepts needed to communicate effectively with Spanish-speaking patients.
Use flashcards	Use the included digital flashcards as a bonus to help reinforce your learning. In addition, create flashcards for each chapter's vocabulary and phrases and review them regularly. This will help you memorize the terms and recall them quickly when needed.
Practice with a partner	Find a partner, such as a colleague or friend who also wants to learn medical Spanish, and practice conversations together. Role-playing exercises in the Additional Practice Exercises chapter are also great for practicing with a partner.
Use the glossary and dictionary	The appendices include a glossary of medical Spanish terms and a Spanish-English and English-Spanish medical dictionary. Use these resources to expand your vocabulary and improve your understanding of medical terminology.
Use the answer key	Check your answers in the exercises with the answer key provided in each chapter. This will help you identify any areas where you need more practice.

Chapter II: Spanish Basics

Cada idioma es un modo diferente de ver la vida

- Federico Fellini

As the healthcare industry becomes more diverse, it's essential for medical professionals to understand the Spanish language. In this chapter, we will provide an overview of the Spanish language for medical professionals. We will begin with the basics of the Spanish alphabet, including pronunciation, and then move on to important medical phrases for greetings and introductions. We will also cover some essential medical vocabulary to help healthcare providers better communicate with their Spanish-speaking patients.

The Alphabet

The Spanish alphabet consists of 27 letters, one more than the standard English alphabet. The additional letter is "ñ" (pronounced "enye"). While the Spanish alphabet shares most of its letters with English, the pronunciation of some letters differs between the two languages. It's important to note that each letter in the Spanish alphabet has a consistent sound. Previously, the Spanish alphabet included the letters "ch" and "ll" as distinct letters, making the total number of letters 29. However, as part of a reform to align with the international Latin alphabet, these letters are now treated as digraphs, not individual letters. As a result, words beginning with "ch" or "ll" are now categorized under the letters "c" and "l", respectively.

The Spanish Sounds

Spanish is a phonetic language, meaning each letter has a distinct sound. Unlike English, Spanish is pronounced exactly as it is written [2]. Therefore, learning the sounds of the Spanish language is very important to communicate effectively.

The Spanish Vowel Sounds

Spanish has five vowel sounds, which are "a," "e," "i," "o," and "u." In comparison with English, Spanish vowels always have the same sound and are pronounced in the same way. [3] The pronunciation of each vowel is as follows:

Vowel	Pronunciation	Notes
A	Ah	as in "father"
E	Eh	as in "pet"

I	Ee	as in "me"
O	Oh	as in "go"
U	Oo	as in "cool"

The Spanish Consonant Sounds

Spanish has 22 consonant sounds. It is important to note that some consonant sounds are different from those in English. Therefore, it is crucial to practice these sounds to ensure effective communication with Spanish-speaking patients. The Spanish consonant sounds are as follows:

Consonant	Pronunciation	Notes
B	"beh"	as in "be"
C	1.- Before "a," "o," or "u," it's pronounced as a hard "k" 2.- Before "e" or "i," it's pronounced as a soft "s" as in "cent."	1.- Example: "casa" (kah-sah) 2.- Example: "ciudad" (see-oo-dahd)
D	"deh"	as in "dog"
F	"efeh"	as in "fun"
G	"ge" 1.- Before "a," "o," or "u," it's pronounced as a hard "g" sound, like the "g" in "go." 2.- Before "e" or "i," it's pronounced as a soft "h" sound, like the "h" in "hot."	1.- Example: "gato" (gah-toh) 2.- Example: "gente" (hen-teh)
H	"hache" No sound	"h" is always silent in Spanish.
J	jota "h"	as in "hallelujah"

K	"Ka"	as in "kilogram"
L	"ele"	as in "love"
M	"eme"	as in "moon"
N	"ene"	as in "no"
Ñ	"ny" "gn"	as in "onion"
P	"peh"	as in "pen"
Q	"cu"	as in "quit." However, when followed by an "e" or "i," it is always followed by a "u" and pronounced like the English "k" in "kite"
R	"ere o erre"	is pronounced with a rolling sound, similar to the Scottish "r"
S	"ese"	as in "sun"
T	"te"	as in "time"
V	"uve"	as in "victory"
W	"doble uve"	
X	"equis"	as in "extra"
Y	"i griega o ye"	as in "yellow." However, when used as a vowel, it is pronounced like the English "ee" in "bee"
Z	"zeta"	as in "zebra"

Medical Spanish for Greetings & Introductions

It is essential for healthcare professionals to make a positive first impression when communicating with Spanish-speaking patients. Greetings and introductions play a crucial role in building rapport. Additionally, accents, vocabulary, and expressions can vary depending on the patient's Spanish-speaking region of origin. Below are some essential medical Spanish phrases for greetings and introductions:

Greeting	Spanish pronunciation	Meaning
Hola	oh-lah	Hello
¿Cómo está?	koh-moh ehs-tah	How are you? (Formal)
¿Cómo estás?	koh-moh ehs-tahs	How are you? (Informal)
Bien, gracias	bee-ehn, grah-see-yahs	Well, thank you
¿Cómo se llama?	koh-moh seh yah-mah	What is your name? (Formal)
¿Cómo te llamas?	koh-moh teh yah-mahs	What is your name? (Informal)
Me llamo	meh yah-moh	My name is
Encantado/a	ehn-kahn-tah-doh/dah	Nice to meet you (male/female)
Mucho gusto	moo-choh goo-stoh	Nice to meet you
Soy un/a doctor/a	soy oon/ah dohk-tohr/ah	I am a doctor (male/female)
Soy un/a enfermero/a	soy oon/oon-ah en-fer-meh-ro/rah	I am a nurse (male/female)
¿Habla inglés?	ah-blah een-glehs	Do you speak English?
Necesito su ayuda	neh-seh-see-toh soo ah-yoo-dah	I need your help
¿Dónde está el hospital?	dohn-deh ehs-tah ehl oh-spee-tahl	Where is the hospital?
¿Cómo puedo ayudarle?	koh-moh pweh-doh ah-yoo-dahr-leh	How can I help you? (Formal)
¿Cómo puedo ayudarte?	koh-moh pweh-doh ah-yoo-dahr-teh	How can I help you? (Informal)

Notes:

The phrases "¿Cómo está?" and "¿Cómo estás?" both translate to "How are you?" in English, but they have grammatical differences in Spanish.

- "¿Cómo está?" is in the third person singular, which is used to address someone formally or respectfully. This form is appropriate when addressing someone you do not know or someone of higher status, such as an elderly person, a professor, or a superior at work.
- "¿Cómo estás?" is in the second person singular, which is used to address someone informally or casually. This form is appropriate when addressing someone you know well, someone of the same age or social status, or someone younger than you.

The phrases "¿Cómo se llama?" and "¿Cómo te llamas?" both translate to "What's your name?" in English, but they have grammatical differences in Spanish.

- "¿Cómo se llama?" is in the third person singular, which is used to address someone formally or respectfully. This form is appropriate when addressing someone you do not know or someone of higher status, such as an elderly person, a professor, or a superior at work.
- "¿Cómo te llamas?" is in the second person singular, which is used to address someone informally or casually. This form is appropriate when addressing someone you know well, someone of the same age or social status, or someone younger than you.

In Spanish, the words "doctor" and "doctora" both mean "doctor" in English, but they have gender differences.

- "Doctor" is the masculine form and is used to address a male doctor or a female doctor when addressing a group that includes both men and women.

  For example: El doctor González es muy amable (Doctor González is very kind).

- "Doctora" is the feminine form and is used to address a female doctor.

  For example: La doctora Ramírez es una excelente cirujana (Doctor Ramírez is an excellent surgeon).

- Additional examples:
  - ✔ Masculine: Enfermero (nurse), Farmacéutico (Pharmacist), Trabajador social, (Social worker), nutriólogo (nutritionist), camillero (stretcher-bearer), psicólogo (psychologist)
  - ✔ Femenine: Enfermera (nurse), Farmacéutica (Pharmacist), Trabajadora social (Social worker), nutrióloga (nutritionist), camillera (stretcher-bearer), psicóloga (psychologist)

On the inclusion of the pronoun "elle" to refer to the subject of neutral gender in Spanish

Additionally, non-binary individuals—those who do not identify strictly as male or female—advocate for the use of the pronoun "elle" instead of "él" or "ella," as well as the gender-neutral ending "-e." Examples:

- Elle está cansade (They is tired)

- Trabajadore social (Social worker)

It's essential to use the correct gender when addressing someone in Spanish, as it shows respect and consideration for their gender identity.

Some Useful Phrases

Now, let's practice some conversations using the phrases we learned:

Conversation 1:

Spanish

Doctor: ¡Hola! ¿Cómo está?

Paciente: Hola, bien gracias, ¿y usted?

Doctor: Estoy bien, gracias. ¿Cómo se llama?

Paciente: Me llamo Ana.

Doctor: Encantado, Ana. El día de hoy seré su médico tratante. ¿En qué puedo ayudarle?

Paciente: Vengo por que tengo mucho dolor de cabeza desde ayer y a pesar de que tomé medicamentos el dolor no mejora.

Doctor: Claro, vamos a revisarla. Sígame, por favor.

Translation

Doctor: Hello! How are you?

Patient: Hi, I'm good. And you?

Doctor: I'm good, thank you. What is your name?

Patient: My name is Ana.

Doctor: Nice to meet you, Ana. Today I will be your attending physician. How can I help you?

Patient: I am here because I have had a headache since yesterday and even though I have taken medication, the pain is not getting better.

Doctor: Sure, let's check it. Follow me, please.

Conversation 2:

Spanish

Enfermera: ¡Hola! ¿Cómo está?

Paciente: Hola, estoy un poco nervioso.

Enfermera: ¿Cómo se llama?

Paciente: Me llamo Miguel.

Translation

Nurse: Hello! How are you?

Patient: Hi, I'm a little nervous.

Nurse: What is your name?

Patient: My name is Miguel.

Enfermera: Mucho gusto, Miguel. Soy enfermera. ¿Habla inglés?

Nurse: Nice to meet you, Miguel. I am a nurse. Do you speak English?

Paciente: Sí, hablo inglés.

Patient: Yes, I speak English.

Enfermera: Perfecto. ¿Dónde le duele?

Nurse: Perfect. Where is the pain?

Paciente: Me duele el estómago.

Patient: My stomach hurts.

Enfermera: Entiendo. Vamos a tomarle la temperatura y la presión arterial para ver cómo se encuentra.

Nurse: I understand. Let's take your temperature and blood pressure to see how we're doing.

Conversation 3:

Spanish

Translation

Doctor: ¡Hola! ¿Cómo está?

Doctor: Hello! How are you?

Paciente: Hola, no me siento bien.

Patient: Hi, I don't feel well.

Doctor: ¿Cómo se llama?

Doctor: What is your name?

Paciente: Me llamo Juan.

Patient: My name is Juan.

Doctor: Encantado, Juan. ¿Qué le duele?

Doctor: Nice to meet you, Juan. What hurts you?

Paciente: Me duele la garganta y tengo fiebre.

Patient: My throat hurts and I have a fever.

Doctor: Entiendo. ¿Habla inglés?

Doctor: I understand. Do you speak English?

Paciente: No mucho.

Patient: Not much.

Doctor: No hay problema, yo y la enfermera hablamos español y podemos asistirlo y responder sus dudas. Voy a examinarle para ver qué está sucediendo.

Doctor: No problem, me and the nurse speak Spanish and we can assist you and answer your questions. I will examine you to see what is going on.

The best way to learn and retain Spanish

Learning Spanish can be challenging, especially if you have never been exposed to the language or have interacted with Spanish speakers. However, as a healthcare professional, knowing Spanish can be a valuable asset that can help you communicate better with your patients and provide better care. Here are some tips to help you learn and retain Spanish effectively:

Set goals	Do you want to be able to understand basic medical terms and phrases, or do you want to be able to have full conversations with your patients? Having clear goals will help you focus your learning efforts and measure your progress.
Use Multiple Resources	Use a combination of textbooks, workbooks, podcasts, online resources, and apps to help you learn Spanish. Each resource can offer a different approach to learning and reinforce the concepts you are studying.
Practice Regularly	Set aside time each day to practice your Spanish, even if it's just for a few minutes. Consistency is key, and regular practice can help you retain what you've learned and improve your skills.
Immerse Yourself	Listen to Spanish music, watch Spanish movies, TV shows, and podcasts, and read Spanish books and news articles. With the widespread use of social media, you can also follow medical Spanish influencers and learn from their informative content in Spanish. Consistent exposure to the language will improve your comprehension and pronunciation while immersing you in the culture.
Speak and Listen	Language learning involves both speaking and listening. Practice speaking with native speakers or other healthcare professionals who are learning Spanish. This will help you improve your pronunciation and fluency. Slowly, you can also start practicing a few words with your patients. Listening to Spanish conversations or recordings can also help you improve your comprehension and vocabulary.
Use Mnemonics	Mnemonics are memory aids that can help you remember new words and phrases. Create your own mnemonics or use existing ones to help you remember medical terms and phrases in Spanish. For example, to remember the Spanish word for "stomach," you could use the mnemonic "ESTO-mago," which sounds similar to the English word.
Seek Feedback	Ask native speakers or other healthcare professionals to provide feedback on your pronunciation and speaking skills. Constructive feedback can help you identify areas for improvement and refine your language skills.

Key Takeaways

In this chapter, we covered the basics of the Spanish language, including the Spanish alphabet and sounds. We also provided you with some essential medical Spanish phrases for greetings and introductions. The key takeaways from this chapter are:

- The Spanish alphabet has 27 letters, including one additional letter "ñ."
- Spanish is a phonetic language, which means that each letter has a distinct sound.
- Spanish has five vowel sounds and 22 consonant sounds.
- It is important to learn the basic Spanish sounds to communicate effectively in medical settings.
- Essential medical Spanish phrases for greetings and introductions include "Hola," "¿Cómo está?" and "Soy un/a doctor/a."

Exercises

Exercise 1

Write the Spanish pronunciation for the following English words:

No.	English	Spanish
1	Father	
2	Pet	
3	Me	
4	Boat	
5	Blue	

Exercise 2

Write the English pronunciation for the following Spanish words:

No.	Spanish	English
1	Perro	
2	Gato	
3	Médico	
4	Hospital	
5	Enfermera	

Exercise 3

Complete the following sentences in Spanish:

_____ es tu nombre? (What is your name?)

_____ es un/a doctor/a. (He/She is a doctor/nurse.)

¿_____ está el hospital? (Where is the hospital?)

_____ puedo ayudarle? (How can I help you?)

Mucho _____. (Nice to meet you.)

Answer Key

Exercise 1

Write the Spanish pronunciation for the following English words:

No.	English	Spanish
1	Father	**padre (pah-dreh)**
2	Pet	**mascota (mahs-koh-tah)**
3	Me	**yo (yoh)**
4	Boat	**barco (bar-koh)**
5	Blue	**azul (ah-sool)**

Exercise 2

Write the English pronunciation for the following Spanish words:

No.	Spanish	English
1	Perro	**dog (peh-roh)**
2	Gato	**cat (gah-toh)**
3	Médico	**doctor (meh-dee-koh)**
4	Hospital	**hospital (oh-spee-tahl)**
5	Enfermera	**nurse (en-fehr-meh-rah)**

Exercise 3

Complete the following sentences in Spanish:

¿Cuál es tu nombre? (What is your name?)

Él/Ella es un/a doctor/a. (He/She is a doctor/nurse.)

¿Dónde está el hospital? (Where is the hospital?)

¿Cómo puedo ayudarle? (How can I help you?)

Mucho gusto. (Nice to meet you.)

Chapter III: Basic Medical Terminology

La medicina no es sólo una ciencia, sino también el arte de dejar que nuestra individualidad se relacione con la de nuestros pacientes

William Osler

Introduction to Medical Terminology in Spanish

Medical terminology is an essential part of healthcare, and being proficient in it is crucial for healthcare professionals who interact with Spanish-speaking patients. In this chapter, we will provide you with an introduction to medical terminology in Spanish, which will help you communicate more effectively with your Spanish-speaking patients.

Knowing the proper medical terms in Spanish is particularly important when communicating with patients who may not speak English fluently. Language barriers can lead to misunderstandings, affecting patient care and outcomes. By having a solid foundation of essential medical terms and phrases in Spanish, healthcare professionals can ensure that they can communicate clearly and effectively with their Spanish-speaking patients.

This chapter will cover the most common medical terms and phrases in Spanish, including body parts, symptoms, diseases, and treatments. We will also discuss how to properly use these terms in a medical context to ensure accurate communication. By the end of this chapter, you will have a better understanding of medical terminology in Spanish, which will improve your ability to provide high-quality care to Spanish-speaking patients.

In addition to being beneficial for healthcare professionals, this chapter may also be useful for students studying medical terminology or anyone interested in learning more about the Spanish language in a medical context. Whether you are just starting to learn Spanish or have been speaking it for years, this chapter will provide you with a solid foundation in medical terminology.

Common Medical Terms and Phrases in Spanish

Medical terminology is a specialized language used in the healthcare industry. Knowing common medical terms and phrases in Spanish will help you understand patient needs, provide instructions, and explain medical procedures. Here are some of the most common medical terms and phrases in Spanish:

Medical terms in Spanish	Medical terms in English
Corazón	Heart
Riñón	Kidney
Pulmón	Lung
Hígado	Liver
Cerebro	Brain
Sangre	Blood
Hueso	Bone
Cáncer	Cancer
Infección	Infection
Diabetes	Diabetes
Enfermedad	Disease
Fiebre	Fever
Dolor	Pain
Presión arterial	Blood pressure
Vacuna	Vaccine
Tratamiento	Treatment
Antibiótico	Antibiotic
Inflamación	Inflammation
Radiografía	X-ray
Nutrición	Nutrition
Paciente	Patient
Terapia	Therapy

Síntomas	Symptoms
Salud	Health
Cirugía	Surgery
Emergencia	Emergency
Dosis	Dose
Medicamento	Medication
Venas	Veins
Músculo	Muscle
Hormona	Hormone
Terapeuta	Therapist
Especialista	Specialist
Epidemia	Epidemic
Contagio	Contagion
Medicina	Medicine
Órganos	Organs
Enfermera	Nurse
Deshidratación	Dehydration
Asma	Asthma
Infarto	Heart attack
Anestesia	Anesthesia
Trasplante	Transplant
Hemorragia	Hemorrhage
Psiquiatría	Psychiatry

Traumatismo	Trauma
Síndrome	Syndrome
Virus	Virus
Quimioterapia	Chemotherapy
Radioterapia	Radiation therapy

Pronunciation and Spelling Rules for Medical Spanish

Pronunciation is a critical component of communication, and it is especially important in the healthcare industry. Knowing the correct pronunciation of medical terms in Spanish will help you communicate more effectively with your Spanish-speaking patients. Here are some pronunciation and spelling rules for medical Spanish:

- "J" in Spanish is pronounced like the "h" in "hot."

  For example, the Spanish word "juego" (game) is pronounced "wey-go," and the word "jirafa" (giraffe) is pronounced "hee-rah-fah."

- "G" in Spanish is pronounced differently depending on the letter that follows it. Before "e" or "i," it is pronounced like the "h" in "hot." Before "a," "o," or "u," it is pronounced like the "g" in "go."

  For example, the Spanish word "ginecólogo" (gynecologist) is pronounced "hee-neh-koh-loh-goh."

- "C" in Spanish is also pronounced differently depending on the letter that follows it. Before "e" or "i," it is pronounced like the "s" in "sit." Before "a," "o," or "u," it is pronounced like the "k" in "kite."

  For example, the Spanish word "cirugía" (surgery) is pronounced "see-roo-hee-yah."

- "H" in Spanish is always silent.

  For example, the Spanish word "hígado" (liver) is pronounced "ee-gah-doh."

- In some Spanish-speaking regions, such as Argentina and Uruguay, the pronunciation of 'LL' is similar to 'Y' (often sounding like a 'sh' or 'zh' sound). However, 'LL' and 'Y' are not interchangeable in spelling.

  Examples of Different Pronunciations:

  Calle (Street) – In most regions, pronounced as "ka-yeh," but in Argentina, it may sound like "ka-she" or "ka-zhe."

  Lluvia (Rain) – In many places, pronounced "yoo-vyah," but in Argentina, often "shoo-vyah" or "zhoo-vyah."

Caballo (Horse) – Generally pronounced "kah-ba-yo," but may sound like "kah-ba-sho" or "kah-ba-zho" in Argentina or Uruguay.

- Accents are used in Spanish to indicate where the stress falls on a word.

  For example, the word "médico" (doctor) is stressed on the second-to-last syllable, but the word "quirúrgico" (surgical) is stressed on the third-to-last syllable, so it has an accent mark on the "u."

By following these pronunciation and spelling rules, you will be better equipped to communicate with your Spanish-speaking patients and colleagues in a clear and effective manner.

Examples of Conversations between Doctors/Nurses and Patients

Understanding medical terminology is essential, but knowing how to use it in patient conversations is equally important. Here are some examples of conversations between doctors/nurses and patients:

Conversation 1:

Spanish	Translation
Doctor: Hola, ¿cómo te sientes hoy?	*Doctor*: Hi, how are you feeling today?
Paciente: No me siento bien. Tengo fiebre y dolor en el pecho.	*Patient*: I don't feel well. I have a fever and chest pain.
Doctor: ¿Has tenido problemas en el corazón antes?	*Doctor*: Have you had any heart problems before?
Paciente: Sí, tengo la presión alta.	*Patient*: Yes, I have high blood pressure.
Doctor: Entiendo, necesito hacerte una revisión general, un electrocardiograma, y una radiografía de tórax para ver qué podría estar causando el dolor en tu pecho. Después podremos decidir mejor tu tratamiento.	*Doctor*: I understand, I need to do a general check-up, electrocardiogram, and a chest x-ray to see what could be causing your chest pain. Then we can better decide on your treatment.

Conversation 2:

Spanish	Translation
Enfermera: Hola, ¿cómo te sientes hoy?	*Nurse*: Hi, how are you feeling today?

Paciente: Me duele mucho el riñón.	Patient: My kidney hurts a lot.
Enfermera: ¿Has estado tomando tus medicamentos para la infección del riñón?	Nurse: Have you been taking your medication for the kidney infection?
Paciente: No, olvidé tomarlos ayer.	*Patient*: No, I forgot to take them yesterday.
Enfermera: Es muy importante que tomes tus medicamentos para que puedas recuperarte rápidamente.	*Nurse*: It's very important that you take your medication so you can recover quickly.

Conversation 3:

Spanish	Translation
Doctor: Hola, ¿cómo te ha ido desde la última vez que nos vimos?	*Doctor*: Hi, how have you been since the last time we saw each other?
Paciente: Me he sentido bien en general, pero todavía tengo dolores de cabeza y mareos.	*Patient*: I've been feeling good overall, but I still have headaches and dizziness.
Doctor: ¿Te has sentido deprimido o ansioso recientemente?	Doctor: Have you been feeling depressed or anxious recently?
Paciente: Sí, me he sentido muy ansioso últimamente.	*Patient*: Yes, I've been feeling very anxious lately.
Doctor: Te voy a dar una interconsulta con un especialista en psiquiatría para que evalúe tu caso.	*Doctor*: I will give you a consultation with a psychiatric specialist to evaluate your case.

Conversation 4:

Spanish	Translation
Enfermera: Hola, ¿cómo has estado desde tu cirugía?	*Nurse*: Hi, how have you been since your surgery?
Paciente: Me he estado recuperando bien, pero todavía tengo dolores en los huesos y los músculos.	*Patient*: I've been recovering well, but I still have pains in my bones and muscles.

Enfermera: ¿Has estado tomando tus medicamentos para el dolor?	*Nurse*: Have you been taking your pain medication?
Paciente: Sí, pero no parecen estar funcionando tan bien como antes.	*Patient*: Yes, but they don't seem to be working as well as before.
Enfermera: Puedo hablar con el médico para que te recete un medicamento diferente si es necesario.	*Nurse*: I can talk to the doctor to prescribe a different medication for you if needed.

Key Takeaways

- Medical terminology is essential in healthcare, and knowing the proper medical terms in Spanish is crucial for healthcare professionals who interact with Spanish-speaking patients.

- Language barriers can lead to misunderstandings, which can affect patient care and outcomes, but having a solid foundation of essential medical terms and phrases in Spanish can ensure clear and effective communication.

- The chapter covers the most common medical terms and phrases in Spanish, including body parts, symptoms, diseases, and treatments.

- Pronunciation is a critical component of communication, and knowing the correct pronunciation of medical terms in Spanish can help healthcare professionals communicate more effectively with their Spanish-speaking patients.

Exercises

Exercise 1

Write the Spanish equivalent for the following English medical terms:

English	Spanish
Heart	
Kidney	
Lung	
Liver	
Brain	
Blood	
Bone	
Cancer	
Infection	
Diabetes	

Exercise 2

Match the following Spanish medical terms with their corresponding English meanings:

Spanish	English
Fiebre	Fever
Presión arterial	Antibiotic
Vacuna	Treatment
Tratamiento	Blood pressure
Antibiótico	Vaccine

Exercise 3

Choose the correct pronunciation of the following medical terms:

1.- Corazón

      a. ko-rah-zon
      b. ko-rah-thohn
      c. ko-rah-sohn

2.- Ginecólogo

      a. gih-neh-koh-loh-goh
      b. gee-neh-koh-loh-goh
      c. hee-neh-koh-loh-goh

3.- Cirugía

      a. see-roo-gyah
      b. see-roo-hee-yah
      c. kee-roo-gyah

Exercise 4

Fill in the blank with the correct pronunciation of the medical term:

Spanish word	Pronunciation
Hígado	ee-gah-_____
Enfermedad	en-fer-meh-_____
Hemorragia	eh-moh-rah-_____

Answer Key

Exercise 1

Write the Spanish equivalent for the following English medical terms:

English	Spanish
Heart	Corazón
Kidney	Riñón
Lung	Pulmón
Liver	Hígado
Brain	Cerebro
Blood	Sangre
Bone	Hueso
Cancer	Cáncer
Infection	Infección
Diabetes	Diabetes

Exercise 2

Match the following Spanish medical terms with their corresponding English meanings:

Spanish	English
Fiebre	Fever
Presión arterial	Blood pressure
Vacuna	Vaccine
Tratamiento	Treatment
Antibiótico	Antibiotic

Exercise 3

Choose the correct pronunciation of the following medical terms:

1.- b. ko-rah-thohn

2.- c. hee-neh-koh-loh-goh

3.- b. see-roo-hee-yah

Exercise 4

Fill in the blank with the correct pronunciation of the medical term:

Spanish word	Pronunciation
Hígado	ee-gah-__**doh**____
Enfermedad	en-fer-meh-__**dahd**____
Hemorragia	eh-moh-rah-_ **hee-ah**_

BOOK 2

Spanish Medical Communication: Anatomy, Procedures, Prescription, and Emergencies

¡ Fluency for Better Care: Discovering Medical Spanish Language, Human Body, and Practices!

Explore to Win

Book 2 Description

Welcome to the second part of our series, 'Medical Terminology, Anatomy, and Procedures.' As a dedicated healthcare professional, your journey to becoming a proficient Spanish speaker continues, propelling you toward delivering exceptional patient care and fostering genuine connections.

You will learn common medical terms, phrases, and pronunciations specific to medical Spanish. From basic anatomy and physiology terms to in-depth knowledge of the body's systems and apparatuses, we've got you covered.

Communication is vital in medical settings, especially during procedures and exams. That's why this book provides you with the vocabulary needed to conduct medical procedures and exams in Spanish. You'll also learn essential patient consultation phrases and how to give instructions in Spanish.

Furthermore, we understand the significance of medication management. To help you in this area, we've compiled a list of Spanish terms related to prescription and medication. You'll be able to inquire about allergies and side effects, clarify dosage, and accurately communicate medication information.

Real-life examples of conversations between medical professionals and patients are woven throughout the book, reinforcing your learning and practical application of medical Spanish. Are you ready to expand your horizons and embrace the world of medical communication in Spanish? Let's start!

Chapter I: Anatomy and Physiology

La belleza del cuerpo es muchas veces indicio de la hermosura del alma

Miguel de Cervantes

Basic anatomy and physiology terms in Spanish

As a healthcare professional, your ability to communicate effectively with your patients is crucial to providing quality care. In a multicultural and multilingual society, it is essential to understand basic anatomy and physiology terms in Spanish to bridge the language barrier and ensure patients understand their medical conditions and treatment plans. This chapter aims to equip healthcare professionals with the necessary vocabulary to communicate with Spanish-speaking patients confidently. We will delve into the various body systems and their functions, explore common medical conditions related to each system, and provide practical examples of conversations between healthcare professionals and patients. By the end of this chapter, you will have a solid foundation in medical Spanish, enabling you to provide better care to your Spanish-speaking patients.

To effectively communicate with Spanish-speaking patients, it is important to know basic anatomy and physiology terms in Spanish. Here are important terms to keep in mind:

Spanish	English
Anatomía	Anatomy
Fisiología	Physiology
Sistema nervioso	Nervous system
Sistema cardiovascular	Cardiovascular system
Sistema respiratorio	Respiratory system
Sistema digestivo	Digestive system
Sistema endocrino	Endocrine system
Sistema muscular	Muscular system
Sistema óseo	Skeletal system

Sistema linfático	Lymphatic system
Sistema urinario	Urinary system
Sistema reproductor	Reproductive system
Tejido	Tissue
Célula	Cell
Glóbulo rojo	Red blood cell
Glóbulo blanco	White blood cell
Plaqueta	Platelet
Epitelio	Epithelium
Cartílago	Cartilage
Hueso	Bone
Músculo	Muscle
Ligamento	Ligament
Tendón	Tendon
Articulación	Joint
Neurona	Neuron
Sinapsis	Synapse
Cerebro	Brain
Médula espinal	Spinal cord
Ganglio	Ganglion
Nervio	Nerve
Corazón	Heart
Vena	Vein

Arteria	Artery
Capilar	Capillary
Pulmón	Lung
Tráquea	Trachea
Bronquio	Bronchus
Diafragma	Diaphragm
Estómago	Stomach
Hígado	Liver
Páncreas	Pancreas
Intestino delgado	Small intestine
Intestino grueso	Large intestine
Vesícula biliar	Gallbladder
Glándula tiroides	Thyroid gland
Glándula suprarrenal	Adrenal gland
Glándula pituitaria	Pituitary gland
Riñón	Kidney
Vejiga	Bladder
Ovario	Ovary

Parts of the body and their functions

Here are some key body parts and their functions, organized by systems and apparatuses:

Skeletal System: It provides support and structure to the body through bones, ligaments, and cartilage.

1. Hueso: Bone
2. Cartílago: Cartilage

3. Tendón: Tendon
4. Ligamento: Ligament
5. Músculo: Muscle
6. Vértebras: Vertebrae
7. Cráneo: Skull
8. Articulación: Joint
9. Médula ósea: Bone marrow
10. Fémur: Femur

Muscular System*:* It is responsible for movement and posture through muscles and tendons.

1. Músculo: Muscle
2. Sistema muscular esquelético: The skeletal muscular system
3. Músculos lisos: Smooth muscles
4. Músculos cardíacos: Cardiac muscles
5. Masa muscular: Muscle mass
6. Contracción muscular: Muscle contraction
7. Fibra muscular: Muscle fiber
8. Tono muscular: Muscle tone
9. Miopatía: Myopathy
10. Miembro inferior: Lower limb

Nervous System*:* It controls and coordinates the body's functions and responses to stimuli through the brain, spinal cord, and nerves.

1. Cerebro: Brain
2. Médula espinal: Spinal cord
3. Nervios: Nerves
4. Neuronas: Neurons
5. Sistemas sensoriales: Sensory systems
6. Sistema nervioso autónomo: The autonomic nervous system
7. Neurotransmisores: Neurotransmitters
8. Sinapsis: Synapses
9. Corteza cerebral: Cerebral cortex
10. Sistema nervioso periférico: Peripheral nervous system

Circulatory System*:* Responsible for transporting blood, nutrients, and oxygen throughout the body through the heart, blood vessels, and blood.

1. Corazón: Heart
2. Arteria: Artery
3. Vena: Vein
4. Capilar: Capillary
5. Sistema cardiovascular: The cardiovascular system
6. Plasma sanguíneo: Blood plasma
7. Glóbulos rojos: Red blood cells
8. Glóbulos blancos: White blood cells
9. Hemoglobina: Hemoglobin
10. Circulación sanguínea: Blood circulation

Respiratory System: Its function is to exchange gases (oxygen and carbon dioxide) between the body and the environment.

1. Pulmón: Lung
2. Tráquea: Trachea
3. Bronquio: Bronchus
4. Alvéolo: Alveolus
5. Diafragma: Diaphragm
6. Vía aérea: Airway
7. Intercambio gaseoso: Gas exchange
8. Respiración: Breathing
9. Capacidad pulmonar: Lung capacity
10. Cavidad nasal: Nasal cavity

Digestive System: Its function is to break down food into smaller molecules that can be absorbed by the body and to eliminate waste products.

1. Boca: Mouth
2. Esófago: Esophagus
3. Estómago: Stomach
4. Recto: Rectum
5. Ano: Anus
6. Hígado: Liver
7. Vesícula biliar: Gallbladder
8. Páncreas: Pancreas
9. Intestino delgado: Small intestine

10. Intestino grueso: Large intestine

Urinary System*:* Its function is to remove waste products from the blood and to regulate fluid and electrolyte balance in the body.

1. Riñón: Kidney
2. Uretra: Urethra
3. Vejiga: Bladder
4. Tracto urinario: Urinary tract
5. Filtración renal: Renal filtration
6. Orina: Urine
7. Sistema excretor: The excretory system
8. Regulación del equilibrio ácido-base: Regulation of acid-base balance
9. Sistema renina-angiotensina-aldosterona: Renin-angiotensin-aldosterone system
10. Sistema urinario masculino/femenino: Male/female urinary system.

Reproductive System*:* Its function is to produce and transport gametes (sperm and eggs) and to facilitate reproduction.

1. Ovario: Ovary
2. Útero: Uterus
3. Vagina: Vagina
4. Pene: Penis
5. Testículo: Testicle
6. Epidídimo: Epididymis
7. Próstata: Prostate
8. Glándulas de Bartolino: Bartholin's glands
9. Células de Leydig: Leydig cells
10. Trompas de Falopio: Fallopian tubes

Endocrine system*:* Its function is to regulate various bodily functions, such as growth, metabolism, and reproduction.

1. Glandula: Gland
2. Hormonas: Hormones
3. Hipotálamo: Hypothalamus
4. Pituitaria: Pituitary gland
5. Tiroides: Thyroid gland
6. Paratiroides: Parathyroid gland

7. Páncreas: Pancreas

8. Adrenalina: Adrenaline

9. Glucagon: Glucagon

10. Insulina: Insulin

Integumentary system: Its function is to protect the body from external damage and to regulate body temperature.

1. Piel: Skin

2. Cabello: Hair

3. Uñas: Nails

4. Glándulas sudoríparas: Sweat glands

5. Glándulas sebáceas: Sebaceous glands

6. Estrato córneo: Stratum corneum

7. Epidermis: Epidermis

8. Dermis: Dermis

9. Hipodermis: Hypodermis

10. Termorregulación: Thermoregulation

Lymphatic system: Its function is to help defend the body against infection and disease by transporting immune cells and filtering harmful substances from the blood.

1. Linfocitos: Lymphocytes

2. Ganglios linfáticos: Lymph nodes

3. Sistema linfático: The lymphatic system

4. Vasos linfáticos: Lymphatic vessels

5. Bazo: Spleen

6. Amígdalas: Tonsils

7. Timo: Thymus

8. Linfoma: Lymphoma

9. Inflamación linfática: Lymphadenitis

10. Cáncer linfático: Lymphatic cancer

Spanish / English diagrams of the human body systems and apparatuses

Sistema Esquelético / Skeletal System

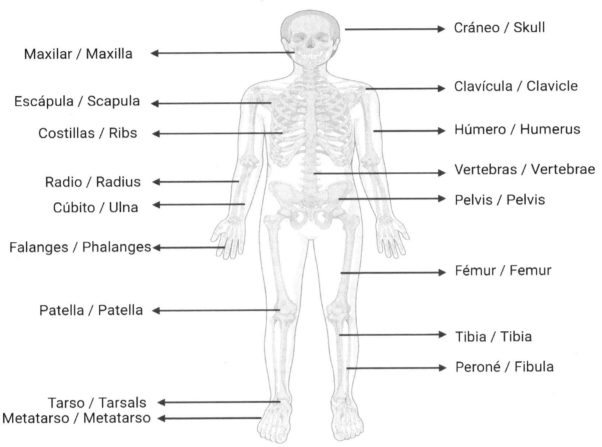

Cráneo / Skull

Maxilar / Maxilla

Clavícula / Clavicle

Escápula / Scapula

Húmero / Humerus

Costillas / Ribs

Vertebras / Vertebrae

Radio / Radius

Pelvis / Pelvis

Cúbito / Ulna

Falanges / Phalanges

Fémur / Femur

Patella / Patella

Tibia / Tibia

Peroné / Fibula

Tarso / Tarsals
Metatarso / Metatarso

The skeletal system, anterior view, Created with BioRender.com

Sistema Muscular / Muscular Systems　　**Sistema Cardiovascular / Cardiovascular System**

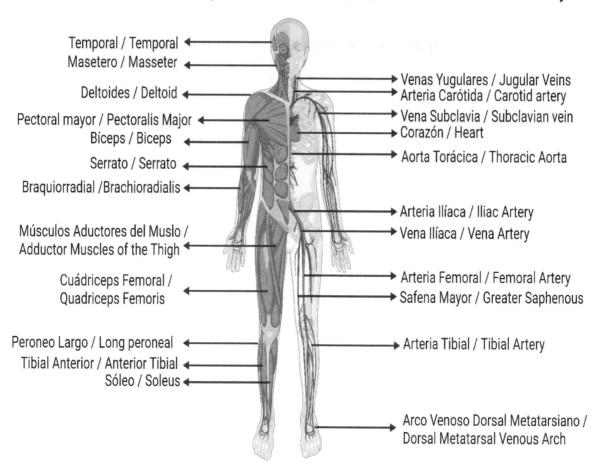

Temporal / Temporal

Masetero / Masseter

Deltoides / Deltoid

Pectoral mayor / Pectoralis Major

Bíceps / Biceps

Serrato / Serrato

Braquiorradial /Brachioradialis

Músculos Aductores del Muslo / Adductor Muscles of the Thigh

Cuádriceps Femoral / Quadriceps Femoris

Peroneo Largo / Long peroneal

Tibial Anterior / Anterior Tibial

Sóleo / Soleus

Venas Yugulares / Jugular Veins

Arteria Carótida / Carotid artery

Vena Subclavia / Subclavian vein

Corazón / Heart

Aorta Torácica / Thoracic Aorta

Arteria Ilíaca / Iliac Artery

Vena Ilíaca / Vena Artery

Arteria Femoral / Femoral Artery

Safena Mayor / Greater Saphenous

Arteria Tibial / Tibial Artery

Arco Venoso Dorsal Metatarsiano / Dorsal Metatarsal Venous Arch

The muscular and cardiovascular systems, anterior view,

Created with BioRender.com

Sistema Digestivo / Digestive System

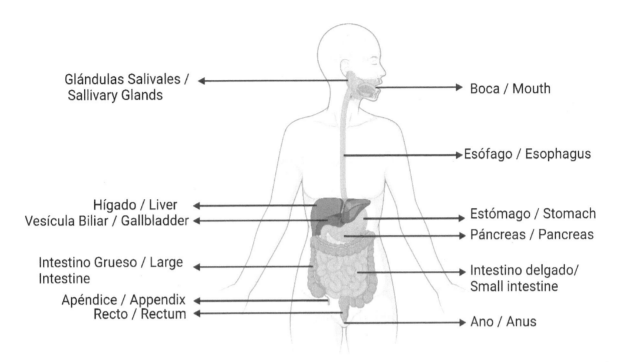

Glándulas Salivales / Sallivary Glands

Boca / Mouth

Esófago / Esophagus

Hígado / Liver
Vesícula Biliar / Gallbladder

Estómago / Stomach
Páncreas / Pancreas

Intestino Grueso / Large Intestine

Intestino delgado/ Small intestine

Apéndice / Appendix
Recto / Rectum

Ano / Anus

The digestive system, anterior view, Created with BioRender.com

Sitema Respiratorio / Respiratory System

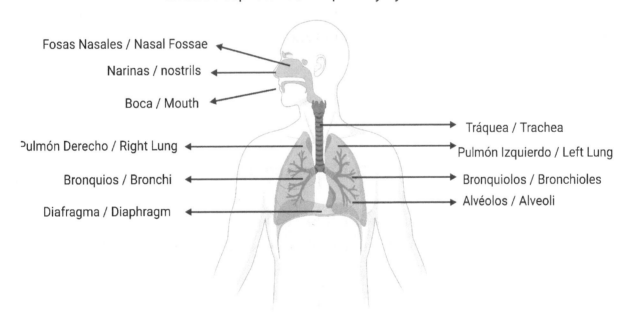

Fosas Nasales / Nasal Fossae

Narinas / nostrils

Boca / Mouth

Tráquea / Trachea

Pulmón Derecho / Right Lung

Pulmón Izquierdo / Left Lung

Bronquios / Bronchi

Bronquiolos / Bronchioles

Alvéolos / Alveoli

Diafragma / Diaphragm

The respiratory system, anterior view, Created with BioRender.com

Medical conditions and diseases related to the body systems

Now that you have a good grasp of the various systems of the human body, it is important to understand the different medical conditions and diseases that can affect these systems [3]. Below are some of the most common medical conditions and diseases that healthcare professionals may encounter in their work, along with their corresponding Spanish terms:

Respiratory System

1. Asthma (asma)
2. Chronic obstructive pulmonary disease (enfermedad pulmonar obstructiva crónica or EPOC)
3. Pneumonia (neumonía)
4. Bronchitis (bronquitis)
5. Emphysema (enfisema)

Cardiovascular System

1. Hypertension (hipertensión)
2. Coronary artery disease (enfermedad de las arterias coronarias)
3. Heart failure (insuficiencia cardíaca)
4. Myocardial infarction (infarto de miocardio)
5. Arrhythmia (arritmia)

Digestive System

1. Gastroesophageal reflux disease (enfermedad por reflujo gastroesofágico or ERGE)
2. Irritable bowel syndrome (síndrome de intestino irritable or SII)
3. Hepatitis (hepatitis)
4. Cirrhosis (cirrosis)
5. Gallstones (cálculos biliares)

Urinary System

1. Urinary tract infection (infección del tracto urinario or ITU)
2. Kidney stones (cálculos renales)
3. Urinary incontinence (incontinencia urinaria)
4. Chronic kidney disease (enfermedad renal crónica or ERC)
5. Bladder cancer (cáncer de vejiga)

Musculoskeletal System

1. Osteoarthritis (osteoartritis)
2. Rheumatoid arthritis (artritis reumatoide)
3. Fractures (fracturas)

4. Sprains (esguinces)

5. Herniated disc (hernia de disco)

Nervous System

1. Alzheimer's disease (enfermedad de Alzheimer)

2. Parkinson's disease (enfermedad de Parkinson)

3. Epilepsy (epilepsia)

4. Multiple sclerosis (esclerosis múltiple)

5. Stroke (accidente cerebrovascular or ACV)

Examples of conversations between doctor/nurses and patients

Here are some sample conversations between healthcare professionals and patients to help you practice using the anatomy and physiology terms, medical conditions and diseases, and vocabulary you have learned in this chapter:

Conversation 1: Musculoskeletal System

Spanish	Translation
Doctor: Hola, ¿cómo te sientes hoy?	*Doctor:* Hello, how are you feeling today?
Paciente: Hola, Doctor. Me duele la rodilla derecha.	*Patient:* Hi, Doctor. My right knee hurts.
Doctor: ¿Desde cuándo te duele?	*Doctor:* How long has it been hurting?
Paciente: Desde hace unos días.	*Patient:* For a few days.
Doctor: Debe ser algo relacionado con los músculos o los huesos. ¿Has tenido algún golpe o caída reciente?	*Doctor:* It must be something related to the bone or muscle. Have you had any recent hits or falls?
Paciente: No, no que yo recuerde.	*Patient:* No, not that I remember.
Doctor: Entonces puede ser una lesión en el cartílago o el tendón. Vamos a programar una radiografía y una resonancia magnética para obtener una imagen más clara.	*Doctor:* Then it could be an injury to the cartilage or tendon. Let's schedule an X-ray and an MRI to get a clearer picture.
Paciente: De acuerdo, Doctor. ¿Qué debo hacer mientras tanto?	Patient: Okay, Doctor. What should I do in the meantime?

Spanish	Translation
Doctor: Te recetaré algunos analgésicos y te recomiendo que evites hacer ejercicio o actividades físicas que puedan empeorar el dolor.	*Doctor:* I will prescribe you some painkillers and recommend that you avoid exercising or physical activities that may worsen the pain.

Conversation 2: Respiratory System

Spanish	Translation
Doctor: Hola, ¿cómo te sientes hoy?	*Doctor:* Hello, how are you feeling today?
Paciente: Hola, Doctor. Tengo problemas para respirar.	Patient: Hi, Doctor. I'm having trouble breathing.
Paciente: Desde hace unos días.	*Patient:* For a few days.
Doctor: Es posible que tengas asma. ¿Tienes algún historial de asma en tu familia?	*Doctor:* It's possible that you have asthma. Do you have any history of asthma in your family?
Paciente: No, no que yo sepa.	*Patient:* No, not that I know of.
Doctor: Te recetaré un inhalador para el asma y te recomiendo que evites el humo del tabaco y otros irritantes. Si no mejora, volveremos a evaluar tu caso y podemos hacer pruebas adicionales.	*Doctor:* I will prescribe you an inhaler for asthma and recommend that you avoid tobacco smoke and other irritants. If it doesn't improve, we will reassess your case and can do additional testing.
Paciente: De acuerdo, Doctor	*Patient:* Okay, Doctor.

Conversation 3: Urinary Tract Infection (UTI)

Spanish	Translation
Doctor: Hola, ¿cómo estás hoy?	*Doctor:* Hi, how are you today?
Paciente: Hola, no muy bien. Tengo dolor al orinar y muchas ganas de ir al baño.	*Patient:* Hi, not very well. I have pain when urinating and a strong urge to go to the bathroom.
Doctor: Entiendo, esos síntomas pueden indicar una infección urinaria. ¿Ha tenido esto antes?	*Doctor:* I understand, those symptoms can indicate a urinary infection. Have you had this before?

Spanish	Translation
Paciente: Sí, una vez antes hace unos años.	*Patient:* Yes, once before a few years ago.
Doctor: Bien, vamos a hacer un examen de orina y si es necesario, le prescribiré antibióticos para tratar la infección. Mientras tanto, asegúrese de beber mucha agua y evitar los irritantes de la vejiga como la cafeína y el alcohol.	*Doctor:* Alright, we're going to do a urine test and if necessary, I'll prescribe antibiotics to treat the infection. In the meantime, make sure to drink plenty of water and avoid bladder irritants like caffeine and alcohol.
Paciente: De acuerdo, gracias.	*Patient:* Okay, thank you.
Doctor: Los resultados del examen de orina muestran que tiene una infección del tracto urinario. Le recetaré un antibiótico para tomar durante los próximos cinco días. Asegúrese de tomarlo según las indicaciones y siga bebiendo mucha agua.	*Doctor:* The urine test results show that you have a urinary tract infection. I'll prescribe an antibiotic for you to take for the next five days. Make sure to take it as directed and continue drinking plenty of water.
Paciente: De acuerdo, lo haré. ¿Hay algo más que pueda hacer para prevenir futuras infecciones del tracto urinario?	*Patient:* Alright, I will. Is there anything else I can do to prevent future urinary tract infections?
Doctor: Sí, asegúrese de orinar después de tener relaciones sexuales y siempre limpiarse de adelante hacia atrás después de ir al baño para evitar la propagación de bacterias desde el ano a la uretra.	*Doctor:* Yes, make sure to urinate after sexual intercourse and always wipe from front to back after using the bathroom to avoid the spread of bacteria from the anus to the urethra.
Paciente: Gracias, tomaré nota de eso.	*Patient:* Thank you, I'll take note of that.

Conversation 4: Rheumatoid Arthritis

Spanish	Translation
Doctor: Hola, ¿cómo ha estado desde la última vez que nos vimos?	*Doctor:* Hi, how have you been since the last time we saw each other?
Paciente: No muy bien, tengo mucho dolor en las articulaciones y me cuesta moverme.	*Patient:* Not very well, I have a lot of joint pain, and it's hard for me to move.
Doctor: Entiendo. Por lo que me dijo, creo que puede estar experimentando síntomas de	*Doctor:* I understand. Based on what you told me, I think you may be experiencing the

artritis reumatoide. Vamos a hacer algunas pruebas para confirmar el diagnóstico.	symptoms of rheumatoid arthritis. Let's do some tests to confirm the diagnosis.
Paciente: De acuerdo, espero que pueda ayudarme a sentirme mejor.	*Patient:* Okay, I hope you can help me feel better.
Doctor: Los resultados de las pruebas confirman que tiene artritis reumatoide. Hay varias opciones de tratamiento que podemos explorar, como medicamentos antiinflamatorios y terapia física. También puede ser útil hacer algunos cambios en su estilo de vida, como hacer más ejercicio y comer una dieta saludable.	*Doctor:* The test results confirm that you have rheumatoid arthritis. There are several treatment options we can explore, such as anti-inflammatory medication and physical therapy. It may also be helpful to make some changes to your lifestyle, such as exercising more and eating a healthy diet.
Paciente: ¿Puedo seguir trabajando mientras estoy en tratamiento?	*Patient:* Can I continue working while I'm undergoing treatment?
Doctor: Depende de su trabajo y de la gravedad de sus síntomas. Podríamos tener que hacer algunos ajustes a su horario o tareas para que pueda manejar mejor el dolor.	*Doctor:* It depends on your job and the severity of your symptoms. We may need to make some adjustments to your schedule or tasks so that you can better manage the pain.
Paciente: Entiendo, gracias por su ayuda.	*Patient:* I understand, thank you for your help.

Key Takeaways:

- Basic anatomy and physiology terms are essential to communicate effectively in a medical setting.

- Knowing the parts of the body and their functions is crucial to understanding and diagnosing medical conditions and diseases.

- Medical professionals need to be able to communicate with their patients in their language to provide the best possible care.

- Active listening and clear communication are essential to establishing trust and providing accurate diagnoses and treatments.

- The Spanish language is rich in medical vocabulary and expressions that can help healthcare professionals communicate more effectively with Spanish-speaking patients.

Exercises

Exercise 1

Translate the following medical conditions and diseases from English to Spanish.

No.	English	Spanish
1	Asthma	
2	Diabetes	
3	Arthritis	
4	High blood pressure	
5	Migraine	
6	Osteoporosis	
7	Stroke	
8	Breast cancer	
9	Prostate cancer	
10	Alzheimer's disease	

Exercise 2

Match the medical terms in Spanish with their English translations.

1. El corazón   a. Liver

2. El hígado   b. Brain

3. El estómago   c. Heart

4. El cerebro   d. Stomach

5. El riñón   e. Kidney

Exercise 3

Translate the following medical phrases from English to Spanish.

No.	English	Spanish
1	Can you describe your symptoms?	
2	How long have you been feeling this way?	
3	Have you been taking any medication for this?	
4	Please lie down on the examination table.	
5	Take a deep breath and hold it.	

Exercise 4

Create a dialogue between a doctor and a patient. Use at least five body parts and medical terms in Spanish.

Exercise 5

Choose the appropriate medical condition to match the given symptoms.

No.	Symptoms	Medical condition in Spanish
1	A patient complains of chest pain and difficulty breathing.	
2	A patient experiences frequent urination and increased thirst.	
3	A patient has joint pain and stiffness.	
4	A patient has a persistent cough and wheezing.	
5	A patient has sudden weakness or numbness on one side of the body.	

Answer Key

Exercise 1

No.	English	Spanish
1	Asthma	Asma
2	Diabetes	Diabetes
3	Arthritis	Artritis
4	High blood pressure	Hipertensión arterial
5	Migraine	Migraña
6	Osteoporosis	Osteoporosis
7	Stroke	Accidente cerebrovascular
8	Breast cancer	Cáncer de mama
9	Prostate cancer	Cáncer de próstata
10	Alzheimer's disease	Enfermedad de Alzheimer

Exercise 2

1. c
2. a
3. d
4. b
5. e

Exercise 3

No.	English	Spanish
1	Can you describe your symptoms?	¿Puede describir sus síntomas?
2	How long have you been feeling this way?	¿Cuánto tiempo ha estado sintiéndose así?

3	Have you been taking any medication for this?	¿Ha estado tomando algún medicamento para esto?
4	Please lie down on the examination table.	Por favor, acuéstese en la mesa de examen.
5	Take a deep breath and hold it.	Tome una respiración profunda y manténgala.

Exercise 4

Example of possible dialogue:

Doctor: Buenos días, ¿cómo se encuentra hoy?

Paciente: Hola, doctor. Me duele la cabeza y tengo náuseas.

Doctor: Entiendo. ¿Tiene también dolor en el estómago o en el abdomen?

Paciente: Sí, tengo un dolor abdominal y he estado vomitando.

Doctor: De acuerdo, parece que tiene una gastroenteritis. Le recetaré unos medicamentos para aliviar el dolor abdominal y las náuseas. También le sugiero que beba mucho líquido y descanse lo suficiente para que su cuerpo pueda recuperarse.

Paciente: Doctor, también tengo dolor en la espalda y en el cuello.

Doctor: Esto puede ser debido a la tensión muscular. Le recetaré unos relajantes musculares para aliviar el dolor. Además, asegúrese de mantener una buena postura mientras está sentado o de pie para evitar la tensión muscular en el futuro.

Paciente: Muchas gracias, doctor.

Exercise 5

No.	Symptoms	Medical condition in Spanish
1	A patient complains of chest pain and difficulty breathing.	Infarto al miocardio
2	A patient experiences frequent urination and increased thirst.	Diabetes
3	A patient has joint pain and stiffness.	Artritis
4	A patient has a persistent cough and wheezing.	Asma

5	A patient has sudden weakness or numbness on one side of the body.	Accidente cerebrovascular

Chapter II. Medical Procedures and Exams

La agonía física, biológica, natural, de un cuerpo por hambre, sed o frío, dura poco, muy poco, pero la agonía del alma insatisfecha dura toda la vida

Federico García Lorca

In this chapter, we will cover essential medical vocabulary, common questions and phrases, instructions for patients, and examples of conversations to help healthcare professionals learn medical Spanish. This knowledge is vital for communicating with Spanish-speaking patients and providing them with the best care possible. [1, 2]

We will begin by introducing key medical terminology, including terms like "prueba de sangre" (blood test), "radiografía de tórax" (chest x-ray), "resonancia magnética" (MRI), and more. Next, we will provide common questions and phrases to help healthcare professionals establish a rapport with patients and understand their medical history and symptoms. Additionally, we will offer instructions to help healthcare professionals communicate effectively with their patients during and after medical procedures and exams.

Vocabulary for medical procedures and exams in Spanish

Spanish	English
Tomografía computarizada	CT scan
Radiografía	X-ray
Resonancia magnética	MRI
Electrocardiograma	ECG
Examen de sangre	Blood tests
Examen de orina / urinálisis	Urine test
Examen de heces	Stool test
Endoscopía	Endoscopy
Colonoscopía	Colonoscopy

Biopsia	Biopsy
Cirugía	Surgery
Anestesia	Anesthesia
Terapia física	Physical therapy
Terapia ocupacional	Occupational therapy
Terapia del habla	Speech therapy
Terapia respiratoria	Respiratory therapy
Hemodiálisis	Hemodialysis
Quimioterapia	Chemotherapy
Radioterapia	Radiation therapy
Trasplante	Transplant

Common questions and phrases for patient consultations

Asking questions and using phrases in medical Spanish can help patients feel more comfortable and improve communication. Here are some common questions and phrases that can be useful during a patient consultation:

Questions:

Spanish	English
¿Qué síntomas tiene?	What symptoms do you have?
¿Desde cuándo ha tenido estos síntomas?	How long have you had these symptoms?
¿Ha tenido esto antes?	Have you had this before?
¿Está tomando algún medicamento actualmente?	Are you currently taking any medication?
¿Tiene alguna alergia a algún medicamento?	Do you have any allergies to medication?
¿Ha tenido alguna cirugía antes?	Have you had any surgery before?

Spanish	English
¿Ha tenido alguna enfermedad importante en el pasado?	Have you had any significant illness in the past?
¿Tiene algún problema médico crónico?	Do you have any chronic medical condition?
¿Ha estado en contacto con alguien que tenga COVID-19?	Have you been in contact with someone who has COVID-19?
¿Está vacunado contra COVID-19?	Are you vaccinated against COVID-19?

Phrases:

Spanish	English
Hablemos sobre su historial médico.	Let's talk about your medical history.
Vamos a realizar algunos exámenes para diagnosticar su problema.	We will perform some tests to diagnose your problem.
Por favor, siéntese aquí.	Please, have a seat here.
Por favor, respire profundamente.	Please, take a deep breath.
No se preocupe, estamos aquí para ayudarlo.	Don't worry, we are here to help you.
Voy a examinarlo ahora.	I am going to examine you now.
Es posible que sienta un poco de molestia.	You may feel some discomfort.
Necesito que se quite la ropa.	I need you to take off your clothes.
Por favor, espere aquí.	Please, wait here.
Vamos a necesitar que venga para más exámenes.	We will need you to come back for more tests.

How to give instructions to patients in Spanish

Providing clear instructions in medical Spanish is crucial to ensuring patients understand what they need to do. Here are some examples of how to give instructions to patients:

Spanish	English
Tomar la medicación dos veces al día después de las comidas.	Take the medication twice a day after meals.
Beber mucha agua antes del ultrasonido pélvico.	Drink plenty of water before the pelvic ultrasound.
No comer nada después de la medianoche antes de la cirugía.	Do not eat anything after midnight before surgery.
Mantener el área limpia y seca después de la cirugía.	Keep the area clean and dry after surgery.
Descansar y evitar actividades físicas pesadas después de la cirugía.	Rest and avoid heavy physical activities after surgery.
Usar la silla de ruedas si tiene dificultades para caminar.	Use the wheelchair if you have difficulty walking.
Cambiar el vendaje y aplicar la crema en la herida según las instrucciones.	Change the bandage and apply the cream to the wound as directed.
Hacer ejercicios de terapia física según lo indicado.	Do physical therapy exercises as directed.
Evitar comer alimentos grasosos y picantes después de la endoscopia.	Avoid eating fatty and spicy foods after endoscopy.
No tomar nada por vía oral después de la medianoche antes de la colonoscopia.	Do not take anything orally after midnight before colonoscopy.
Realizar ejercicios de respiración profunda después de la cirugía del pecho.	Perform deep breathing exercises after chest surgery.
Usar la máscara de oxígeno según lo indicado.	Use the oxygen mask as directed.
Aplicar hielo en la zona lesionada para reducir la hinchazón.	Apply ice to the injured area to reduce swelling.
Usar un protector solar con un alto factor de protección después de la terapia de radiación.	Use a high SPF sunscreen after radiation therapy.
Evitar conducir después de recibir anestesia.	Avoid driving after receiving anesthesia.

Examples of conversations between doctor/nurses and patients

Conversation 1:

Spanish	Translation
Doctor: Hola, ¿cómo está hoy?	Doctor: Hi, how are you feeling today?
Paciente: Estoy bien, gracias.	Patient: I'm fine, thank you.
Doctor: ¿Qué síntomas tiene?	Doctor: What symptoms do you have?
Paciente: Tengo dolor de cabeza y fiebre.	Patient: I have a headache and a fever.
Doctor: ¿Desde cuándo ha tenido estos síntomas?	Doctor: How long have you had these symptoms?
Paciente: Desde ayer por la noche.	Patient: Since last night.
Doctor: Bien, vamos a realizar algunos exámenes para ver qué está causando su dolor de cabeza y fiebre. También le daré medicamentos para reducir su dolor y fiebre. ¿Tiene alguna alergia a algún medicamento?	Doctor: Alright, we're going to run some tests to see what's causing your headache and fever. I'll also give you medication to help reduce your pain and fever. Do you have any allergies to any medication?
Paciente: Sí, soy alérgico a la penicilina.	Patient: Yes, I'm allergic to penicillin.
Doctor: Muy bien, tendremos en cuenta su alergia al elegir su medicina. ¿Tiene alguna otra pregunta o preocupación?	Doctor: Okay, we'll take note of your allergy when choosing your medication. Do you have any other questions or concerns?
Paciente: No, eso es todo. Gracias, doctor.	Patient: No, that's all. Thank you, doctor

Conversation 2:

Spanish	Translation
Enfermero: Hola, soy el enfermero que lo va a preparar para su cirugía. ¿Está listo para que empecemos?	*Nurse:* Hello, I'm the nurse who will be preparing you for your surgery. Are you ready to begin?
Paciente: Sí, estoy listo.	*Patient:* Yes, I'm ready.

Enfermero: Antes de la cirugía, necesitará quitarse toda la ropa y ponerse esta bata de hospital. También necesitará quitarse cualquier joya o prótesis dental. ¿Hay algo más que necesite saber?	*Nurse:* Before the surgery, you'll need to remove all your clothing and put on this hospital gown. You'll also need to remove any jewelry or dental prostheses. Is there anything else you need to know?
Paciente: No, eso está bien.	*Patient:* No, that's okay.
Enfermero: Bien, ahora vamos a ponerle una vía intravenosa para administrarle los medicamentos durante la cirugía. También le daremos algunos medicamentos para ayudarlo a relajarse antes de la cirugía. ¿Tiene alguna pregunta o preocupación?	*Nurse:* Okay, now we're going to insert an intravenous line to administer medications during the surgery. We'll also give you some medication to help you relax before the surgery. Do you have any questions or concerns?
Paciente: No, estoy un poco nervioso, pero confío en que todo saldrá bien.	*Patient:* No, I'm a little nervous, but I trust everything will go well.
Enfermero: No se preocupe, estará en buenas manos. Vamos a prepararlo para la cirugía ahora.	*Nurse:* Don't worry, you'll be in good hands. Let's prepare you for the surgery now.

Conversation 3:

Spanish	**Translation**
Doctor: Hola, ¿cómo ha estado desde su última visita?	*Doctor:* Hello, how have you been since your last visit?
Paciente: He estado bien, gracias.	*Patient:* I've been good, thank you.
Doctor: Hoy vamos a realizar una endoscopia para ver si hay algún problema en su estómago. ¿Ha seguido las instrucciones para prepararse para la prueba?	*Doctor:* Today we're going to perform an endoscopy to see if there's any problem in your stomach. Have you followed the instructions to prepare for the test?
Paciente: Sí, he seguido las instrucciones y no he comido nada en las últimas 12 horas.	*Patient:* Yes, I have followed the instructions and haven't eaten anything in the last 12 hours.
Doctor: Muy bien, eso es importante para que podamos obtener una imagen clara de su estómago. Durante la prueba, le daremos un	*Doctor:* Very good, that's important so we can get a clear image of your stomach. During the test, we'll give you a sedative to make you more

Spanish	Translation
sedante para que se sienta más cómodo. ¿Tiene alguna pregunta o preocupación?	comfortable. Do you have any questions or concerns?
Paciente: ¿Cómo será la prueba?	*Patient:* What will the test be like?
Doctor: Le insertaremos un tubo flexible en su boca y lo guiaremos hacia su estómago para verlo con una cámara. No sentirá dolor, pero puede sentir algo de presión. La prueba suele durar unos 30 minutos. ¿Tiene alguna otra pregunta?	*Doctor:* We'll insert a flexible tube through your mouth and guide it down to your stomach to see it with a camera. You won't feel any pain, but you may feel some pressure. The test usually lasts about 30 minutes. Do you have any other questions?
Paciente: No, eso está bien. Gracias, doctor.	*Patient:* No, that's okay. Thank you, doctor.

Conversation 4:

Spanish	Translation
Enfermera: Hola, soy la enfermera encargada de su cuidado después de la cirugía. ¿Cómo se siente?	*Nurse:* Hi, I'm the nurse in charge of your care after surgery. How are you feeling?
Paciente: Me duele mucho el área donde me operaron.	*Patient:* The area where I was operated on hurts a lot.
Enfermera: Eso es normal después de la cirugía. Le daremos medicamentos para el dolor. ¿Ha estado respirando profundamente como le indicamos?	*Nurse:* That's normal after surgery. We will give you pain medication. Have you been breathing deeply as instructed?
Paciente: Sí, he estado haciendo los ejercicios de respiración.	*Patient:* Yes, I have been doing the breathing exercises.
Enfermera: Muy bien, eso es importante para prevenir complicaciones después de la cirugía. También necesitamos que se mueva un poco para prevenir coágulos de sangre. ¿Puede levantarse y caminar un poco con nuestra ayuda?	*Nurse:* Very good, that's important to prevent complications after surgery. We also need you to move a little to prevent blood clots. Can you try to get up and walk a bit with our help?
Paciente: Sí, puedo intentarlo.	*Patient:* Yes, I can try.

Enfermera: Muy bien, vamos a ayudarlo a levantarse y caminar. ¿Tiene alguna otra pregunta o preocupación?	*Nurse:* Great, we'll help you get up and walk. Do you have any other questions or concerns?
Paciente: No, eso es todo por ahora. Gracias, enfermera.	*Patient:* No, that's all for now. Thank you, nurse.

Key Takeaways

- Medical Spanish vocabulary for procedures and exams is essential for healthcare professionals working with Spanish-speaking patients.

- Common questions and phrases for patient consultations can help establish clear communication with patients.

- Giving instructions to patients in Spanish requires clear and concise language to ensure they understand what they need to do.

- Conversations between healthcare professionals and patients can vary depending on the situation, but clear communication is key. [3, 4]

Exercises

Exercise 1

Translate the following medical procedures into Spanish:

No.	English	Spanish
1	Blood test	
2	Chest X-ray	
3	MRI	
4	Physical therapy	
5	Endoscopy	

Exercise 2

Complete the following sentences with the correct vocabulary:

a. Después de la cirugía, es importante mantener el área _____ y _____.

b. La endoscopia es un procedimiento para examinar el _____.

c. La _____ es un tipo de terapia que ayuda a mejorar la movilidad

d. La _____ se utiliza para obtener imágenes detalladas del cuerpo.

e. Durante la radiografía de tórax, el paciente debe _____.

Exercise 3

Match the following questions with their appropriate answers:

a. ¿Cómo se siente?

b. ¿Ha seguido las instrucciones?

c. ¿Qué le duele?

d. ¿Cuánto tiempo durará la prueba?

e. ¿Qué vamos a hacer hoy?

i. Vamos a realizar una endoscopia para ver si hay algún problema en su estómago.

ii. Me duele mucho el área donde me operaron.

iii. Hoy vamos a ponerle una vía intravenosa para administrarle los medicamentos durante la cirugía.

iv. La prueba suele durar unos 30 minutos.

v. Sí, he seguido las instrucciones y no he comido nada en las últimas 12 horas.

Exercise 4

Write instructions in Spanish for the following situations:

No.	English	Spanish
1	Instruct a patient to take their medication twice a day with food.	
2	Instruct a patient to drink plenty of water before their MRI.	
3	Instruct a patient to avoid eating or drinking anything after midnight before their surgery.	

Exercise 5

Write a conversation between a doctor and a patient about the patient's upcoming surgery. Use at least 10 vocabulary words related to medical procedures and exams.

Answer Key

Exercise 1

No.	English	Spanish
1	Blood test	Prueba de sangre
2	Chest X-ray	Radiografía de tórax
3	MRI	Resonancia magnética
4	Physical therapy	Terapia física
5	Endoscopy	Endoscopía

Exercise 2

a. Después de la cirugía, es importante mantener el área **limpia** y **seca**.

b. La endoscopia es un procedimiento para examinar el **estómago**.

c. La **terapia física** es un tipo de terapia que ayuda a mejorar la movilidad

d. La **resonancia magnética** se utiliza para obtener imágenes detalladas del cuerpo.

e. Durante la radiografía de tórax, el paciente debe **respirar profundamente**.

Exercise 3

a-ii, b-v, c-ii, d-iv, e-i

Exercise 4

No.	English	Spanish
1	Instruct a patient to take their medication twice a day with food.	Tome su medicamento dos veces al día con comida.
2	Instruct a patient to drink plenty of water before their MRI.	Beba mucha agua antes de su resonancia magnética.
3	Instruct a patient to avoid eating or drinking anything after midnight before their surgery.	Evite comer o beber cualquier cosa después de medianoche antes de su cirugía.

Exercise 5

Example of possible dialogue:

Doctor: Hola, ¿cómo se siente hoy?

Paciente: Un poco nervioso sobre mi cirugía la próxima semana.

Doctor: No se preocupe, todo irá bien. ¿Ha seguido las instrucciones antes de la cirugía?

Paciente: Sí, he dejado de comer o beber desde la noche anterior.

Doctor: Perfecto. Durante la cirugía, le administraremos anestesia para que no sienta dolor. También le pondremos una vía intravenosa para administrarle medicamentos durante la cirugía. Después de la cirugía, necesitará descansar y recuperarse. ¿Tiene alguna otra pregunta?

Paciente: ¿Cuánto tiempo durará la cirugía?

Doctor: La cirugía debería durar unas dos horas. Estaremos monitoreando su condición durante todo el procedimiento. ¿Tiene alguna otra pregunta o preocupación?

Paciente: No, eso es todo. Gracias, doctor.

Chapter III. Prescription and Medication

El buen médico trata la enfermedad; el gran médico trata al paciente que tiene la enfermedad.

William Osler

In this chapter, we will delve into the essential Spanish vocabulary and phrases related to prescription and medication. This is a crucial part of communicating with patients in a healthcare setting, as proper understanding and administration of medications can greatly impact a patient's well-being. By the end of this chapter, you will learn:

- Spanish terms for prescription and medication
- How to ask about allergies and side effects in Spanish
- How to explain dosage and instructions in Spanish
- Common prescription (R.X.) and over-the-counter (OTC) medications in Spanish
- Examples of conversations between doctors/nurses and patients

Spanish terms for prescription and medication

In Spanish, the word for prescription is "receta médica," and medication is "medicamento." Prescriptions may be written by a doctor, "médico," or prescribed by a nurse practitioner, "enfermero especialista." Here are ten examples of essential terms related to prescriptions and medications in Spanish:

Spanish	English
Antibiótico	Antibiotic
Antiinflamatorio	Anti-inflammatory
Analgésico	Pain reliever
Antihipertensivos	Antihypertensive drug
Insulina	Insulin
Esteroides	Steroids
Vacuna	Vaccine

Antidepresivo	Antidepressant

How to ask about allergies and side effects in Spanish

Inquiring about allergies and potential side effects of medications is essential for safeguarding your patient's well-being. It is important to be able to confidently and accurately ask these questions to prevent any adverse reactions and provide appropriate care. Here are ten comprehensive examples of questions in Spanish pertaining to allergies and side effects, along with their English translations:

Spanish	English
¿Es alérgico a algún medicamento?	Are you allergic to any medication?
¿Ha tenido alguna reacción alérgica a algún medicamento en el pasado?	Have you ever had an allergic reaction to any medication in the past?
¿Ha experimentado algún efecto secundario con este medicamento?	Have you experienced any side effects with this medication?
¿Tiene alergia al gluten, lactosa o algún otro componente?	Are you allergic to gluten, lactose, or any other ingredient?
¿Le han recetado este medicamento anteriormente?	Have you been prescribed this medication before?
¿Hay algún medicamento que no pueda tomar?	Is there any medication you cannot take?
¿Experimentó náuseas, vómitos o mareos con este medicamento?	Did you experience nausea, vomiting, or dizziness with this medication?
¿Siente algún dolor o molestia después de tomar el medicamento?	Do you feel any pain or discomfort after taking the medication?
¿Ha notado alguna mejora desde que comenzó a tomar este medicamento?	Have you noticed any improvement since you started taking this medication?

How to explain dosage and instructions in Spanish

Appropriately conveying dosage and instructions for medication is of utmost importance to guarantee that patients adhere to the prescribed treatment regimen accurately and safely. This not only enhances the effectiveness of the medication but also helps in preventing potential side effects or complications. For healthcare professionals working with Spanish-speaking patients, clear communication is key. To assist you in providing accurate and concise information, we have compiled a list of ten essential phrases for explaining dosage and instructions in Spanish:

Spanish	English
Tome una pastilla cada ocho horas.	Take one pill every eight hours.
Tome dos pastillas al día, una por la mañana y otra por la noche.	Take two pills a day, one in the morning and one at night.
Aplique el ungüento en la zona afectada dos veces al día.	Apply the ointment to the affected area twice a day.
Use el inhalador según sea necesario, pero no más de cuatro veces al día.	Use the inhaler as needed, but no more than four times a day.
Inyecte la insulina antes de cada comida.	Inject insulin before each meal.
Agite bien el medicamento antes de usarlo.	Shake the medication well before using it.
No tome este medicamento con el estómago vacío.	Do not take this medication on an empty stomach.
Beba un vaso lleno de agua con cada dosis.	Drink a full glass of water with each dose.
No consuma alcohol mientras toma este medicamento.	Do not consume alcohol while taking this medication.
Si experimenta efectos secundarios graves, comuníquese con su médico de inmediato.	If you experience severe side effects, contact your doctor immediately.

Common R.X. and OTC medications in Spanish

In the world of medicine, there are two main types of medications: prescription medications (R.X.) and over-the-counter medications (OTC).

Prescription medications are those that can only be obtained with a prescription from a licensed healthcare professional. The reason is because these medications are typically more potent and have more potential side effects than over-the-counter medications. They are prescribed for a specific medical condition, and the dosage and duration of treatment are carefully determined by the healthcare provider.

On the other hand, over-the-counter medications are available without a prescription and can be purchased directly from a pharmacy or store. These medications are typically used for mild to moderate symptoms, such as pain, fever, allergies, and indigestion, which are non-serious conditions in most cases. They are generally considered safe when used according to the recommended dosage and for the intended purpose.

In this medical book, we will focus on the most common prescription (R.X.) and over-the-counter (OTC) medications in Spanish. It is very important to know the names of these medications in Spanish for effective communication with Spanish-speaking patients. This knowledge can help ensure that patients receive the appropriate medication and dosage for their medical condition and help prevent potentially harmful medication interactions.

Here are 20 examples of common prescription and over-the-counter medications in Spanish:

R.X. Medications:

Spanish	English
Amoxicilina	Amoxicilin
Cefalexina	Cephalexin
Paracetamol Acetaminofén	Paracetamol (Acetaminophen)
Ibuprofeno	Ibuprofen
Diazepam	Diazepam
Omeprazol	Omeprazole
Enalapril	Enalapril
Metformina	Metformin
Simvastatina	Simvastatin
Insulina	Insulin
Prednisona	Prednisone
Furosemida	Furosemide
Alprazolam	Alprazolam
Ranitidina	Ranitidine
Atorvastatina	Atorvastatin

Losartán	Losartan
Amoxicilina con Ácido Clavulánico	Amoxicillin with Clavulanic Acid
Metoprolol	Metoprolol
Clonazepam	Clonazepam
Levotiroxina	Levothyroxine

OTC Medications:

Spanish	English
Aspirina	Aspirin
Loratadina	Loratadine
Ranitidina	Ranitidine
Naproxeno	Naproxen
Antiácidos	Antiacids
Vitamina C	Vitamin C
Dextrometorfano	Dextromethorphan
Salbutamol	Salbutamol
Ibuprofeno con Pseudoefedrina	Ibuprofen with Pseudoephedrine
Ketoprofeno	Ketoprofen
Paracetamol con Pseudoefedrina	Paracetamol with Pseudoephedrine
Acetaminofén con Codeína	Acetaminophen with Codeine
Clorfeniramina	Chlorpheniramine
Loperamida	Loperamide
Lansoprazol	Lansoprazole

Metamizol	Metamizole
Magnesio	Magnesium

Examples of conversations between doctor/nurses and patients

Conversation 1:

Spanish	Translation
Doctor: Hola, ¿cómo se siente hoy?	*Doctor:* Hi, how are you feeling today?
Paciente: Hola doctor, me duele mucho la garganta y tengo fiebre.	*Patient:* Hi doctor, my throat hurts a lot and I have a fever.
Doctor: Entiendo. ¿Cuántos días lleva con estos síntomas?	*Doctor:* I understand. How long have you had these symptoms?
Paciente: Aproximadamente tres días.	*Patient:* About three days.
Doctor: ¿Ha tomado algún medicamento para aliviar el dolor o la fiebre?	*Doctor:* Have you taken any medication to relieve the pain or fever?
Paciente: Solo he tomado paracetamol, pero no me ha ayudado mucho.	*Patient:* I've only taken paracetamol, but it hasn't helped much.
Doctor: Bien, podría ser una infección bacteriana. ¿Es alérgico a algún medicamento?	*Doctor:* Okay, it could be a bacterial infection. Are you allergic to any medication?
Paciente: Sí, soy alérgico a la penicilina.	*Patient:* Yes, I'm allergic to penicillin.
Doctor: De acuerdo, le recetaré un antibiótico diferente llamado azitromicina. Tome una tableta al día durante cinco días. También puede seguir tomando paracetamol para aliviar el dolor y la fiebre.	Doctor: Alright, I'll prescribe a different antibiotic called azithromycin. Take one tablet a day for five days. You can also continue taking paracetamol to relieve the pain and fever.
Paciente: ¿Hay algún efecto secundario que deba tener en cuenta?	*Patient:* Are there any side effects I should watch out for?
Doctor: Los efectos secundarios más comunes de la azitromicina incluyen náuseas, vómitos, diarrea y dolor de estómago. Si experimenta	*Doctor:* The most common side effects of azithromycin include nausea, vomiting, diarrhea, and stomach pain. If you experience

Spanish	Translation
algún efecto secundario grave, como dificultad para respirar o erupción cutánea, comuníquese con nuestra oficina de inmediato.	any severe side effects, such as difficulty breathing or a rash, please contact our office immediately.
Paciente: Entiendo. Gracias, doctor.	*Patient:* I understand. Thank you, doctor.

Conversation 2:

Spanish	Translation
Enfermera: Buenos días, ¿cómo puedo ayudarle hoy?	*Nurse:* Good morning, how can I assist you today?
Paciente: Hola, estoy aquí para recoger mi receta para la insulina.	*Patient:* Hi, I'm here to pick up my prescription for insulin.
Enfermera: De acuerdo, permítame verificar su información. Mientras tanto, ¿tiene alguna pregunta sobre cómo administrar la insulina?	*Nurse:* Alright, let me check your information. In the meantime, do you have any questions about how to administer insulin?
Paciente: Sí, ¿puede recordarme cuántas unidades debo inyectar antes de las comidas?	*Patient:* Yes, can you remind me how many units I should inject before meals?
Enfermera: Claro, según la receta de su médico, debe inyectarse 10 unidades de insulina antes de cada comida. Asegúrese de seguir las instrucciones al pie de la letra.	*Nurse:* Sure, according to your doctor's prescription, you should inject 10 units of insulin before each meal. Make sure to follow the instructions carefully.
Paciente: También tengo una pregunta sobre cómo almacenar la insulina.	*Patient:* I also have a question about how to store insulin.
Enfermera: Guarde la insulina en el refrigerador hasta que esté lista para usarla. Una vez que la empiece a utilizar, puede guardarla a temperatura ambiente durante un máximo de 28 días. Recuerde no exponerla a temperaturas extremas o luz solar directa.	*Nurse:* Store the insulin in the refrigerator until you are ready to use it. Once you start using it, you can store it at room temperature for a maximum of 28 days. Remember not to expose it to extreme temperatures or direct sunlight.
Paciente: Gracias por la información.	*Patient:* Thank you for the information.

Conversation 3:

Spanish	Translation
Doctor: Hola, ¿cómo ha estado desde nuestra última cita?	*Doctor:* Hi, how have you been since our last appointment?
Paciente: Hola doctor, he estado siguiendo las recomendaciones para mi presión arterial, pero todavía no veo mucha mejoría.	*Patient:* Hi doctor, I have been following the recommendations for my blood pressure, but I still don't see much improvement.
Doctor: Entiendo, ¿ha estado tomando el medicamento para la presión arterial según las indicaciones?	*Doctor:* I understand. Have you been taking the blood pressure medication as directed?
Paciente: Sí, tomo una pastilla de losartán todos los días por la mañana.	*Patient:* Yes, I take one losartan pill every morning.
Doctor: Bien, también es importante mantener una dieta baja en sal y hacer ejercicio regularmente. ¿Ha estado haciendo cambios en su estilo de vida?	*Doctor:* Good. It is also important to maintain a low-salt diet and exercise regularly. Have you been making lifestyle changes?
Paciente: He intentado, pero me cuesta mantener una rutina.	*Patient:* I have tried, but I find it hard to maintain a routine.
Doctor: Comprendo que puede ser difícil, pero es crucial para controlar su presión arterial. Podemos considerar ajustar su medicina si es necesario, pero antes, sigamos trabajando en cambios en su estilo de vida. Puedo recomendarle a un dietista y un especialista en ejercicio para ayudarle en este proceso.	*Doctor:* I understand that it can be difficult, but it is crucial for controlling your blood pressure. We can consider adjusting your medication if necessary, but let's keep working on lifestyle changes first. I can recommend a dietitian and an exercise specialist to help you in this process.
Paciente: Eso sería de gran ayuda, gracias doctor	*Patient:* That would be very helpful, thank you, doctor.

Conversation 4:

Spanish	Translation
Enfermera: Hola, ¿en qué puedo ayudarle hoy?	*Nurse:* Hello, how can I assist you today?

Paciente: Hola, mi médico me recetó un inhalador para el asma, pero no estoy seguro de cómo usarlo correctamente.	*Patient:* Hi, my doctor prescribed me an inhaler for asthma, but I'm not sure how to use it properly.
Enfermera: Claro, puedo mostrarte cómo hacerlo. Primero, agite el inhalador durante unos segundos. Luego, saque el aire de sus pulmones y coloque el inhalador en la boca, asegurándose de que esté bien sellado alrededor de sus labios. Presione la parte superior del inhalador para liberar la medicina mientras inhala lentamente y profundamente.	*Nurse:* Sure, I can show you how to do it. First, shake the inhaler for a few seconds. Then, exhale all the air from your lungs and place the inhaler in your mouth, making sure it is well sealed around your lips. Press the top of the inhaler to release the medicine while inhaling slowly and deeply.
Paciente: ¿Cuánto tiempo debo inhalar?	*Patient:* How long should I inhale for?
Enfermera: Intente inhalar durante unos cinco segundos, luego sostenga la respiración durante 10 segundos para permitir que la medicina se distribuya en los pulmones. Si necesita más de una inhalación, espere al menos un minuto antes de repetir el proceso.	*Nurse:* Try inhaling for about five seconds, then hold your breath for 10 seconds to allow the medicine to distribute into your lungs. If you need more than one inhalation, wait at least one minute before repeating the process.
Paciente: Gracias por la explicación, ahora me siento más seguro al usar mi inhalador.	*Patient:* Thank you for the explanation, I now feel more confident using my inhaler.

Key Takeaways

- Familiarize yourself with essential terms related to prescriptions and medications in Spanish, such as "receta médica" (prescription) and "medicamento" (medication).

- Learn to ask about allergies and side effects in Spanish to ensure patient safety and improve communication.

- Be able to explain dosage and instructions in Spanish, as proper understanding and administration of medications can greatly impact a patient's well-being.

- Know common prescription (R.X.) and over-the-counter (OTC) medications in Spanish to help patients understand their prescribed treatments.

- Practice conversation examples to improve your communication skills in real-life healthcare situations.

Exercises

Exercise 1

Match the Spanish medication name with its English translation.

Spanish	English
Ibuprofeno	A. Ibuprofen
Enalapril	B. Insulin
Insulina	C. Amoxicillin
Amoxicilina	D. Enalapril
Diazepam	E. Diazepam

Exercise 2

Fill in the blank with the appropriate Spanish term.

Antibióticos, Medicamentos, Analgésico, Antihipertensivos, Esteroides, Vacunas, Antiinflamatorios, Antidepresivos.

Los _____ son utilizados para tratar la inflamación y el dolor.

Las _____ se utiliza para prevenir enfermedades infecciosas.

Los _____ se utilizan para tratar el dolor.

Los _____ son utilizados para tratar la presión arterial alta.

Los _____ se utilizan para tratar la inflamación y el dolor.

Los _____ se utilizan para tratar enfermedades mentales como la depresión.

Los _____ se utilizan para tratar infecciones bacterianas.

Los _____ se utilizan para reducir la inflamación y la hinchazón.

Exercise 3

Choose the correct Spanish term to complete the sentence.

1. ¿_____es el medicamento que está tomando?
    A. Cuál
    B. Cómo
    C. Dónde

D. Por qué

2. El médico me recetó un _____ para el dolor de cabeza.

    A. Analgésico
    B. Antiinflamatorio
    C. Antibiótico
    D. Vacuna

3. Tome una pastilla de _____ cada cuatro horas para la fiebre.

    A. Antibiótico
    B. Paracetamol
    C. Antihipertensivos
    D. Esteroides

4. ¿_____ algún efecto secundario con este medicamento?

    A. Tiene
    B. Hace
    C. Come
    D. Necesita

5. El _____ se aplica en la piel para tratar la inflamación.

    A. Antibiótico
    B. Antiinflamatorio
    C. Analgésico
    D. Antidepresivo

Exercise 4

Translate the following sentences into Spanish.

English	Spanish
Take one pill every eight hours.	
Apply the ointment to the affected area twice a day.	
Do not take this medication on an empty stomach.	

Exercise 5

Identify and correct the mistakes in the following Spanish sentences:

Spanish sentence	Correction
Tome una pastilla cada ocha oras.	
Aplique el unguento dos veses al día.	
La vacuna no es necesario para adultos.	
El medicamento se debe tomar antes de la comida.	
Yo necesito comprar un analgésico para mi dolor de cabeza.	

Answer Key

Exercise 1

1. A
2. D
3. B
4. C
5. E

Exercise 2

Los **antiinflamatorios** son utilizados para tratar la inflamación y el dolor.

Las **vacunas** se utilizan para prevenir enfermedades infecciosas.

Los **analgésicos** se utilizan para tratar el dolor.

Los **antihipertensivos** son utilizados para tratar la presión arterial alta.

Los **esteroides** se utilizan para tratar la inflamación y el dolor.

Los **antidepresivos** se utilizan para tratar enfermedades mentales como la depresión.

Los **antibióticos** se utilizan para tratar infecciones bacterianas.

Los **antiinflamatorios** se utilizan para reducir la inflamación y la hinchazón.

Exercise 3

1. ¿_____es el medicamento que está tomando?
   - **A. <u>Cuál</u>**
   - B. Cómo
   - C. Dónde
   - D. Por qué

2. El médico me recetó un _____ para el dolor de cabeza.
   - **A. <u>Analgésico</u>**
   - B. Antiinflamatorio
   - C. Antibiótico
   - D. Vacuna

3. Tome una pastilla de _____ cada cuatro horas para la fiebre.
   - A. Antibiótico
   - **B. <u>Paracetamol</u>**
   - C. Antihipertensivos
   - D. Esteroides

4. ¿_____ algún efecto secundario con este medicamento?

    A. <u>Tiene</u>
    B. Hace
    C. Come
    D. Necesita

5. El _____ se aplica en la piel para tratar la inflamación.

    A. Antibiótico
    B. Antiinflamatorio
    C. Analgésico
    D. Antidepresivo

Exercise 4

English	Spanish
Take one pill every eight hours.	Tome una pastilla cada ocho horas.
Apply the ointment to the affected area twice a day.	Aplique la pomada en la zona afectada dos veces al día.
Do not take this medication on an empty stomach.	No tome este medicamento con el estómago vacío.

Exercise 5

Spanish sentence	Correction
Tome una pastilla cada ocha oras.	Tome una pastilla cada ocho horas. (The correct spelling for "ocho" is with "h", meaning "eight" in English)
Aplique el unguento dos veses al día.	Aplique el ungüento dos veces al día. (The correct spelling is "ungüento" with "ü" and "veces" instead of "veses". "Dos veces al día" means "twice a day" in English)
La vacuna no es necesario para adultos.	La vacuna no es necesaria para adultos. (The correct form is "necesaria" in feminine form, meaning "necessary" in English)
El medicamento se debe tomar antes de la comida.	El medicamento se debe tomar después de la comida. (The correct word is "después" meaning "after" in English. "Antes" means "before".)
Yo necesito comprar un analgésico para mi dolor de cabeza.	The sentence is correct.

Chapter IV. Medical Emergencies

El médico competente, antes de dar una medicina a su paciente, se familiariza no sólo con la enfermedad que desea curar, sino también con los hábitos y la constitución del enfermo.

Marco Tulio Cicerón

This chapter will focus on vocabulary and phrases for emergency situations, which are essential for healthcare professionals when providing care to Spanish-speaking patients. It will cover how to give directions to first responders, communicate with patients during an emergency, and present examples of conversations between healthcare professionals and patients. Key takeaways and interactive exercises will help you learn and practice these critical skills.

As you learn from this chapter, you will be able to make informed decisions and respond rapidly to emergencies involving Spanish-speaking patients. Real-life examples and interactive exercises are included to reinforce your understanding of the vocabulary and phrases, enabling you to handle medical emergencies with greater competence.

Vocabulary and phrases for emergency situations

Medical emergencies can occur unexpectedly, and healthcare professionals must be prepared to provide care to patients from diverse linguistic and cultural backgrounds. Effective communication is essential in these high-pressure situations, especially when time is of the essence. Being proficient in essential Spanish vocabulary and phrases can make all the difference in delivering appropriate care and responding to emergencies competently.

In this chapter, our goal is to equip you with the skills you need to confidently navigate emergency scenarios. You'll learn to give clear directions to first responders, communicate effectively with patients during critical moments, and understand their needs and concerns. We recognize that in emergencies, every second counts. The ability to communicate swiftly and efficiently with first responders is crucial—guiding them to the patient's location and relaying vital information about the patient's condition can significantly impact outcomes.

To support you in these emergency situations, we have compiled a carefully curated list of 20 key phrases that you may find invaluable when providing directions to first responders in Spanish.

Spanish	English
Necesitamos una ambulancia en [dirección].	We need an ambulance at [address].
Hay una emergencia en el tercer piso.	There is an emergency on the third floor.

El paciente está en la sala de espera.	The patient is in the waiting room.
Por favor, sigan a [nombre].	Please follow [person's name].
La entrada principal está bloqueada, usen la entrada lateral.	The main entrance is blocked, use the side entrance.
El paciente se desmayó.	The patient fainted.
La persona herida está en la esquina de [calle] y [calle].	The injured person is at the corner of [street] and [street].
El paciente no puede respirar.	The patient cannot breathe.
El paciente tiene una hemorragia.	The patient is bleeding.
El accidente de tráfico ocurrió en [ubicación].	The car accident occurred at [location].
La persona está inconsciente.	The person is unconscious.
El paciente tiene un dolor intenso en el pecho.	The patient has severe chest pain.
La persona está atrapada en el vehículo.	The person is trapped in the vehicle.
Hay un incendio en [dirección].	There is a fire at [address].
El paciente tiene una reacción alérgica grave.	The patient has a severe allergic reaction.
Por favor, traigan una camilla.	Please bring a stretcher.
El paciente necesita oxígeno.	The patient needs oxygen.
La persona ha sufrido quemaduras.	The person has suffered burns.
Hay múltiples heridos.	There are multiple injured people.
El paciente está en shock.	The patient is in shock.

How to give directions to first responders in Spanish

In an emergency situation, every second is critical. Healthcare professionals must be able to communicate quickly and effectively with first responders, guiding them to the patient's location and providing crucial information about the patient's condition. Here are 20 examples of phrases you might use when giving directions to first responders in Spanish:

Spanish	English
La emergencia es en el segundo piso.	The emergency is on the second floor.
El paciente está en la sala de espera.	The patient is in the waiting room.
Por favor, dirígete a la habitación 210.	Please go to room 210.
Hay un accidente en la entrada principal.	There is an accident at the main entrance.
Necesitamos una ambulancia en el estacionamiento.	We need an ambulance in the parking lot.
El paciente está inconsciente en el pasillo.	The patient is unconscious in the hallway.
La persona herida está al final del pasillo.	The injured person is at the end of the hallway.
Dirígete a la sala de emergencias.	Head to the emergency room.
El paciente tiene dificultad para respirar.	The patient is having difficulty breathing.
Hay una situación crítica en el área de pediatría.	There is a critical situation in the pediatrics area.
Vengan al quirófano lo más rápido posible.	Come to the operating room as quickly as possible.
Necesitamos más personal en el área de trauma.	We need more staff in the trauma area.
El paciente requiere oxígeno de inmediato.	The patient requires oxygen immediately.
Trae un desfibrilador a la habitación 305.	Bring a defibrillator to room 305.
Necesitamos una camilla en el pasillo.	We need a stretcher in the hallway.
Por favor, evalúa la situación en la sala de rayos X.	Please assess the situation in the X-ray room.
Necesitamos un médico en la sala de partos.	We need a doctor in the delivery room.
La víctima del accidente automovilístico acaba de llegar.	A car accident victim has just arrived.

Por favor, envía a un médico a la sala de terapia intensiva.	Please send a doctor to the intensive care unit.
Hay un incendio en el tercer piso; evacúa a los pacientes.	There is a fire on the third floor; evacuate the patients.

How to communicate with patients during an emergency in Spanish

Effective communication with patients during an emergency is essential for ensuring they receive the best possible care when it matters most. In high-stress situations, where emotions may run high and clarity is paramount, being able to connect with Spanish-speaking patients can significantly impact their experience and outcomes.

When communicating with patients in the midst of a crisis, it's important not only to convey medical information but also to provide reassurance and empathy. Patients may be frightened or confused, so using simple, clear language can help them understand what is happening and feel supported throughout the process.

Here are some examples of phrases you might use when talking to a Spanish-speaking patient during an emergency:

Spanish	English
¿Puedes respirar bien?	Can you breathe well?
¿Cuánto tiempo llevas sintiéndote así?	How long have you been feeling like this?
¿Tienes alguna alergia?	Do you have any allergies?
Voy a revisar tus signos vitales.	I'm going to check your vital signs.
¿Puedes decirme tu nombre completo?	Can you tell me your full name?
¿Tienes alguna enfermedad preexistente?	Do you have any pre-existing conditions?
¿Estás tomando algún medicamento?	Are you taking any medication?
Vamos a llevarte al hospital.	We're going to take you to the hospital.
¿Puedes mover tus dedos de los pies y las manos?	Can you move your fingers and toes?
No te preocupes, estás en buenas manos.	Don't worry, you're in good hands.
Voy a ponerte oxígeno.	I'm going to put you on oxygen.

Spanish	Translation
¿Puedes describir el dolor?	Can you describe the pain?
Necesito que te quedes tranquilo/a.	I need you to stay calm.
Voy a realizar una evaluación rápida.	I'm going to perform a quick assessment.
¿Has sufrido alguna lesión en la cabeza?	Have you suffered any head injury?
¿Qué sucedió?	What happened?
¿Tienes algún familiar o amigo a quien podamos llamar?	Do you have any family or friend we can call?
Te estamos llevando al hospital ahora mismo.	We are taking you to the hospital right now.

The ability to communicate effectively in such situations is a valuable skill for any healthcare professional, fostering trust and promoting better patient outcomes.

Examples of conversations between doctor/nurses and patients

Conversation 1:

Spanish	Translation
Doctor: Hola, soy el Dr. Pérez. ¿Cómo te encuentras?	*Doctor:* Hello, I am Dr. Pérez. How are you feeling?
Paciente: Hola, me duele mucho la cabeza y me siento mareado.	*Patient*: Hi, I have a severe headache and feel dizzy.
Doctor: ¿Cuándo empezaron estos síntomas?	*Doctor:* When did these symptoms start?
Paciente: Comenzaron hace unas dos horas.	*Patient:* They began about two hours ago.
Doctor: ¿Has tenido fiebre o escalofríos?	*Doctor*: Have you had a fever or chills?
Paciente: Sí, tuve fiebre alta anoche.	*Patient:* Yes, I had a high fever last night.
Doctor: ¿Has estado en contacto con alguien enfermo recientemente?	*Doctor:* Have you been in contact with anyone sick recently?
Paciente: Mi hermana tuvo gripe la semana pasada.	*Patient:* My sister had the flu last week.

Spanish	Translation
Doctor: ¿Has experimentado algún otro síntoma, como dolor muscular, tos o congestión nasal?	*Doctor*: Have you experienced any other symptoms, such as muscle pain, cough, or nasal congestion?
Paciente: Sí, he tenido tos y dolor en todo el cuerpo.	*Patient*: Yes, I have had a cough and pain all over my body.
Doctor: Vamos a realizar algunas pruebas para determinar la causa de tus síntomas. Mientras tanto, te administraremos medicamentos para aliviar el dolor y la fiebre. Si los resultados indican una infección viral, podríamos recetarte antivirales.	*Doctor:* We will perform some tests to determine the cause of your symptoms. In the meantime, we will administer medications to relieve the pain and fever. If the results indicate a viral infection, we might prescribe antivirals.
Paciente: ¿Cuánto tiempo tardarán los resultados?	*Patient*: How long will the results take?
Doctor: Usualmente, los resultados están disponibles en unas pocas horas. La enfermera te informará cuando estén listos.	*Doctor*: Usually, the results are available in a few hours. The nurse will inform you when they are ready.

Conversation 2:

Spanish	Translation
Enfermera: Hola, soy la enfermera García. ¿Qué te trae al hospital?	*Nurse:* Hello, I am Nurse García. What brings you to the hospital?
Paciente: Me torcí el tobillo mientras jugaba fútbol.	*Patient*: I twisted my ankle while playing soccer.
Enfermera: ¿Puedes describir el dolor? ¿Es constante o intermitente?	*Nurse*: Can you describe the pain? Is it constant or intermittent?
Patient: Es un dolor constante y punzante.	*Patient*: It's a constant, sharp pain.
Nurse: ¿Has aplicado hielo en el área lesionada?	*Nurse*: Have you applied ice to the injured area?
Patient: Sí, pero el dolor sigue siendo intenso.	*Patient*: Yes, but the pain is still intense.
Nurse: Vamos a revisar tu tobillo y realizar algunas pruebas para determinar si hay una	*Nurse*: We will examine your ankle and perform some tests to determine if there is a fracture or

Spanish	Translation
fractura o esguince. Mientras tanto, te proporcionaremos analgésicos y te daremos instrucciones sobre cómo cuidar tu tobillo en casa.	sprain. In the meantime, we will provide painkillers and give you instructions on how to care for your ankle at home.
Patient: ¿Necesitaré una radiografía?	*Patient:* Will I need an X-ray?
Nurse: Sí, una radiografía nos ayudará a evaluar el alcance de la lesión y a descartar cualquier fractura.	*Nurse:* Yes, an X-ray will help us assess the extent of the injury and rule out any fractures.
Patient: ¿Cuánto tiempo tardaré en recuperarme?	*Patient:* How long will it take for me to recover?
Nurse: Dependiendo de la gravedad de la lesión, podrías tardar unas pocas semanas en recuperarte completamente. Te proporcionaremos un plan de tratamiento y posiblemente te vamos a referir a un fisioterapeuta para una rehabilitación adecuada.	*Nurse:* Depending on the severity of the injury, it could take a few weeks to fully recover. We will provide a treatment plan and possibly refer you to a physical therapist for proper rehabilitation.

Conversation 3:

Spanish	Translation
Doctor: ¿Cuál es el problema?	*Doctor:* What is the problem?
Paciente: No puedo respirar bien y me duele el pecho.	*Patient:* I can't breathe well, and my chest hurts.
Doctor: ¿Cuánto tiempo lleva con estos síntomas?	*Doctor:* How long have you had these symptoms?
Paciente: Empezaron hace unas horas.	*Patient:* They started a few hours ago.
Doctor: ¿Tiene antecedentes de problemas cardíacos en su familia?	*Doctor:* Do you have a family history of heart problems?
Paciente: Sí, mi padre tuvo un infarto.	*Patient:* Yes, my father had a heart attack.
Doctor: Vamos a realizar un electrocardiograma y unos análisis de sangre para evaluar su situación.	*Doctor:* We will perform an electrocardiogram and some blood tests to assess your situation.

Spanish	Translation
Paciente: ¿Podría ser algo grave?	*Patient:* Could it be something serious?
Doctor: Podría serlo, pero también podrían ser síntomas de estrés o ansiedad. Es importante que nos aseguremos.	*Doctor:* It could be, but it could also be symptoms of stress or anxiety. It's important that we make sure.
Paciente: Entiendo. ¿Cuánto tiempo tardarán los resultados?	*Patient:* I understand. How long will the results take?
Doctor: Los resultados del electrocardiograma estarán listos en unos minutos. Los análisis de sangre pueden tardar un poco más.	*Doctor:* The electrocardiogram results will be ready in a few minutes. The blood tests may take a bit longer.

Conversation 4:

Spanish	Translation
Enfermera: ¿Qué le sucedió?	*Nurse:* What happened?
Paciente: Me corté con un cuchillo mientras cocinaba.	*Patient:* I cut myself with a knife while cooking.
Enfermera: ¿Sangra mucho?	*Nurse:* Is it bleeding a lot?
Paciente: Sí, no puedo detener la hemorragia.	*Patient:* Yes, I can't stop the bleeding.
Enfermera: Voy a limpiar la herida y luego la suturaré.	*Nurse:* I will clean the wound and then suture it.
Paciente: ¿Duele mucho?	*Patient:* Will it hurt a lot?
Enfermera: Aplicaremos anestesia local antes de suturar para que no sienta dolor. Pero puede sentir algo de incomodidad después.	*Nurse:* We will apply local anesthesia before suturing so you won't feel pain. But you might feel some discomfort afterward.
Paciente: ¿Cuánto tiempo tardará en sanar?	*Patient:* How long will it take to heal?
Enfermera: Dependerá de la profundidad de la herida y cómo la cuides. Por lo general, una herida como esta puede sanar en unas dos semanas.	*Nurse:* It will depend on the depth of the wound and how well you care for it. Typically, a wound like this can heal in about two weeks.

Paciente: ¿Hay algo que deba evitar mientras se cura?	*Patient:* Is there anything I should avoid while it's healing?
Enfermera: Evita mojar la herida y asegúrate de mantenerla limpia y seca. Te daré instrucciones sobre cómo cuidarla adecuadamente.	*Nurse:* Avoid getting the wound wet and make sure to keep it clean and dry. I will give you instructions on how to properly care for it.

Key Takeaways

1. In emergency situations, it's crucial to be able to communicate quickly and effectively with first responders and patients. Mastering Spanish vocabulary and phrases related to emergencies will help you provide better care to Spanish-speaking patients.

2. Giving clear directions to first responders in Spanish can save valuable time during an emergency. Practice using phrases to describe locations and patients' conditions to ensure you can communicate effectively when needed.

3. Communicating with patients in Spanish during an emergency involves asking questions about their symptoms, medical history, and current medications. Understanding and responding to their concerns is essential for providing appropriate care.

4. Familiarize yourself with conversational examples between healthcare professionals and patients to better understand how to communicate in emergency situations.

5. Regular practice and application of the Spanish vocabulary and phrases learned in this chapter will help you become more confident and prepared when faced with medical emergencies involving Spanish-speaking patients.

Exercises

Exercise 1

Translate the following English instructions from Spanish to English.

English	Spanish
Call an ambulance.	
Apply pressure to the wound.	
Perform cardiopulmonary resuscitation (CPR).	
Administer oxygen to the patient.	
Place the patient in the recovery position.	

Exercise 2

Complete the sentences with the appropriate Spanish vocabulary related to medical emergencies.

a) Necesitamos _____ médica urgente. (help)

b) _____ los signos vitales del paciente. (monitor)

c) Use un _____ para detener la hemorragia. (tourniquet)

d) Estabilice el paciente antes de _____. (transport)

e) Tenga listo el equipo de _____. (emergency)

Exercise 3

Role-playing exercise: In pairs, practice a conversation between a healthcare professional and a patient during a medical emergency. One person will act as the healthcare professional, while the other will act as the patient. Switch roles and practice the conversation again.

Exercise 4

Choose the correct Spanish translation for each English phrase.

1. Immobilize the injured area.

    Inmovilice el área lesionada.

    Inmovilice el área cortada.

    Inmovilice el área quemada.

2. Take the patient to the nearest hospital.

> Lleve al paciente al hospital más cercano.

> Lleve al paciente al hospital más al sur.

> Lleve al paciente al hospital más lejano.

3. Have the emergency equipment ready.

> Tenga listo el equipo de emergencia.

> Tenga lejos el equipo de urgencia.

> Tenga fuera el equipo de primeros auxilios.

4. Prepare the automated external defibrillator (AED).

> Prepare el desfibrilador externo automático (DEA).

> Prepare el desfibrilador automático externo (DAE).

> Prepare el desfibrilador externo automático (AED).

5. Perform cardiopulmonary resuscitation (CPR).

> Realice la reanimación cardiopulmonar (RCP).

> Realice la resucitación cardiopulmonar (RCP).

> Realice la reanimación cardiovascular (RCV).

Exercise 5

Translate the following medical emergency instructions from Spanish to English.

Spanish	English
Evacue el área.	
Pida refuerzos si es necesario.	
Comuníquese con el centro de control de envenenamientos.	
Notifique a la familia del paciente.	

Answer Key

Exercise 1

Translate the following English instructions from Spanish to English.

English	Spanish
Call an ambulance.	Llame a una ambulancia.
Apply pressure to the wound.	Aplique presión en la herida.
Perform cardiopulmonary resuscitation (CPR).	Realice la reanimación cardiopulmonar (RCP).
Administer oxygen to the patient.	Administre oxígeno al paciente.
Place the patient in the recovery position.	Coloque al paciente en posición de recuperación.

Exercise 2

Complete the sentences with the appropriate Spanish vocabulary related to medical emergencies.

a) Necesitamos **ayuda** médica urgente. (help)
b) **Monitorice** los signos vitales del paciente. (monitor)
c) Use un **torniquete** para detener la hemorragia. (tourniquet)
d) Estabilice el paciente antes de **transportarlo**. (transport)
e) Tenga listo el equipo de **emergencia**. (emergency)

Exercise 3

Example of a Medical Emergency Conversation

Scenario: A patient has been brought to the emergency room with symptoms of a heart attack. The healthcare professional (Doctor) is assessing the patient's condition and providing initial care.

Doctor: Hola, soy el Dr. López. ¿Puede decirme qué síntomas tiene?

Patient: Hola, doctor. Tengo un fuerte dolor en el pecho y me falta el aliento.

Doctor: ¿Cuánto tiempo hace que comenzaron estos síntomas?

Patient: Empezaron hace aproximadamente una hora.

Doctor: ¿Ha tenido algún episodio similar antes?

Patient: No, esto nunca me había pasado.

Doctor: Vamos a realizar un electrocardiograma (ECG) para evaluar su corazón. Mientras tanto, voy a administrarle medicamentos para aliviar el dolor y mejorar el flujo sanguíneo.

Patient: ¿Qué medicamentos me va a administrar?

Doctor: Le daré aspirina, nitroglicerina y posiblemente un anticoagulante.

Patient: ¿Cuál es el siguiente paso después del electrocardiograma?

Doctor: Si el ECG confirma un ataque cardíaco, podríamos realizar un cateterismo cardíaco para identificar bloqueos y tratar de abrir las arterias bloqueadas.

Patient: ¿Qué puedo hacer para prevenir otro ataque cardíaco en el futuro?

Doctor: Es importante llevar un estilo de vida saludable, que incluya una dieta equilibrada, ejercicio regular, no fumar, controlar el estrés y hacerse revisiones.

[Now, switch roles and practice the conversation again.]

Translation

Doctor: Hello, I am Dr. Lopez. Can you tell me what symptoms you are experiencing?

Patient: Hello, doctor. I have a strong pain in my chest and shortness of breath.

Doctor: How long have you been experiencing these symptoms?

Patient: They started about an hour ago.

Doctor: Have you had any similar episodes before?

Patient: No, this has never happened to me before.

Doctor: We're going to perform an electrocardiogram (ECG) to evaluate your heart. Meanwhile, I'm going to give you medication to relieve the pain and improve blood flow.

Patient: What medication will you give me?

Doctor: I'll give you aspirin, nitroglycerin, and possibly an anticoagulant.

Patient: What's the next step after the electrocardiogram?

Doctor: If the ECG confirms a heart attack, we could perform a cardiac catheterization to identify any blockages and try to open any blocked arteries.

Patient: What can I do to prevent another heart attack in the future?

Doctor: It's important to maintain a healthy lifestyle, which includes a balanced diet, regular exercise, not smoking, managing stress, and getting regular check-ups.

Exercise 4

Choose the correct Spanish translation for each English phrase.

1. Immobilize the injured area.

   Inmovilice el área lesionada.

   Inmovilice el área cortada.

   Inmovilice el área quemada.

2. Take the patient to the nearest hospital.

   Lleve al paciente al hospital más cercano.

   Lleve al paciente al hospital más al sur.

   Lleve al paciente al hospital más lejano.

3. Have the emergency equipment ready.

   Tenga listo el equipo de emergencia.

   Tenga lejos el equipo de urgencia.

   Tenga fuera el equipo de primeros auxilios.

4. Prepare the automated external defibrillator (AED).

   Prepare el desfibrilador externo automático (DEA).

   Prepare el desfibrilador automático externo (DAE).

   Prepare el desfibrilador externo automático (AED).

5. Perform cardiopulmonary resuscitation (CPR).

   Realice la reanimación cardiopulmonar (RCP).

   Realice la resucitación cardiopulmonar (RCP).

   Realice la reanimación cardiovascular (RCV).

Exercise 5

Translate the following medical emergency instructions from Spanish to English.

Spanish	English
Evacue el área	Evacuate the area.
Pida refuerzos si es necesario	Call for backup if necessary.
Comuníquese con el centro de control de envenenamientos	Contact the poison control center.

| Notifique a la familia del paciente | Notify the patient's family. |

BOOK 3

Cultural Competence in Healthcare and Additional Practice

¡ Building Bridges of Understanding: Cultivating Cultural Competence in Healthcare and Beyond!

Explore to Win

Book 3 Description

Welcome to the third part of our series, 'Cultural Competence in Healthcare and Additional Practice.' If you have reached this point, your journey to becoming a truly inclusive and culturally sensitive caregiver continues here, enriching your understanding and skills in medical Spanish.

In this comprehensive guide, you will understand the significance of cultural competence in healthcare interactions with Spanish-speaking patients. As the global landscape becomes increasingly diverse, mastering medical Spanish is not just about language proficiency but also about fostering genuine connections and providing equitable care.

Chapter by chapter, you'll enhance your communication abilities during critical moments, such as medical emergencies, learning essential vocabulary and compassionate phrases to navigate these situations seamlessly. Real-life conversations between doctors/nurses and patients will further solidify your expertise and preparedness.

Beyond language, you'll explore the depths of Hispanic healthcare practices, understanding traditional healing methods, cultural concepts, and the complexities of the Latino family. You'll emerge with a profound appreciation for cultural diversity and the importance of building trust with patients from different backgrounds.

Practice exercises throughout the book will fine-tune your pronunciation, expand your medical vocabulary by specialty, and immerse you in cultural competence scenarios. From mastering the Spanish naming system to utilizing region-specific expressions, these exercises will elevate your language abilities and cultural awareness.

In the appendices, you'll find a wealth of valuable resources at your fingertips, including medical abbreviations, a glossary of medical Spanish terms, conjugations, pronunciation guides, and a Spanish-English and English-Spanish medical dictionary for quick reference.

As you go through this enriching journey, you'll celebrate your milestones and accomplishments in mastering medical Spanish and cultural competence. Embrace diversity and elevate your practice as a culturally competent healthcare professional, empowering yourself to provide truly inclusive care and create meaningful connections with your Spanish-speaking patients.

Are you ready to embark on this transformative path, shaping compassionate and equitable healthcare experiences for all? Let 'Cultural Competence in Healthcare and Additional Practice' be your guide to becoming a true healthcare ally, transcending language barriers, and embracing diversity in the world of medicine.

Chapter I. Introduction

Vivir es extraerse del corazón cada mañana una brasa de sueño para seguir creando.

Josefina Plá

In this third book, we explore the significance of cultural competence in effectively engaging with diverse people and communities, embracing understanding and empathy to bridge differences and foster an inclusive global community.

Step into the realm of 'Cultural Knowledge,' immersing yourself in the rich tapestry of distinct characteristics, histories, values, and behaviors of various ethnic and cultural groups. This essential groundwork sets the stage for the thrilling next phase - 'Cultural Awareness.' Here, embark on a fearless journey of self-exploration, reevaluating and reshaping pre-existing cultural attitudes.

The metamorphosis that unfolds is the very essence of fostering profound understanding and respect between cultures, leading to a lasting impact on your approach to life beyond the pages of this book.

With this foundation, we move into "Cultural Sensitivity." This stage illuminates the rich diversity between cultures without imposing value judgments, highlighting the essence of maintaining respect amidst diversity. It acknowledges cultural differences and mitigates potential conflicts arising from clashing customs and beliefs, a crucial aspect in a multicultural world where internal conflicts can stem from this complex intercultural interaction.

Moving to Cultural Competence, this stage encompasses the appreciation of diversity, which is about respecting differences within and across cultures. It dispels the common misconception that members of the same racial, linguistic, or religious groups share a homogeneous culture. While sharing certain commonalities, individuals within a group can embody unique cultural experiences, particularly apparent when societies merge, and individuals assimilate into new areas, fostering a vibrant mix of subcultures.

Let's illustrate this with the example of healthcare. A medical professional treating a Hispanic patient must comprehend that the Hispanic culture, while united by shared historical and geographical experiences, is far from homogeneous. Each patient brings a unique set of beliefs and norms shaped by their individual experiences. Recognizing and respecting these nuances can enhance communication, promote mutual respect, and foster improved healthcare outcomes.

Dr. Maria was treating Mr. Garcia, an older patient of Mexican descent, for Type 2 Diabetes. Recognizing the importance of individual cultural nuances, she tailored her approach. Instead of imposing a standard diet, she consulted with a nutritionist familiar with Mexican cuisine, creating a customized diet that accommodated Mr. Garcia's cultural food preferences.

She also acknowledged his traditional belief that diseases were a divine test, integrating this belief into her counseling to increase his acceptance of the diagnosis. By involving his family in the treatment process, she leveraged his strong sense of familial responsibility.

Dr. Maria's ability to understand the unique aspects of Mr. Garcia's cultural background fostered improved communication, mutual respect, and more effective healthcare outcomes. This example underscores the importance of recognizing that the Hispanic culture while sharing common roots, consists of diverse individual experiences that healthcare providers must take into account.

At its essence, culture is a dynamic entity shaped by communities or societies. It influences our worldview and outlines our norms, values, and beliefs regarding relationships, lifestyle, environment and organization. Therefore, individuals often belong to multiple cultural groups within any nation, race, or community, each with its distinct set of norms.

"Cultural Identity" encapsulates this fluidity, illustrating an individual's connection to various groups. It's a dynamic entity that continually evolves over an individual's lifetime. Its diverse nature, even among people who identify with the same culture, emphasizes the necessity for an individualized approach in the pursuit of cultural competence.

Through this book, we aim to guide you in comprehending these intricacies and enhancing your cultural competence, facilitating improved communication and understanding in healthcare and beyond.

Chapter II. Enhancing Cultural Competence in Healthcare

Vinieron. Ellos tenían la Biblia y nosotros teníamos la tierra. Nos dijeron: 'Cierren los ojos y recen'.
Cuando abrimos los ojos, ellos tenían la tierra y nosotros teníamos la Biblia.

Eduardo Galeano

In today's diverse healthcare landscape, providing culturally competent care is essential for healthcare professionals. This chapter will focus on enhancing cultural competence in healthcare, specifically for Spanish-speaking patients. The chapter will cover topics such as cultural diversity, effective communication strategies, understanding common patient responses, and the Spanish naming system. By the end of this chapter, readers will have a deeper understanding of how to provide culturally competent care to Spanish-speaking patients.

Cultural Diversity in Healthcare

The Hispanic population is a heterogeneous group of individuals with varying cultural origins and life experiences. While the term "Hispanic" may be used to refer to people with roots in Latin America or Spain, this group encompasses a broad range of cultures, languages, and traditions. For healthcare professionals, it is crucial to understand that the Hispanic population is not monolithic and that cultural differences can significantly impact healthcare outcomes.

In certain Hispanic cultures, the participation of family members in healthcare decision-making may be given precedence. In certain cultural contexts, it is customary to seek the input of family members prior to a patient's decision-making regarding treatment options or to involve them directly in the provision of care. Diverse cultural groups may exhibit a notable inclination towards customary therapeutic interventions or may harbor distinct convictions regarding the etiology and management of illnesses. For instance, some Hispanic patients may prefer herbal remedies or may be hesitant to take medications.

Understanding cultural diversity among Hispanics can help healthcare professionals provide more effective care that is tailored to the unique needs of each patient. This involves not only speaking the patient's language but also being aware of their cultural background and values. By doing so, healthcare professionals can build trust with patients and work collaboratively to achieve positive health outcomes.

To give a few examples of the cultural diversity within the Hispanic population, let's consider the following:

Mexican Americans	Puerto Ricans	Cuban Americans
They are the largest Hispanic subgroup in the United States. Their culture is heavily influenced by indigenous and Spanish traditions, and they may have specific beliefs about health and illness. They may place a strong emphasis on the concept of "hot" and "cold" foods and how they can impact health.	Their culture is a blend of Taíno, African, and Spanish influences, and they may have specific beliefs about health and wellness. They may use "susto," a condition caused by a frightening experience, to explain certain illnesses.	They are a smaller Hispanic subgroup in the United States, and their culture is heavily influenced by Spanish and Afro-Caribbean traditions. They may have specific beliefs about health, curanderismo and wellness, such as the use of santería, a syncretic religion that blends African and Catholic beliefs.

Overall, understanding the cultural diversity among Hispanics is essential to providing culturally competent care in healthcare settings. By recognizing and respecting cultural differences, healthcare professionals can better engage with patients, build trust, and ultimately improve health outcomes.

Providing Culturally Competent Care for Spanish-Speaking Patients

Providing culturally competent care for Spanish-speaking patients requires medical doctors to take the time to understand and respect their patients' cultural backgrounds. Cultural competence involves being aware of cultural differences and how they can impact healthcare, as well as tailoring care to meet the unique needs of each patient.

One way that medical doctors can improve their understanding of Hispanic culture is by working with bilingual staff or medical interpreters. These professionals can help bridge the language barrier and ensure that patients receive accurate information and understand their treatment options. In addition, medical doctors can take the time to learn key phrases in Spanish, such as greetings, medical terms, and common phrases used during medical consultations.

Another important aspect of providing culturally competent care for Spanish-speaking patients is incorporating patient preferences and beliefs into treatment plans. Medical doctors should take the time to understand their patients' beliefs about health and wellness and work to find treatment options that align with these beliefs.

Here are some more examples of different Hispanic cultures and their beliefs in medical care:

Ecuadorian Americans	Dominican Americans	Colombian Americans
They may have a belief in "mal aire," which is a condition caused by exposure to cold or wind. They may also use natural remedies, such as herbs or plant extracts, for common illnesses or seek treatment from traditional healers.	They may have a belief in "mal de ojo," which is a condition caused by being looked at by someone with envy or jealousy. They may also have a strong belief in the healing power of prayer or use natural remedies, such as herbs and teas.	They may have a belief in "limpias," which is a form of spiritual cleansing that is used to rid the body of negative energy. "Susto" is a condition caused by trauma that can cause both physical and mental health problems.

Overall, providing culturally competent care for Spanish-speaking patients requires medical doctors to take a patient-centered approach that is respectful, compassionate, and responsive to their unique needs. By working to understand and respect Hispanic culture, medical doctors can build trust with their patients, improve communication, and ultimately provide better healthcare outcomes.

Effective Communication Strategies for Spanish-Speaking Patients

Effective communication is essential in healthcare, especially when working with Spanish-speaking patients. Some effective communication strategies for Spanish-speaking patients include:

- Using simple and clear language
- Speaking slowly and enunciating clearly
- Avoiding medical jargon and technical terms
- Using visual aids such as diagrams or illustrations
- Checking for understanding by asking patients to repeat or summarize information
- Using interpreters or bilingual staff when necessary
- Using culturally appropriate nonverbal communication, such as eye contact and hand gestures
- Being aware of language barriers and adapting communication strategies accordingly.

Understand common patient responses

Understanding common patient responses is also essential when working with Spanish-speaking patients. Healthcare professionals should be aware of potential responses to certain questions or situations and how to respond appropriately. Some common patient responses in Spanish include:

"Sí" (Yes)

"No" (No)

"No lo sé" (I don't know)

"Me duele aquí" (It hurts here)

"Estoy mareado" (I am dizzy)

"Tengo calor" (I am hot)

"Tengo frío" (I am cold)

"Tengo hambre" (I am hungry)

"Tengo sed" (I am thirsty)

"No puedo respirar" (I can't breathe)

"Me siento débil" (I feel weak)

"Me siento enfermo" (I feel sick)

"Me siento cansado" (I feel tired)

"Me siento mejor" (I feel better)

"Me siento peor" (I feel worse)

"Me duele la cabeza" (I have a headache)

"Me siento triste" (I feel sad)

"Me siento ansioso/a" (I feel anxious)

"Me falta el aire" (I am short of breath)

"Me duele el estómago" (I have stomach pain)

"Me duele el pecho" (I have chest pain)

"Me duele la espalda" (I have back pain)

"Me duele la garganta" (I have a sore throat)

"Me duele la pierna" (I have leg pain)

"Me duele el brazo" (I have arm pain)

"Me duele el oído" (I have ear pain)

"Me duele el diente" (I have a toothache)

"Me duele el cuerpo" (I have body pain)

"Tengo un resfriado" (I have a cold)

"Tengo la gripe" (I have the flu)

"Tengo alergia a" (I have allergy to)

"Tengo una infección" (I have an infection)

"Tengo una herida aquí" (I have a wound here)

"Me fracturé el brazo" (I broke my arm)

"Gracias" (Thank you)

"De nada" (You're welcome)

"Lo siento" (I'm sorry)

"No hay problema" (No problem)

"Adiós" (Goodbye)

Understand the Spanish naming system and identify common errors made by Spanish-speaking patients

Understanding the Spanish naming system is crucial for healthcare professionals working with Spanish-speaking patients. While the typical Spanish surname includes both a paternal and maternal surname, there are variations among different Hispanic cultures. For example, in some cultures, such as Mexican and Colombian, it is common for individuals to use both their paternal and maternal surnames, while in other cultures, such as Cuban and Puerto Rican, it is more common to use only the paternal surname.

Furthermore, there are common errors that Spanish-speaking patients may make when providing their names to healthcare professionals. These errors can include omitting a surname, using a surname that is not legally recognized, or providing an incorrect spelling of their name. Healthcare professionals should take the time to confirm and verify the patient's name, using identification documents if necessary, to ensure accurate medical record keeping.

It is also important for healthcare professionals to be aware of the potential impact of cultural differences on patients' names. For example, some Hispanic cultures may have different naming traditions for children, such as using family names or names of religious significance. Healthcare professionals should be sensitive to these differences and respect the patient's naming preferences.

Here, you can find some examples of differences in the Spanish naming system among different Hispanic cultures:

Region	Naming system

Mexican Americans	They often use both paternal and maternal surnames, such as Rodriguez Garcia.
Puerto Ricans	They typically use only the paternal surname, such as Rodriguez.
Cuban Americans	They may use both paternal and maternal surnames, but the paternal surname is typically listed first, such as Rodriguez Garcia.
Salvadoran Americans	They often use both paternal and maternal surnames, but the paternal surname is typically listed first, such as Rodriguez Garcia.
Dominican Americans	They typically use both paternal and maternal surnames, such as Rodriguez Garcia, but may also use a maternal surname as a middle name, such as Rodriguez de Garcia.
Colombian Americans	They often use both paternal and maternal surnames, such as Garcia Rodriguez.
Ecuadorian Americans	They may use both paternal and maternal surnames, but the paternal surname is typically listed first, such as Rodriguez Garcia.
Venezuelan Americans	They may use both paternal and maternal surnames, but the paternal surname is typically listed first, such as Rodriguez Garcia.
Peruvian Americans	They may use both paternal and maternal surnames, such as Garcia Rodriguez.
Argentinian Americans	Argentinian Americans, like most Hispanic groups, typically use both paternal and maternal surnames, with the paternal surname listed first, such as Rodriguez Garcia.

Overall, understanding the Spanish naming system and identifying common errors is essential for healthcare professionals working with Spanish-speaking patients. By being aware of cultural differences and respecting patients' naming preferences, healthcare professionals can build trust and rapport with their patients and provide more effective and culturally competent care.

Key Takeaways

- Understanding cultural diversity among Hispanics is essential to providing culturally competent care.
- Communicating in Spanish and understanding cultural differences can improve healthcare outcomes.

- Effective communication strategies for Spanish-speaking patients include using simple language, visual aids, and nonverbal communication.
- Healthcare professionals should be aware of common patient responses in Spanish and how to respond appropriately.
- Understanding the Spanish naming system and common errors made by Spanish-speaking patients can improve the accuracy of patient information.

Exercises

Exercise 1

Choose the correct answer for the following questions:

1. What is an effective communication strategy for Spanish-speaking patients?
    A. Using complex medical terminology
    B. Speaking quickly
    C. Using visual aids such as diagrams or illustrations
    D. Not checking for understanding

2. Why is it important for healthcare professionals to understand the cultural diversity among Hispanics?
    A. It is not important
    B. To provide effective care that is tailored to the unique needs of each patient
    C. To discriminate against certain cultures
    D. To provide ineffective care

3. What is one way that medical doctors can improve their understanding of Hispanic culture?
    A. Avoiding working with bilingual staff
    B. Speaking only English
    C. Learning key phrases in Spanish
    D. Disrespecting patients' cultural beliefs

4. What is the typical naming convention for Cuban Americans?
    A. They typically use both paternal and maternal surnames, with the paternal surname listed first.
    B. They typically use only the paternal surname.
    C. They typically use both paternal and maternal surnames, but the maternal surname is typically listed first.
    D. They typically use both paternal and maternal surnames, with the maternal surname listed first.

5. Why is it important for healthcare professionals to understand common patient responses in Spanish?
    A. It is not important
    B. To provide inaccurate information
    C. To ignore the patient's concerns
    D. To respond appropriately to certain questions or situations

Exercise 2

Fill in the blanks with the appropriate word(s) from the chapter:

1. Understanding cultural diversity among Hispanics can help healthcare professionals provide more _____ care that is tailored to the unique needs of each patient.

2. One way that medical doctors can improve their understanding of Hispanic culture is by working with _____ or medical interpreters.

3. _____ are often consulted before a patient makes a decision about treatment or may play an active role in the care process in some Hispanic cultures.

4. Understanding the Spanish naming system is crucial for healthcare professionals working with Spanish-speaking patients to ensure accurate _____.

5. Effective communication is essential in healthcare, especially when working with _____ patients.

Words: Spanish speaking, bilingual staff, medical record-keeping, family members, effective

Exercise 3

Indicate whether the following statements are true or false:

1. Healthcare professionals should use complex medical terminology when communicating with Spanish-speaking patients.

2. Understanding the cultural diversity among Hispanics is not important when providing healthcare.

3. Using visual aids such as diagrams or illustrations is an effective communication strategy for Spanish-speaking patients.

4. Healthcare professionals should disregard the cultural beliefs and values of their patients.

5. The typical naming convention for Mexican Americans is to use only the paternal surname.

Exercise 4

Match the Hispanic culture with their typical naming convention (they are not in order):

Hispanic Culture	Naming convention
Mexican Americans	They typically use only the paternal surname.
Puerto Ricans	They typically use both paternal and maternal surnames, with the paternal surname listed first.
Cuban Americans	They typically use both paternal and maternal surnames, but the maternal surname is typically listed first.
Salvadoran Americans	They typically use both paternal and maternal surnames, with the paternal surname listed first.

Exercise 5

Provide a short answer to the following questions:

1. Why is it important for healthcare professionals to check for understanding when communicating with Spanish-speaking patients?

2. What is an example of a cultural difference that may impact healthcare outcomes for Hispanic patients?

3. What are some effective communication strategies for Spanish-speaking patients?

4. Why is it important for healthcare professionals to understand common patient responses in Spanish?

5. What is the typical naming convention for Colombian Americans?

Answer Key

Exercise 1

1. What is an effective communication strategy for Spanish-speaking patients?

    A. Using complex medical terminology
    B. Speaking quickly
    C. Using visual aids such as diagrams or illustrations
    D. Not checking for understanding

2. Why is it important for healthcare professionals to understand the cultural diversity among Hispanics?

    A. It is not important
    B. To provide effective care that is tailored to the unique needs of each patient
    C. To discriminate against certain cultures
    D. To provide ineffective care

3. What is one way that medical doctors can improve their understanding of Hispanic culture?

    A. Avoiding working with bilingual staff
    B. Speaking only English
    C. Learning key phrases in Spanish
    D. Disrespecting patients' cultural beliefs

4. What is the typical naming convention for Cuban Americans?

    A. They typically use both paternal and maternal surnames, with the paternal surname listed first.
    B. They typically use only the paternal surname.
    C. They typically use both paternal and maternal surnames, but the maternal surname is typically listed first.
    D. They typically use both paternal and maternal surnames, with the maternal surname listed first.

5. Why is it important for healthcare professionals to understand common patient responses in Spanish?

    A. It is not important
    B. To provide inaccurate information
    C. To ignore the patient's concerns
    D. To respond appropriately to certain questions or situations

Exercise 2

1. Understanding cultural diversity among Hispanics can help healthcare professionals provide more **effective** care that is tailored to the unique needs of each patient.

2. One way that medical doctors can improve their understanding of Hispanic culture is by working with **bilingual** staff or medical interpreters.

3. **Family members** are often consulted before a patient makes a decision about treatment or may play an active role in the care process in some Hispanic cultures.

4. Understanding the Spanish naming system is crucial for healthcare professionals working with Spanish-speaking patients to ensure accurate **medical record keeping.**

5. Effective communication is essential in healthcare, especially when working with **Spanish-speaking** patients.

Exercise 3

1. False
2. False
3. True
4. False
5. False

Exercise 4

Hispanic Culture	Naming convention
Mexican Americans	They typically use both paternal and maternal surnames, with the paternal surname listed first.
Puerto Ricans	They typically use only the paternal surname
Cuban Americans	They typically use both paternal and maternal surnames, with the paternal surname listed first.
Salvadoran Americans	They typically use both paternal and maternal surnames, but the paternal surname is typically listed first.

Exercise 5

1. What is an example of a cultural difference that may impact healthcare outcomes for Hispanic patients?

   Answer: One example of a cultural difference that may impact healthcare outcomes for Hispanic patients is the preference for traditional healing practices over Western medicine, which may lead to noncompliance with treatment plans.

2. What are some effective communication strategies for Spanish-speaking patients?

Answer: Effective communication strategies for Spanish-speaking patients include using simple and clear language, speaking slowly and enunciating clearly, avoiding medical jargon and technical terms, using visual aids such as diagrams or illustrations, checking for understanding by asking patients to repeat or summarize information, and using interpreters or bilingual staff when necessary.

3. Why is it important for healthcare professionals to understand common patient responses in Spanish?

   Answer: It is important for healthcare professionals to understand common patient responses in Spanish to respond appropriately to certain questions or situations, which can help ensure accurate diagnosis and treatment.

4. What is the typical naming convention for Colombian Americans?

   Answer: The typical naming convention for Colombian Americans is to use both paternal and maternal surnames, such as Garcia Rodriguez.

Chapter III. Cultural Concepts in Hispanic Healthcare

La atención médica efectiva requiere una comprensión de los conceptos y prácticas culturales

Elena Rios

In this chapter, we will explore cultural concepts that are important for healthcare professionals to understand when working with Hispanic patients. We will discuss how to build trust in the Hispanic community, traditional healing practices such as curanderismo and chamanismo, common ailments such as el empacho, mal de ojo, and susto, navigating formal and familiar settings in Hispanic healthcare, cultural considerations for healthcare in the United States, the importance of the Latino family in healthcare, and finally, key takeaways and exercises to reinforce your understanding of these concepts.

Building Trust

Building trust is crucial in the Hispanic community. Hispanics place a great deal of importance on personal relationships, and building a relationship with your patient can go a long way towards developing trust. In order to build trust, it is important to take the time to listen to your patient and address their concerns. This means taking the time to explain procedures and treatments in a way that is easy to understand and being open to answering any questions they may have. In addition, it is important to be respectful and culturally sensitive when working with Hispanic patients.

Traditional Healing Practices: Curanderismo and Chamanismo

Curanderismo and chamanismo are traditional healing practices that are still used by many Hispanics today. While both practices involve the use of herbs and natural remedies, they have distinct differences. Curanderismo is a Mexican folk healing practice that combines indigenous healing methods with Catholicism. It is often used to treat physical, emotional, and spiritual ailments. Chamanismo, on the other hand, is a spiritual practice that originated in the Andes and Amazon regions of South America. It involves the use of shamanic rituals and ceremonies to heal both physical and emotional ailments.

While both practices have some similarities, they also have some notable differences:

Similarities	Differences
• Both practices have their roots in indigenous traditions and beliefs.	• Curanderismo is primarily focused on healing physical, emotional, and spiritual

- Both practices are based on the idea of maintaining balance and harmony between the body, mind, and spirit.
- Both practices view illness as a result of imbalance, either physical or spiritual.
- Both practices use natural remedies such as herbs and plants to promote healing.
- Both practices emphasize the importance of spiritual connection and involve rituals and ceremonies to achieve this connection.

ailments, while Chamanismo is focused mainly on spiritual healing.
- Curanderismo is heavily influenced by Catholicism, while Chamanismo has its roots in indigenous beliefs from the Andes and Amazon regions of South America.
- Curanderismo practitioners are known as curanderos, while Chamanismo practitioners are known as shamans.
- Curanderismo often involves the use of objects such as candles, amulets, and crosses in rituals, while Chamanismo involves the use of music and dance.
- Curanderismo is more prevalent in Mexico and other parts of Central America, while Chamanismo is more prevalent in South America.

In summary, while both Curanderismo and Chamanismo share some commonalities, such as a focus on natural remedies, spiritual connection, and the importance of maintaining balance, they also have some distinct differences, such as their primary focus, cultural roots, and specific practices.

Understanding Common Ailments: El Empacho, Mal de Ojo, and Susto

In Hispanic communities, there are several common ailments that have spiritual and cultural roots. It is important for healthcare professionals to understand these ailments in order to provide effective care to Hispanic patients. Three of the most common ailments are El Empacho, Mal de Ojo, and Susto.

Empacho	El Empacho is a condition caused by overeating or eating something that is difficult to digest. It can cause stomach pain, nausea, and vomiting. The traditional treatment for El Empacho involves a curandero, or traditional healer, who will use massage techniques to help move the food through the digestive system. For example, a curandero may use a technique called "sobar el estómago," which involves massaging the stomach in a circular motion to help ease the symptoms of El Empacho.
Mal de ojo	Mal de Ojo, or the evil eye, is a condition believed to be caused by a person with negative energy or bad intentions. It can cause headaches, stomach pain, and general malaise. The traditional treatment for Mal de Ojo involves a curandero who will use various methods to remove the bad energy from the

	patient. For example, a curandero may use an egg to draw out the negative energy, or perform a cleansing ritual involving herbs and prayer.
Susto	Susto is a condition that is believed to be caused by a traumatic event or scare. It can cause a variety of physical and emotional symptoms, including insomnia, loss of appetite, and anxiety. The traditional treatment for Susto involves a curandero who will use various methods to help the patient recover their lost soul. For example, a curandero may perform a cleansing ritual or use herbs and other natural remedies to help the patient regain their strength.

It is important for healthcare professionals to be aware of these common ailments and to approach them with cultural sensitivity and respect. While these ailments may have spiritual and cultural roots, it is also important to address any physical symptoms that may be present and to provide appropriate medical treatment as necessary.

Navigating Formal and Familiar Settings in Hispanic Healthcare

Hispanics in the USA: Cultural Considerations for Healthcare

When working with Hispanic patients in the United States, it is important to be aware of cultural differences and to be sensitive to them; this will provide better care and communication towards Hispanic patients. In the US, all Hispanics come from a variety of countries and cultural backgrounds, and it is important to understand, as healthcare professionals, the specific cultural norms and values of the patient you are working with. Take the example mentioned earlier: Hispanics often place a strong emphasis on family and community, and it is important to involve family members in healthcare decisions whenever possible.

Also, it is important in the medical-patient environment to be aware of the specific cultural norms and values of the Hispanic community they are working with. For example, Mexican-Americans may have different cultural norms and values than Puerto Ricans or Cuban-Americans. Understanding these differences can help healthcare professionals provide more effective and culturally sensitive care.

Defining Hispanic or Latino: Understanding Identity

The terms Hispanic and Latino are often used interchangeably, but they actually have different meanings. Understanding the identity of Hispanics and Latinos is important for healthcare professionals who work with these communities.

Hispanic typically refers to people from Spanish-speaking cultures or countries, including Spain and many Latin American countries. However, it generally excludes Brazil since Portuguese, not Spanish, is spoken there. Latino (or Latina for females) refers to people from Latin America, including Brazil, because it's based on geography and cultural ties rather than language. However, it excludes Spain as Spain is in Europe, not Latin America.

Also, remember to recognize that not all Hispanics or Latinos share the same cultural background or identity. Many Hispanics and Latinos also identify with their specific country of origin and may have strong ties to that culture. For example, a person who is Puerto Rican may identify as Hispanic or Latino, but they may also identify specifically as Puerto Rican and have a strong connection to Puerto Rican culture and traditions.

Identity is complex in all cultures, and healthcare professionals need to be aware of their patients' diverse identities and backgrounds. By learning about their patients' cultural norms and values, healthcare professionals can provide more effective and culturally sensitive care.

On the other hand, recognize that identity is fluid, and people may identify with different aspects of their identity at different times in their lives. For example, a person who was born in Mexico and raised in the United States may identify as Mexican-American or Hispanic, but they may also identify as American and have a strong connection to American culture. Any identity Is valid and should be respected.

The Importance of the Latino Family in Healthcare

The Latino family plays a significant role in healthcare decisions. It is common for family members to be involved in healthcare decisions, and they may also be responsible for providing care for their loved ones at home. It is important for healthcare professionals to involve family members in the care process and to be sensitive to the family dynamics and cultural norms that may be at play.

Key Takeaways

- Building trust is crucial in the Hispanic community and involves listening to your patient, being open to answering questions, and being respectful and culturally sensitive.

- Curanderismo and chamanismo are traditional healing practices that emphasize spirituality and the connection between the body, mind, and spirit.

- El empacho, mal de ojo, and susto are common ailments in Hispanic communities that have spiritual and cultural roots.

- Hispanic healthcare settings can be divided into formal and familiar settings, and it is important to be professional and respectful in formal settings and to use informal language in familiar settings.

- Hispanics in the United States come from a variety of countries and cultural backgrounds, and it is important to be aware of cultural differences and to involve family members in healthcare decisions whenever possible.

Exercises

Exercise 1: Building Trust

Match the following actions with the strategies to build trust with Hispanic patients:

Actions	Strategies
1. Take the time to listen to your patient. 2. Address their concerns. 3. Explain procedures and treatments in an easy-to-understand way. 4. Be respectful and culturally sensitive.	a. Develop a personal relationship with your patient. b. Use informal language in familiar settings. c. Involve family members in healthcare decisions. d. Be open to answering any questions your patient may have.

Exercise 2: Traditional Healing Practices

Fill in the blanks with the appropriate words or phrases from the table:

Curanderismo is a Mexican folk healing practice that combines _____ healing methods with _____. It is often used to treat physical, emotional, and spiritual ailments. Chamanismo, on the other hand, is a spiritual practice that originated in the _____ regions of South America. It involves the use of shamanic rituals and ceremonies to heal both physical and emotional ailments. While both practices have their roots in indigenous traditions and beliefs, Curanderismo is primarily focused on healing physical, emotional, and spiritual ailments, while Chamanismo is focused mainly on _____ healing.

Exercise 3: Common Ailments

Choose the appropriate treatment for each of the following common ailments:

1. El Empacho
   a. A curandero will use massage techniques to help move the food through the digestive system.
   b. A curandero will use an egg to draw out the negative energy.
   c. A curandero will use various methods to help the patient recover their lost soul.

2. Mal de Ojo
   a. A curandero will use massage techniques to help move the food through the digestive system.
   b. A curandero will use an egg to draw out the negative energy.
   c. A curandero will use various methods to remove the bad energy from the patient.

3. Susto
   a. A curandero will use massage techniques to help move the food through the digestive system.
   b. A curandero will use an egg to draw out the negative energy.
   c. A curandero will use various methods to help the patient recover their lost soul.

Exercise 4: Cultural Differences

Match the following cultural norms or values with the Hispanic community they are commonly associated with:

Cultural Norms/Values Hispanic Community

1. Strong emphasis on family and community	a. Mexican-Americans
2. Influence of Catholicism on healing practices	b. Puerto Ricans
3. More prevalent in Mexico and Central America	c. Curanderismo
4. More prevalent in South America	d. Chamanismo
5. Different cultural norms and values based on specific country of origin	e. Hispanics/Latinos in general

Exercise 5: Cultural Sensitivity

Match the following actions with the strategies for demonstrating cultural sensitivity in healthcare:

Actions	Strategies
Be aware of cultural differences.	a. Use formal language in formal settings.
Involve family members in healthcare decisions.	b. Understand the specific cultural norms and values of the patient.
Use appropriate language and terminology.	c. Be aware of the cultural significance of certain practices or objects.
Respect personal space and touch boundaries.	d. Recognize that the patient's cultural background may influence their health beliefs and practices.

Answer Key

Exercise 1: Building Trust

1. Develop a personal relationship with your patient. (a)
2. Be open to answering any questions your patient may have. (d)
3. Explain procedures and treatments in an easy-to-understand way. (b)
4. Be respectful and culturally sensitive. (c)

Exercise 2: Traditional Healing Practices

Curanderismo is a Mexican folk healing practice that combines **Mexican folk** healing methods with **Catholicism**. It is often used to treat physical, emotional, and spiritual ailments. Chamanismo, on the other hand, is a spiritual practice that originated in the **Andes and Amazon** regions of South America. It involves the use of shamanic rituals and ceremonies to heal both physical and emotional ailments. While both practices have their roots in indigenous traditions and beliefs, Curanderismo is primarily focused on healing physical, emotional, and spiritual ailments, while Chamanismo is focused mainly on **spiritual** healing.

Exercise 3: Common Ailments

1. El Empacho - a. A curandero will use massage techniques to help move the food through the digestive system.
2. Mal de Ojo - c. A curandero will use various methods to remove the bad energy from the patient.
3. Susto - c. A curandero will use various methods to help the patient recover their lost soul.

Exercise 4: Cultural Differences

1. Strong emphasis on family and community - e. Hispanics/Latinos in general
2. Influence of Catholicism in healing practices - c. Curanderismo
3. More prevalent in Mexico and Central America - a. Mexican-Americans
4. More prevalent in South America - d. Chamanismo
5. Different cultural norms and values based on specific country of origin - b. Puerto Ricans

Exercise 5: Cultural Sensitivity

Actions	Strategies
Be aware of cultural differences.	b. Understand the specific cultural norms and values of the patient.

Involve family members in healthcare decisions.	d. Recognize that the patient's cultural background may influence their health beliefs and practices.
Use appropriate language and terminology.	a. Use formal language in formal settings.
Respect personal space and touch boundaries.	c. Be aware of the cultural significance of certain practices or objects.

Chapter IV. Additional Practice Exercises

Sólo los que tienen la paciencia de hacer cosas simples con precisión y dedicación alcanzarán la habilidad de hacer cosas difíciles con facilidad y excelencia

James J. Corbett

Congratulations on making it this far in your journey to learn medical Spanish! In this chapter, we will explore additional practice exercises that will help you reinforce what you have learned so far and improve your skills in speaking and understanding medical Spanish. The exercises in this chapter will challenge you to apply your knowledge to various contexts, improve your listening comprehension, and review your vocabulary in a fun and engaging way. Let's dive in!

Spanish pronunciation exercises

To effectively speak Spanish, having a good grasp of its pronunciation is crucial. It not only ensures that you are understood but also helps you sound more natural and confident. This section provides a few exercises that can aid you in perfecting your Spanish pronunciation.

Exercise 1: Vowels

As we mentioned in previous chapters, Spanish vowels differ from English vowels in that they have a consistent sound. There are five vowels in Spanish: a, e, i, o, and u. Here are a few exercises to assist you in correctly pronouncing these vowels:

- Begin by saying each vowel sound slowly and clearly: a, e, i, o, u.
- Next, try pronouncing these vowel sounds in various combinations, such as ae, ei, io, ou, and au.
- Finally, practice saying words that contain each vowel sound, like casa (house), perro (dog), libro (book), ojo (eye), and uva (grape).

Exercise 2: Consonants

Although many Spanish consonants sound the same as their English counterparts, some have distinct pronunciations. Here are a few exercises to assist you in correctly pronouncing Spanish consonants:

- To practice the "rr" sound, try saying "perro" (dog) and "ferrocarril" (railroad) slowly while rolling your tongue.
- To practice the "j" sound, emphasize the "j" sound while saying "joven" (young) and "jardín" (garden) slowly.

- To practice the "ñ" sound, emphasize the "ñ" sound while saying "mañana" (tomorrow) and "muñeca" (doll) slowly.

Medical Spanish vocabulary and exercises by specialty

Depending on your specialty, you may need to know more specific medical terms. Here are some examples:

- Cardiology:

    El infarto (heart attack): el in-FAR-toh

    La arritmia (arrhythmia): lah ah-REE-mee-ah

    El cateterismo cardíaco (cardiac catheterization): el kah-teh-teh-REES-moh kar-dee-AH-koh

- Pediatrics:

    La vacuna (vaccine): lah bah-koo-nah

    La diarrea (diarrhea): lah dee-ah-RREH-ah

    El asma (asthma): el AHS-mah

- Obstetrics and Gynecology:

    El embarazo (pregnancy): el em-bah-RAH-soh

    La cesárea (cesarean section): lah seh-SAH-reh-ah

    El parto (birth): el PAHR-toh

- Neurology:

    La migraña (migraine): lah me-GRAH-nyah

    El accidente cerebrovascular (stroke): el ahk-see-DEN-teh seh-reh-broh-vas-KOO-lar

    Epilepsia (epilepsy): lah eh-pee-LEP-see-ah

- Ophthalmology:

    Astigmatismo (astigmatism, ah-steeg-ma-TEES-mo)

    Catarata (cataract, kah-tah-RAH-tah)

    Conjuntivitis (conjunctivitis, kohn-hoon-tee-VEE-tis)

- Dermatology:

    Dermatitis (dermatitis, der-mah-TEE-tis)

    Eczema (eczema, ehk-SEH-ma)

    Melanoma (melanoma, meh-lah-NOH-ma)

- Endocrinology:

Diabetes (diabetes, dee-ah-BEH-tehs)

Tiroides (thyroid, tee-roy-DEHS)

Insulina (insulin, een-SOO-lee-nah)

- Gastroenterology:

Gastroenteritis (gastroenteritis, gas-tro-en-teh-REE-tis),

Ulcera (ulcer, OOL-seh-rah),

Colitis (colitis, koh-LEE-tis)

- Pulmonology:

Neumonía (pneumonia, new-moh-NEE-ah)

Bronquitis (bronchitis, bron-kee-TEES)

Enfisema (emphysema, en-fee-SEH-ma)

- Urology:

Cistitis (cystitis, sis-TYE-tis)

Nefritis (nephritis, neh-FRY-tis)

Prostatitis (prostatitis, proh-stuh-TYE-tis)

- Nephrology:

Insuficiencia renal (renal insufficiency, in-suh-fish-EN-see-uh ree-nuhl)

Nefropatía diabética (diabetic nephropathy, neh-froh-PAY-thee-uh dye-uh-BET-ik-uh)

Síndrome nefrótico (nephrotic syndrome, neh-FROT-ik sin-drohm)

- Infectology:

Sepsis (sepsis, SEP-sis)

Meningitis (meningitis, men-in-JYE-tis)

Tuberculosis (tuberculosis, too-ber-kyoo-LOH-sis)

Exercise 2: Medical Vocabulary Practice

To practice your medical vocabulary in Spanish, try the following exercises:

1. Create flashcards with Spanish medical terms on one side and their definitions on the other. Practice regularly until you can quickly and confidently recall the meanings.

2. Read medical texts or articles in Spanish, and look up any unfamiliar words.

   Some examples include:

- "¿Qué es la presión arterial?" - This is a simple article explaining what blood pressure is and how it is measured. It was published on the Spanish Ministry of Health website.
- "Prevención de enfermedades cardio y cerebrovasculares" - This is a short article with five tips for maintaining good health and preventing diseases. It was published on the website of the Spanish Ministry of Health.
- "Beneficios del ejercicio físico en población sana e impacto sobre la aparición de enfermedad" - This is an article about the health benefits of physical exercise, including tips for getting started. It was published on the website of the Elsevier.

3. Listen to Spanish-language medical podcasts, lectures, or webinars to become more familiar with medical terms and their usage.

   You can find them easily on Youtube, Spotify, Coursera, Doc Molly, etc.

4. Translate English medical terms into Spanish, and vice versa, to build your vocabulary and understanding of medical terminology in both languages.

Exercise 3: Medical Language Exchange

Find a language exchange partner who is a native Spanish speaker and works in healthcare. Practice speaking with each other and taking turns discussing healthcare topics in both languages. This will allow you to improve your fluency, build your vocabulary, and learn about healthcare practices and culture in Spanish-speaking countries.

Role-playing exercises for diverse medical scenarios

By simulating real-life medical scenarios, you can gain confidence in using medical Spanish terminology and phrases. Here are ten role-playing exercises for diverse medical scenarios:

Patient history	You are a medical professional taking a patient's history. The patient is a Spanish speaker who is experiencing stomach pain. Ask the patient about their symptoms, including when the pain started, the location of the pain, and any other relevant information.
Prescription refills	You are a pharmacist speaking with a Spanish-speaking patient about their prescription refill. Confirm the patient's name and date of birth, ask about any allergies or side effects, and provide instructions for taking the medication.
Physical exam	You are a medical professional performing a physical exam on a Spanish-speaking patient. Ask the patient to describe any pain or discomfort, use medical terminology to explain the exam, and provide instructions for follow-up care.

Emergency room	You are a medical professional in the emergency room treating a Spanish-speaking patient who is experiencing chest pain. Ask the patient about their symptoms, take their vital signs, and provide emergency treatment.
Pregnancy check-up	You are a medical professional conducting a check-up on a Spanish-speaking pregnant patient. Ask the patient about their symptoms, take their blood pressure and weight, and provide advice for prenatal care.
Mental health consultation	You are a mental health professional conducting a consultation with a Spanish-speaking patient who is experiencing anxiety. Use medical terminology to explain the diagnosis, provide advice for coping with anxiety, and recommend treatment options.
Vaccine administration	You are a nurse administering a vaccine to a Spanish-speaking patient. Use medical terminology to explain the purpose of the vaccine, confirm the patient's identity, and provide instructions for follow-up care.
Dental exam	You are a dentist performing an exam on a Spanish-speaking patient. Ask the patient about their dental history, use medical terminology to explain the exam, and provide instructions for follow-up care.
Physical therapy session	You are a physical therapist conducting a session with a Spanish-speaking patient who is recovering from an injury. Use medical terminology to explain the exercises, provide advice for recovery, and recommend follow-up care.
Health education	You are a healthcare professional providing health education to a Spanish-speaking patient. Use medical terminology to explain the importance of healthy habits, recommend lifestyle changes, and provide resources for additional information.

Some expressions by region

Spanish is spoken in many countries, and each region has its own unique expressions and slang. Here are some common expressions used in different regions of Latin America:

- Mexico: "Qué onda" - How's it going?
- Guatemala: "Pura vida" - Pure life (used to express positivity)
- Colombia: "Chévere" - Cool or great
- Venezuela: "Chamo" - Dude or guy
- Peru: "Chamba" - Work or job

- Argentina: "Boludo" - Stupid or idiot (can also be used affectionately between friends)
- Chile: "Cachai" - Do you understand?
- Ecuador: "Chévere" - Cool or great (similar to Colombia)
- Costa Rica: "Mae" - Dude or guy (similar to Venezuela)
- Cuba: "Qué bola" - What's up?
- Dominican Republic: "Diache" - Wow or oh my god
- Puerto Rico: "Bregar" - To work hard or hustle
- Uruguay: "Laburar" - To work
- Panama: "Sancocho" - A traditional soup made with chicken, plantains, and other ingredients
- Bolivia: "Achachay" - Expression used to express cold or chilliness
- Honduras: "Galillo" - Traditional Honduran dish made with rice, vegetables, and meat
- Nicaragua: "Nica" - Colloquial term for a Nicaraguan person
- El Salvador: "Pupusa" - Traditional Salvadoran dish made with corn masa and filled with cheese, beans, or meat
- Paraguay: "Chipa" - Traditional Paraguayan bread made with manioc flour and cheese
- Brazil: "Saudade" - A feeling of nostalgia or longing for someone or something

By practicing these role-playing exercises, improving your pronunciation, and learning some common expressions used in different regions of Latin America, you can enhance your ability to communicate with Spanish-speaking patients in a medical setting. Always approach patients with cultural sensitivity and respect and seek out resources to continue improving your medical Spanish skills.

Cultural competence scenarios

One crucial aspect of providing quality healthcare is cultural competence. As a healthcare professional, you must be able to communicate effectively with patients from diverse cultural backgrounds. In this exercise, we will explore some scenarios that require cultural competence.

Scenario 1	You are a nurse working in a pediatric clinic, and a Spanish-speaking mother brings in her child for a routine check-up. During the examination, you notice that the child has a rash on his face. The mother tells you that she has been using a traditional home remedy to treat the rash, and the rash has not improved. How would you handle this situation?
	To handle this scenario effectively, you must first acknowledge the mother's concern and show respect for her cultural practices. You can then explain that the rash may require medical treatment and offer to prescribe a medication that is safe and effective for the child's age.

Scenario 2	You are a physician assistant working in an urgent care clinic, and a Spanish-speaking patient comes in with severe abdominal pain. The patient's family members are also present and insist on staying in the exam room during the consultation. How would you handle this situation?	
	In this scenario, it is essential to be sensitive to the patient's cultural values and preferences. You can explain to the patient and their family members that it is standard practice to examine the patient in a private room to ensure their comfort and confidentiality. You can also offer to provide an interpreter if necessary to ensure that the patient's concerns are fully understood.	
Scenario 3	You are a physical therapist working with a Spanish-speaking patient who has recently immigrated to the United States. During the evaluation, you notice that the patient is hesitant to participate in the therapy exercises and seems uncomfortable. How would you handle this situation?	
	In this scenario, it is essential to recognize the potential cultural barriers that may be impacting the patient's comfort and participation in therapy. You can start by acknowledging the patient's cultural background and asking if there are any cultural practices that you should be aware of. You can also explain the importance of the therapy exercises and offer to modify the exercises to better suit the patient's needs and preferences. Additionally, you can consider enlisting the help of a cultural liaison or interpreter to facilitate communication and ensure that the patient is comfortable and engaged in the therapy process.	

Vocabulary review games

Vocabulary review games can be a fun and engaging way to practice medical terminology in Spanish. Here are a few games that you can try:

Game 1	Flashcard Relay	Divide into teams and create flashcards with medical terms in Spanish on one side and their English translations on the other. The first team member runs to the board and picks up a flashcard, reads the Spanish term aloud, and then passes the card to the next team member, who reads the English translation. The first team to finish the relay wins.
Game 2	Medical Bingo	Create bingo cards with medical terms in Spanish in each square. Call out the English translations, and players must mark off the corresponding square on their bingo card. The first player to get bingo wins.

Game 3	Medical Pictionary	Divide into teams and have one team member draw a medical term in Spanish while the other team members try to guess the term. The first team to guess correctly wins a point. Rotate roles so that each team member gets a chance to draw.

Listening comprehension

Listening comprehension is a crucial skill in medical Spanish. In this exercise, you will listen to audio recordings of medical conversations or lectures in Spanish and answer questions about what you heard. You can find resources online, such as Spanish-language medical podcasts or lectures, or create your own recordings.

Here are a few examples of questions you could ask:

1. What is the patient's chief complaint?
2. What medications is the patient taking?
3. What is the diagnosis?
4. What treatment options are being discussed?
5. What is the patient's prognosis?

This exercise will help you improve your ability to understand spoken medical Spanish, which is especially important when communicating with patients who may not be fluent in English.

Conclusion

In this chapter, we explored additional practice exercises that will help you improve your medical Spanish skills. Cultural competence scenarios, vocabulary review games, and listening comprehension exercises will challenge you to apply your knowledge in different contexts, reinforce your vocabulary, and improve your listening comprehension. Remember to practice regularly, immerse yourself in Spanish-language healthcare contexts, and seek opportunities to speak with native Spanish speakers to continue improving your skills. With dedication and persistence, you will be able to speak medical Spanish confidently and effectively in no time!

Chapter V. Appendices

The patient is the most important person in the hospital.

Sister Mary Jean Dorcy

The appendices contain various resources, such as a list of basic medical abbreviations in Spanish, terms, conjugations, pronunciation guides, and a comprehensive Spanish-English and English-Spanish medical dictionary.

Medical abbreviations in Spanish

In the medical field, abbreviations are commonly used to save time and space. However, it is important to note that not all medical abbreviations in Spanish have the same meaning as their English counterparts. Here are 50 commonly used medical abbreviations in Spanish:

Abbreviation	Spanish meaning	English meaning
AC	Antes de comer	Before eating
BM	Biometría hemática	Complete blood count
CC	Centímetros cúbicos	Cubic centimeters
EKG	Electrocargiograma	Electrocardiogram
IM	Intramuscular	Intramuscularly
IV	Intravenoso	Intravenously
PA	Presión arterial	Blood pressure
Rx	Receta	Prescription
Px	Paciente	Patient
SNG	Sonda nasogástrica	Nasogastric tube
TA	Tensión arterial	Blood pressure
TB	Tuberculosis	Tuberculosis

TBC	Test de tuberculina	Tuberculin test
TPR	Temperatura, pulso, respiración	Temperature, pulse, respiration
UCI	Unidad de cuidados intensivos	Intensive care unit
UCIN	Unidad de Cuidados Intensivos Neonatales	Neonatal Intensive Care Unit
URO	Urología	Urology
VHC	Virus de la hepatitis C	Hepatitis C virus
VO	Vía Oral	Orally
VS	Vía subcutánea	Subcutaneously
VHB	Virus de la hepatitis B	Hepatitis B virus
VIH	Virus de la inmunodeficiencia humana	Human immunodeficiency virus
OMS	Organización Mundial de la Salud	World Health Organization
TC	Tomografía computarizada	Computed tomography
RM	Resonancia magnética	Magnetic resonance
EEG	Electroencefalograma	Electroencephalogram
TO	Terapia ocupacional	Occupational therapy
TH	Terapia del habla	Speech therapy
TF	Terapia física	Physical therapy
AAS	Ácido acetilsalicílico	Acetylsalicylic acid
AB	Aborto	Abortion
ACTH	Hormona adrenocorticótropa	Adrenocorticotropic hormone
AGA	Adecuado para la edad gestacional	Adequate for gestational age
ALAT	Alanina aminotransferasa	Alanine aminotransferase

BCG	Bacilo de Calmette y Guérin	Bacillus of Calmette and Guérin
BPD	Displasia broncopulmonar	Bronchopulmonary dysplasia
EPOC	Enfermedad Pulmonar Obstructiva Crónica	Chronic Obstructive Pulmonary Disease
GGT	Gamma glutamil transferasa	Gamma glutamyl transferase
Hb	Hemoglobina	Hemoglobin
HCG	Gonadotropina coriónica humana	Human chorionic gonadotropin
HTA	Hipertensión arterial	Arterial hypertension
DM	Diabetes mellitus	Diabetes mellitus
IVU	Infección de vías urinarias	Urinary tract infection
PCR	Reacción en cadena de la polimerasa	Polymerase Chain Reaction
PTH	Hormona paratiroidea	Parathyroid hormone
TSH	Hormona estimulante de la tiroides	Thyroid-stimulating hormone

Glossary of basic medical Spanish terms

In this glossary, we have compiled a list of the basic medical Spanish terms studied in the first three books. We have also included their English translations.

Spanish	English
Corazón	Heart
Riñón	Kidney
Pulmón	Lung
Hígado	Liver
Cerebro	Brain
Sangre	Blood

Hueso	Bone
Cáncer	Cancer
Infección	Infection
Diabetes	Diabetes
Enfermedad	Disease
Fiebre	Fever
Dolor	Pain
Presión arterial	Blood pressure
Vacuna	Vaccine
Tratamiento	Treatment
Antibiótico	Antibiotic
Inflamación	Inflammation
Radiografía	X-ray
Nutrición	Nutrition
Paciente	Patient
Terapia	Therapy
Síntomas	Symptoms
Salud	Health
Cirugía	Surgery
Emergencia	Emergency
Dosis	Dose
Medicamento	Medication
Venas	Veins

Músculo	Muscle
Hormona	Hormone
Terapeuta	Therapist
Especialista	Specialist
Epidemia	Epidemic
Contagio	Contagion
Medicina	Medicine
Órganos	Organs
Enfermera	Nurse
Deshidratación	Dehydration
Asma	Asthma
Infarto	Heart attack
Anestesia	Anesthesia
Trasplante	Transplant
Hemorragia	Hemorrhage
Psiquiatría	Psychiatry
Traumatismo	Trauma
Síndrome	Syndrome
Virus	Virus
Quimioterapia	Chemotherapy
Radioterapia	Radiation therapy

Human body systems and apparatuses

Sistema circulatorio	Circulatory system

Sistema digestivo	Digestive system
Sistema endocrino	Endocrine system
Sistema inmunológico	Immune system
Sistema nervioso	Nervous system
Sistema respiratorio	Respiratory system
Sistema urinario	Urinary system

Prescription and Medication

Antibiótico	Antibiotic
Antiinflamatorio	Anti-inflammatory
Analgésico	Pain reliever
Antihipertensivos	Antihypertensive drug
Insulina	Insulin
Esteroides	Steroids
Vacuna	Vaccine
Antidepresivo	Antidepressant

Rx Medication

Amoxicilina	Amoxicillin
Cefalexina	Cephalexin
Paracetamol Acetaminofén	Paracetamol (Acetaminophen)
Ibuprofeno	Ibuprofen
Diazepam	Diazepam
Omeprazol	Omeprazole

Enalapril	Enalapril
Metformina	Metformin
Simvastatina	Simvastatin
Insulina	Insulin
Prednisona	Prednisone
Furosemida	Furosemide
Alprazolam	Alprazolam
Ranitidina	Ranitidine
Atorvastatina	Atorvastatin
Losartán	Losartan
Amoxicilina con Ácido Clavulánico	Amoxicillin with Clavulanic Acid
Metoprolol	Metoprolol
Clonazepam	Clonazepam
Levotiroxina	Levothyroxine

OTC medication

Aspirina	Aspirin
Loratadina	Loratadine
Ranitidina	Ranitidine
Naproxeno	Naproxen
Antiácidos	Antiacids
Vitamina C	Vitamin C
Dextrometorfano	Dextromethorphan
Salbutamol	Salbutamol

Ibuprofeno con Pseudoefedrina	Ibuprofen with Pseudoephedrine
Ketoprofeno	Ketoprofen
Paracetamol con Pseudoefedrina	Paracetamol with Pseudoephedrine
Acetaminofén con Codeína	Acetaminophen with Codeine
Clorfeniramina	Chlorpheniramine
Loperamida	Loperamide
Lansoprazol	Lansoprazole
Metamizol	Metamizole
Magnesio	Magnesium

Clinical and imaging studies

Tomografía computarizada	CT scan
Radiografía	X-ray
Resonancia magnética	MRI
Electrocardiograma	ECG
Examen de sangre	Blood tests
Examen de orina / urinálisis	Urine test
Examen de heces	Stool test
Endoscopía	Endoscopy
Colonoscopía	Colonoscopy
Biopsia	Biopsy
Cirugía	Surgery
Anestesia	Anesthesia
Terapia física	Physical therapy

Terapia ocupacional	Occupational therapy
Terapia del habla	Speech therapy
Terapia respiratoria	Respiratory therapy
Hemodiálisis	Hemodialysis
Quimioterapia	Chemotherapy
Radioterapia	Radiation therapy
Trasplante	Transplant

Conjugations and Pronunciation guides

To communicate effectively with Spanish-speaking patients, it is essential for healthcare professionals to know the correct conjugations of verbs and the proper pronunciation of words. Here are 20 examples of verb conjugations and pronunciation guides:

Hablar (to speak)	
Yo hablo	I speak
Tú hablas	You speak
Él/ella habla	He/she speaks
Nosotros/as hablamos	We speak
Ellos/ellas hablan	They speak
Ustedes hablan	You all speak
Pronunciation: ah-blahr	

Escuchar (to listen)	
Yo escucho	I listen
Tú escuchas	You listen

Él/ella escucha	He/she listens
Nosotros/as escuchamos	We listen
Ustedes escuchan	You all listen
Ellos/ellas escuchan	They listen

Pronunciation: ess-koo-char

Preguntar (to ask)

Yo pregunto	I ask
Tú preguntas	You ask
Él/ella pregunta	He/she asks
Nosotros/as preguntamos	We ask
Ustedes preguntan	You all ask
Ellos/ellas preguntan	They ask

Pronunciation: preh-goon-tahr

Explicar (to explain)

Yo explico	I explain
Tú explicas	You explain
Él/ella explica	He/she explains
Nosotros/as explicamos	We explain
Ustedes explican	You all explain
Ellos/ellas explican	They explain

Pronunciation: ess-plee-kahr

Comprender (to understand)

Yo comprendo	I understand
Tú comprendes	You understand
Él/ella comprende	He/she understands
Nosotros/as comprendemos	We understand
Ustedes comprenden	You all understand
Ellos/ellas comprenden	They understand
Pronunciation: kohm-prehn-dehr	

Decir (to say)

Yo digo	I say
Tú dices	You say
Él/ella dice	He/she says
Nosotros/as decimos	We say
Ustedes dicen	You all say
Ellos/ellas dicen	They say
Pronunciation: deh-seer	

Hacer (to do/make)

Yo hago	I do/make
Tú haces	(You do/make)

Él/ella hace	He/she does/makes
Nosotros/as hacemos	We do/make
Ustedes hacen	You all do/make
Ellos/ellas hacen	They do/make
Pronunciation: ah-sehr	

Tomar (to take)

Yo tomo	I take
Tú tomas	You take
Él/ella toma	He/she takes
Nosotros/as tomamos	We take
Ustedes toman	You all take
Ellos/ellas toman	They take
Pronunciation: toh-mahr	

Cuidar (to care for)

Yo cuido	I care for
Tú cuidas	You care for
Él/ella cuida	He/she cares for
Nosotros/as cuidamos	We care for
Ustedes cuidan	You all care for
Ellos/ellas cuidan	They care for
Pronunciation: kwee-dahr	

Ayudar (to help)

Yo ayudo	I help
Tú ayudas	You help
Él/ella ayuda	He/she helps
Nosotros/as ayudamos	We help
Ustedes ayudan	You all help
Ellos/ellas ayudan	They help
Pronunciation: ah-yoo-dahr	

Examinar (to examine)

Yo examino	I examine
Tú examinas	You examine
Él/ella examina	He/she examines
Nosotros/as examinamos	We examine
Ustedes examinan	You all examine
Ellos/ellas examinan	They examine
Pronunciation: ess-kah-mee-nahr	

Tratar (to treat)

Yo trato	I treat
Tú tratas	You treat

Él/ella trata	He/she treats
Nosotros/as tratamos	We treat
Ustedes tratan	You all treat
Ellos/ellas tratan	They treat
Pronunciation: trah-tahr	

Recetar (to prescribe)

Yo receto	I prescribe
Tú recetas	You prescribe
Él/ella receta	He/she prescribes
Nosotros/as recetamos	We prescribe
Ustedes recetan	You all prescribe
Ellos/ellas recetan	They prescribe
Pronunciation: reh-seh-tahr	

Curar (to cure)

Yo curo	I cure
Tú curas	You cure
Él/ella cura	He/she cures
Nosotros/as curamos	We cure
Usteden curan	You all cure
Ellos/ellas curan	They cure
Pronunciation: koo-rahr	

Diagnosticar (to diagnose)

Yo diagnostic	I diagnose
Tú diagnosticas	You diagnose
Él/ella diagnostica	He/she diagnoses
Nosotros/as diagnosticamos	We diagnose
Ustedes diagnostican	You all diagnose
Ellos/ellas diagnostican	They diagnose
Pronunciation: dee-ahg-nos-tee-kahr	

Monitorear (to monitor)

Yo monitoreo	I monitor
Tú monitoreas	You monitor
Él/ella monitorea	He/she monitors
Nosotros/as monitoreamos	We monitor
Usteden monitorean	You all monitor
Ellos/ellas monitorean	They monitor
Pronunciation: moh-nee-toh-reh-ahr	

Prevenir (to prevent)

Yo prevengo	I prevent
Tú previenes	You prevent

Él/ella previene	He/she prevents
Nosotros/as prevenimos	We prevent
Ustedes previenen	You all prevent
Ellos/ellas previenen	

Pronunciation: preh-veh-neer

Desinfectar (to disinfect)

Yo desinfecto	I disinfect
Tú desinfectas	You disinfect
Él/ella desinfecta	He/she disinfects
Nosotros/as desinfectamos	We disinfect
Ustedes desinfectan	You all disinfect
Ellos/ellas desinfectan	They disinfect

Pronunciation: deh-seen-fehk-tahr

Operar (to operate)

Yo opero	I operate
Tú operas	You operate
Él/ella opera	He/she operates
Nosotros/as operamos	We operate
Ustedes operan	You all operate
Ellos/ellas operan	They operate

Pronunciation: oh-peh-rahr

Vacunar (vaccinate)	
Yo vacuno	I vaccinate
Tú vacunas	You vaccinate
Él/ella vacuna	He/she vaccinates
Nosotros/as vacunamos	We vaccinate
Ustedes vacunan	You vaccinate
Ellos/ellas vacunan	They vaccinate
Pronunciation: bah-koo-nahr	

Spanish-English and English-Spanish medical dictionary

A medical dictionary can be a valuable resource for healthcare professionals who need to communicate with Spanish-speaking patients. Here are some examples of basic medical terms and their translations:

A	
Abdomen	Abdomen
Aborto	Abortion
Absceso	Abscess
Acné	Acne
Agudo	Acute
Adicción	Addiction
Alergia	Allergy
Ambulancia	Ambulance
Anemia	Anemia

Anestesia	Anesthesia
Aneurisma	Aneurysm
Anorexia	Anorexia
Antibiótico	Antibiotic
Ansiedad	Anxiety
Arritmia	Arrhytmia
Atrofia	Atrophy
Avulsión	Avulsion
Adrenérgico	Adrenergic
Afasia	Aphasia
Aterioesclerosis	Atherosclerosis

B

Bacteria	Bacteria
Bazo	Spleen
Biopsia	Biopsy
Bronquitis	Bronchitis
Boca	Mouth
Brazo	Arm
Bulto	Lump
Bebé	Baby
Bilirrubina	Bilirubin
Benigno	Benign

Bocio	Goiter
Bacteremia	Bacteria in the bloodstream
Brote	Outbreak
Bilis	Bile
Bolo Alimenticio	Bolus Feed

C

Cabeza	Head
Cáncer	Cancer
Células	Cells
Corazón	Heart
Cerebro	Brain
Cirugía	Surgery
Columna vertebral	Spine
Cuerpo	Body
Cicatriz	Scar
Cáncer de mama	Breast cancer
Cáncer de próstata	Prostate cancer
Colecistitis	Cholecystitis
Catarata	Cataract
Cálculo	Stone
Cápsula	Capsule

D

Dolor	Pain
Dedo	Finger
Diente	Tooth
Diarrea	Diarrhea
Depresión	Depression
Digestión	Digestion
Dermatitis	Dermatitis
Dolor de cabeza	Headache
Dolor de espalda	Back pain
Dolor abdominal	Abdominal pain
Deshidratación	Dehydration
Dismenorrea	Dysmenorrhea
Displasia	Dysplasia
Dolor torácico	Chest pain

E

Enfermedad	Illness
Estómago	Stomach
Espalda	Back
Esófago	Esophagus
Enfermedad cardiovascular	Cardiovascular disease
Enfermedad respiratoria	Respiratory disease
Enfermedad infecciosa	Infectious disease

Epidemia	Epidemic
Enfermedad crónica	Chronic disease
Edema	Edema
Encefalitis	Encephalitis
Enfermedad renal	Kidney disease
Eritema	Erythema
Esclerosis multiple	Multiple sclerosis

F

Fiebre	Fever
Fractura	Fracture
Flema	Phlegm
Fatiga	Fatigue
Faringitis	Pharyngitis
Fosas nasales	Nasal cavities
Feto	Fetus
Fibrilación auricular	Atrial fibrillation
Fibroma	Fibroma
Fibrosis	Fibrosis
Fístula	Fistula
Fisioterapia	Physiotherapy
Flatulencia	Flatulence
Flujo vaginal	Vaginal discharge

Fascitis	Fasciitis
G	
Garganta	Throat
Gripe	Flu
Gangrena	Gangrene
Gastroenteritis	Gastroenteritis
Ginecología	Gynecology
Genitales	Genitals
Glaucoma	Glaucoma
Gingivitis	Gingivitis
Gonorrea	Gonorrhea
Granuloma	Granuloma
Glándula	Gland
Glóbulo rojo	Red blood cell
Gota	Gout
H	
Hígado	Liver
Herida	Wound
Hipertensión	Hypertension
Hemorragia	Hemorrhage
Hueso	Bone
Hueso fracturado	Fractured brone

Hemofilia	Hemophilia
Hiperactividad	Hyperactivity
Hipercolesterolemia	Hypercholesterolemia
Hipertermia	Hypertermia
Hematoma	Hematoma
Hidratación	Hydration
Hidrocefalia	Hydrocephalus
Hiperplasia	Hyperplasia
Hipoglucemia	Hypoglucemia

I

Infección	Infection
Immunidad	Immunity
Inflamación	Inflammation
Influenza	Influenza
Insuficiencia cardíaca	Heart failure
Insulina	Insulin
Ictericia	Jaundice
Inyección	Injection
Isquemia	Ischemia
Infarto	Infarction
Incontinencia urinaria	Urinary incontinence
Insuficiencia renal	Renal insufficiency

Intoxicación	Intoxication
Íleo	Ileus
Impétigo	impetigo

J

Jeringa	Syringe
Jugo gástrico	Gastric juice
Joroba	Hump
Jarabe	Syrup
Juanete	Bunion

K

Kinesioterapia	Kinesiotherapy
Kilcaloría	Kilocalorie
Ketonemia	Ketonemia
Ketosis	Ketosis
Kinasa	Kinasa
Ketonuria	Ketonuria

L

Laringe	Larynx
Líquido cefalorraquídeo	Cerebrospinal fluid
Llaga	Sore
Laringitis	Laryngitis
Lengua	Tongue

Lesión	Injury
Linfoma	Lymphoma
Linfoadenopatía	Lymphadenopathy

M

Médico	Physician
Mujer	Woman
Músculo	Muscle
Muela	Tooth
Molestia	Discomfort
Mareo	Dizziness
Muela del juicio	Wisdom tooth
Melanoma	Melanoma
Miastenia	Myasthenia
Miocardio	Myocardium
Miopía	Myopia

N

Nariz	Nose
Neumonía	Pneumonia
Nervio	Nerve
Naúsea	Nausea
Necrosis	Necrosis
Neuritis	Neuritis

Necrotizante	Necrotizing
Nódulo	Nodule
Nefritis	Nephritis
Neoplasia	Neoplasia
Narcolepsia	Narcolepsy

O

Oído	Ear
Osteoporosis	Osteoporosis
Ovario	Ovary
Orina	Urina
Odontología	Dentistry
Oftalmología	Ophthalmology
Ortopedia	Orthopedics
Oclusión	Occlusion
Onicomicosis	Onychomycosis
Orzuelo	Sty
Ortopédico	Orthopedic
Otitis	Otitis

P

Pulmón	Lung
Presión arterial	Blood pressure
Piel	Skin

Parto	Delivery
Páncreas	Pancreas
Parálisis	Paralysis
Parkinson	Parkinson
Pus	Pus
Pericardio	Pericardium
Pancreatitis	Pancreatitis
Poliomielitis	Poliomyelitis
Poliuria	Polyuria
Pseudomonas	Pseudomonas
Psoriasis	Psoriasis

Q

Quimioterapia	Chemotherapy
Quiste	Cyst
Quemadura	Burn
Queratitis	Keratitis
Quilotórax	Chylothorax
Quilotripsina	Chymotrypsin
Quiluria	Chyluria
Quimioembolización	Chemoembolization

R

Riñón	Kidney

Reflujo	Reflux
Rinitis	Rhinitis
Resfriado	Cold
Retina	Retina
Reumatismo	Rheumatism
Ronquido	Snore
Rubeola	Rubella
Rabia	Rabies
Rectorragia	Rectal bleeding
Retinopatía	Retinopathy
Ruptura	Rupture
Ruptura prematura de membranas	Premature rupture of membranes
Riesgo cardiovascular	Cardiovascular risk
Radioterapia	Radiation therapy

S

Sangre	Blood
Síndrome	Syndrome
Sistema nervioso	Nervous system
Sudor	Sweat
Sífilis	Syphilis
Sarampión	Measles
Síndrome de Down	Down syndrome

Sistema inmunológico	Immune system
Sobrepeso	Overweight
Sordera	Deafness
Síndrome metabólico	Metabolic syndrome
T	
Tiroides	Thyroid
Tumor	Tumor
Tratamiento	Treatment
Tuberculosis	Tuberculosis
Terapia	Therapy
Tos	Cough
Trasplante	Transplante
Trombosis	Thrombosis
Triglicéridos	Tryglicerides
Tétanos	Tetanus
Trastorno	Disorder
Trombocitopenia	Thrombocytopenia
Tiroiditis	Thyroiditis
U	
Uretra	Urethra
Urticaria	Urticaria
Úlcera	Ulcer

Uña	Nail
Ultrasonido	Ultrasound
Urgencia	Emergency
Uveítis	Uveitis
Uremia	Uremia
Uropatía	Uropathy
Urolitiasis	Urolithiasis
Úlcera gástrica	Gastric ulcer

V

Vena	Vein
Vacuna	Vaccine
Varicela	Chickenpox
Vesícula	Vesicle
Vómito	Vomit
Virus	Virus
Vértebra	Vertebra
Várices	Varicose Veins
Vesícula bilia	Gallbladder
Vértigo	Vertigo
Vasculitis	Vasculitis
Venopunción	Venipuncture
Vía intravenosa	Intravenous route

Vasoconstricción	Vasoconstriction
X	
Xantomas	Xanthomas
Xerodermia pigmentosa	Xeroderma pigmentosum
Xeroftalmia	Xerophthalmia
Xerostomía	Xerostomia
Xenotrasplante	Xenotransplantation
Xerosis	Xerosis
Xantelasma	Xanthelasma
Xantinuria	Xanthinuria
Y	
Yodo	Iodine
Yersinia	Yersinia
Yeyuno	Jejunum
Yodo radioactivo	Radioactive iodine
Yeso	Plaster
Yunque	Anvil
Z	
Zóster	
Zinc	Zinc
Zoonosis	Zoonosis
Zoofilia	Zoophilia

Zoonótico	Zoonotic
Zumbido en los oidos	Ringing in the ears
Zonza pelúcida	Zona pellucida

Chapter VI. Conclusion

The physician's highest calling, his only calling, is to make sick people healthy - to heal, as it is termed.

Samuel Hahnemann

Summary of the book's content and benefits

As we reach the conclusion of "Cultural Competence in Healthcare and Additional Practice," it's important to reflect on the transformative journey we have embarked upon throughout this book. The emphasis on cultural competence in healthcare is paramount, especially in today's increasingly diverse society, where healthcare professionals must not only understand medical language but also navigate the cultural nuances that influence patient care.

This book has aimed to bridge the gap between language and culture, providing you with the tools to communicate effectively with Spanish-speaking patients. We began by exploring the significance of cultural competence, recognizing that beyond simply speaking Spanish, the ability to understand and respect the cultural backgrounds of patients is crucial to fostering trust and improving health outcomes. By considering factors such as family dynamics, traditional beliefs, and the importance of personal relationships, you will enhance your interactions with Hispanic patients, creating a more inclusive and empathetic healthcare environment.

Throughout the chapters, practical exercises were woven into the fabric of our discussions—each designed to refine your language skills while reinforcing your understanding of cultural contexts. Whether examining traditional healing practices like curanderismo and chamanismo or understanding common ailments rooted in cultural beliefs, each section has illustrated the rich tapestry of Hispanic healthcare practices. These insights encourage you to treat each patient as an individual with unique experiences rather than merely a statistic or a homogenous group member.

Ultimately, the journey toward cultural competence is ongoing. As you embrace the principles outlined in this book, remember that cultural sensitivity is not a destination but a continuous process of learning, adapting, and growing. Engage with your community, seek out diverse experiences, and remain open to the lessons that each patient can provide. By doing so, you contribute to a healthcare system that values diversity and is responsive to the needs of all individuals.

Thank you for taking this journey with us. You are now better equipped to be an advocate for your patients, fostering a healthcare environment where everyone feels seen, heard, and cared for. Together, we can acknowledge and respect the multitude of voices in healthcare, ensuring that each patient's experience is not merely heard but celebrated in the context of their unique cultural identity.

BOOK 4

Advanced Medical Spanish: Specialized Vocabulary for Healthcare Disciplines

Bridging the Gap: Advanced Spanish for Pediatrics, Oncology, Gynecology, and Obstetrics

Explore to Win

Book 4 Description

In this book, we focus on key medical specialties such as oncology, cardiology, pediatrics, and obstetrics and gynecology. Each chapter introduces the terminology and phrases needed to understand and explain symptoms, diagnoses, treatments, and procedures. From discussing cancer treatment options with oncology patients to explaining labor and delivery processes in obstetrics, this book is designed to prepare healthcare providers for the linguistic demands of their profession.

Not only does the book cover routine clinical care, but it also prepares the readers with the tools to handle critical situations where clear and effective communication is required. Whether it's guiding a patient through prenatal care or discussing cardiac surgery options, this guide ensures that healthcare providers can engage in meaningful and clear interactions with Spanish-speaking patients and medical staff alike.

To reinforce learning, this book, just like the previous ones, includes practical examples, real-life conversations, and targeted exercises that simulate common clinical scenarios to reinforce consistency. Through these exercises, readers can practice the specialized vocabulary and phrases they need, building confidence in their ability to speak with patients and colleagues in Spanish.

Once the advanced vocabulary in this book is learned in detail, healthcare providers will improve patient outcomes and build stronger, more compassionate relationships with their Spanish-speaking patients.

Chapter I: Pediatrics

El pediatra es el médico de los niños, el psicólogo de los padres y el psiquiatra de los abuelos porque se vuelven locos por los nietos

José Jordán

Medical Terminology in Pediatrics

According to the American Academy of Pediatrics, Pediatrics refers to "the specialty of medical science concerned with the physical, mental, and social health of children from birth to young adulthood. Pediatrics is a discipline that deals with biological, social, and environmental influences on the developing child and with the impact of disease and dysfunction on development. Children differ from adults anatomically, physiologically, immunologically, psychologically, developmentally, and metabolically."

Pediatric patients are not just smaller versions of adults; they present unique medical conditions, symptoms, and developmental milestones that require clear and compassionate communication. Understanding these nuances builds trust with both the child and their parents or guardians. This chapter will cover medical terms related to childhood growth, common symptoms, conditions, and treatment plans, all while addressing the specific concerns and questions that parents often have.

This chapter also incorporates example conversations, highlighting doctor-parent interactions and doctor-nurse dialogues, to demonstrate how these terms are applied in everyday clinical practice between colleagues and parents/caregivers. Different types of exercises at the end of the chapter will help reinforce your knowledge of pediatric medical Spanish, enabling you to confidently use the language in real-world scenarios.

Basic Terminology in Pediatrics

Pediatrics is a specialized branch of medicine that requires healthcare providers to be adept in using medical terms related to childhood growth, development, and illnesses. Children progress through various stages of physical, emotional, and cognitive development, each of which can be accompanied by unique health challenges. As a result, pediatricians must be prepared to discuss a wide range of topics, from basic health maintenance (such as vaccinations) to more complex medical issues (such as developmental delays or respiratory infections).

Here, you can find a basic vocabulary used in pediatrics. Further vocabulary will be explained later:

Medical terms in Spanish	Medical terms in English

Pediatría	Pediatrics
Neonatología	Neonatology
UCIN / Unidad de Cuidados Intensivos en Neonatología	NICU / Neonatal Intensive Care Unit
Recién nacido / Neonato	Newborn / Neonate
Nacimiento	Birth
Infante	Infant
Niño	Child
Vacunas	Vaccines
Crecimiento	Growth
Desarrollo	Development
Fontanela	Fontanel
Placa de crecimiento	Growth plate
Epífisis	Epiphysis
Cartílago de crecimiento	Growth cartilage
Dientes de leche	Baby teeth
Arcos branquiales	Branchial arches
Perímetro cefálico	Head circumference
Cordón umbilical	Umbilical cord
Reflejo de Moro	Moro reflex
Reflejo de succión	Sucking reflex
Desarrollo infantil	Child development
Peso	Weight

Altura	Height
Nutrición	Nutrition
Sangrado nasal/ Epistaxis	Nosebleed
Osificación	Ossification
Consulta pediátrica	Pediatric consultation
Desarrollo motor	Motor development
Obesidad infantil	Childhood obesity
Desnutrición	Malnutrition

Crecimiento y Desarrollo / Growth and Development

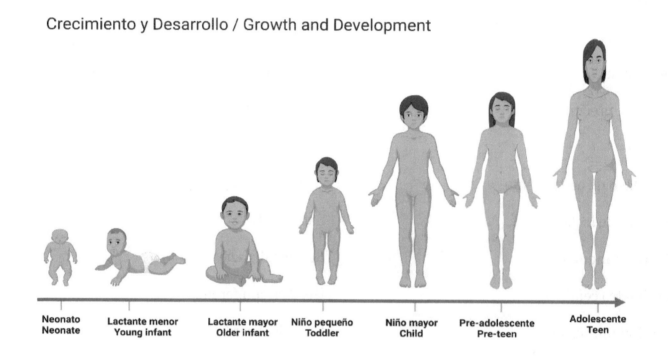

The stages of growth and development

Created with BioRender.com

Explanation:

Pediatric healthcare providers often engage with parents about their children's growth milestones and vaccination schedules, which are integral to a child's overall health. Discussions around a child's growth from their nacimiento (birth) until their adolescencia (teens) or discussing vacunas (vaccines), which help prevent diseases such as measles, polio, and chickenpox, are frequent in pediatric visits. In addition, terms such as infección respiratoria (respiratory infection), fiebre (fever), and tos (cough) are commonly used when assessing illnesses in children. Pediatricians must be well-versed in explaining these symptoms and treatments clearly and compassionately to parents, ensuring that they feel informed and empowered in making decisions for their child's health.

For example, when discussing vaccinations, a pediatrician may say, "El niño necesita recibir sus vacunas según el calendario recomendado," which means "The child needs to receive his vaccines according to the recommended schedule." Similarly, during routine check-ups, doctors often evaluate growth and development, making statements such as "Vamos a evaluar el crecimiento y desarrollo de su hijo durante la consulta" (We are going to evaluate your child's growth and development during the consultation).

Understanding how to ask and respond to questions about symptoms, illnesses, and treatments in Spanish is crucial, especially in communities with high numbers of Spanish-speaking parents. Clear communication ensures parents feel confident and reassured, which in turn enhances patient outcomes.

Common Symptoms & Conditions in Pediatrics

Pediatric patients often present with symptoms that are significantly different from those seen in adults, both in terms of how the symptoms manifest and how they are communicated. In children, symptoms such as fever or a cough can have various underlying causes, from minor infections to more serious illnesses. Therefore, specialists in this area need to recognize and discuss these symptoms in Spanish, particularly when explaining them to parents or caregivers and when communicating with the child or teenager who is sick.

This section focuses on key symptoms and conditions that are frequently encountered in pediatric medicine, such as ear infections, diarrhea, and respiratory issues.

Medical terms in Spanish	Medical terms in English
Erupción cutánea	Skin rash
Dolor de garganta	Sore throat
Bronquitis	Bronchitis
Deshidratación	Dehydration
Infección de oído	Ear infection
Estreñimiento	Constipation

Convulsiones	Seizures
Dermatitis	Dermatitis
Náuseas	Nausea
Faringitis	Pharyngitis
Cólico infantil	Infant colic
Varicela	Chickenpox
Conjuntivitis	Conjunctivitis
Hipotiroidismo congénito	Congenital hypothyroidism
Pie plano	Flat feet
Anemia	Anemia
Hipoxia neonatal	Neonatal hypoxia
Deficiencia de hierro	Iron deficiency
Sarampión	Measles
Rinitis alérgica	Allergic rhinitis
Displasia de cadera	Hip dysplasia
Problemas de Desarrollo	Developmental issues
Criptorquidia	Cryptorchidism
Dermatitis del pañal	Diaper rash
Parotiditis	Mumps
Dislexia	Dyslexia
Hiperactividad	Hyperactivity
Microcefalia	Microcephaly
Retraso del crecimiento	Growth delay

TDAH (Trastorno por déficit de atención e hiperactividad)	ADHD (Attention Deficit Hyperactivity Disorder)
Problemas de audición	Hearing problems
Displasia broncopulmonar	Bronchopulmonary dysplasia
Sinusitis bacteriana	Bacterial sinusitis
Trastorno del espectro autista	Autism spectrum disorder (ASD)
Fibrosis quística	Cystic fibrosis
Enuresis nocturna	Bedwetting (Nocturnal enuresis)
Espina bífida	Spina bifida
Parálisis cerebral	Cerebral palsy
Tos ferina	Whooping cough
Bronquiolitis	Bronchiolitis
Hipoacusia	Hypoacusis

Explanation:

Pediatric patients may have common conditions such as bronquitis (bronchitis), otitis media (middle ear infection), or faringitis (pharyngitis); it might be easier for healthcare providers to ensure that parents fully understand the diagnosis and treatment plans since they will encounter with this diseases relatively often. Moreover, conditions like conjuntivitis (conjunctivitis) or dermatitis del pañal (diaper rash) might be relatively minor but still require clear communication to avoid misunderstandings about treatment.

On the other side, more complex or chronic conditions, such as hipotiroidismo congénito (congenital hypothyroidism) or fibrosis quística (cystic fibrosis), require in-depth conversations where healthcare providers need to explain lifelong care plans and the implications for the child's future overall health. A clear communication channel with Spanish-speaking communities will ensure better health outcomes by fostering understanding, compliance, and trust between providers and parents.

Example Sentences:

"¿Ha notado que el niño tiene fiebre o tos?"

(Have you noticed if the child has fever or cough?)

"Vamos a revisar si tiene una infección en la garganta."

(Let's evaluate if he/she has a throat infection)

"Su hijo tiene una infección de oído. Esto es bastante común en niños pequeños."

(Your child has an ear infection. This is quite common in young children.)

"La erupción en la piel de su hija parece ser dermatitis, probablemente causada por una reacción alérgica."

(The skin rash your daughter has looks like dermatitis, probably caused by an allergic reaction.)

Explaining Pediatric Treatment Plans

In pediatrics, explaining treatment plans involves providing accurate and up-to-date medical information and offering emotional reassurance to caregivers who may feel anxious about their child's health. Healthcare providers might also take different measures if the child is being neglected by their parents. Pediatricians must clearly explain the treatment, whether it involves vaccinations, medications, or long-term management of chronic conditions while addressing any concerns or questions. In addition, providers need to make sure, as much as possible, that treatment is followed in time for an optimal recovery. This section focuses on key language and strategies to effectively communicate pediatric treatment plans in Spanish, with a particular emphasis on vaccines, medication dosage, and follow-up care.

Medical terms in Spanish	Medical terms in English
Calendario de vacunación	Vaccination schedule
Refuerzo	Booster shot
Efectos secundarios	Side effects
Jarabe	Syrup
Prevenir	To prevent
Completar el tratamiento	Complete the treatment
Cita de seguimiento	Follow-up appointment
Plan de tratamiento	Treatment plan
Controlar	To monitor
Progreso	Progress
Revisión pediátrica	Pediatric check-up

Desencadenantes	Triggers
Examen físico	Physical exam
Análisis de sangre	Blood test
Prueba de alergias	Allergy test
Suero oral	Oral rehydration solution

Explanation:

Vaccinations and Immunizations:

Vaccinations are a fundamental part of pediatric care, helping prevent serious diseases in children. It's important for healthcare professionals to explain the benefits of vaccines, address concerns about side effects, and ensure parents understand the calendario de vacunación (vaccination schedule). For example, when discussing the vacuna contra el sarampión (measles vaccine) or refuerzos (booster shots), providers need to provide clear information about the timing and purpose of these vaccines. Parents may ask about the potential efectos secundarios (side effects), such as mild fever or soreness, and it's important to reassure them that these reactions are normal and typically resolve quickly.

Medication Dosage and Usage:

When prescribing medicamentos (medications), especially antibióticos (antibiotics), pediatricians must explain the correct dosis (dosage), how frequently the medication should be taken, and the importance of completar el tratamiento (completing the treatment). Failure to follow the prescribed schedule can lead to incomplete recovery or antibiotic resistance. It's also essential to explain possible efectos adversos (adverse effects), such as allergic reactions, and how to respond if they occur. For example, if the child is prescribed jarabe (syrup) for a cough, the parent needs to understand how much and how often to administer it, and what to do if a dose is missed.

Follow-Up and Long-Term Care:

For chronic conditions such as asma (asthma) or developmental delays, citas de seguimiento (follow-up appointments) are crucial to monitor the child's condition and adjust the plan de tratamiento (treatment plan) as needed. Pediatricians must explain the importance of these appointments and ensure that parents know what symptoms to monitor at home, such as worsening symptoms or adverse reactions to medications. Parents should be informed about when to return for the next examen de control (check-up) and what to expect during these visits. Clear communication about long-term care helps parents feel prepared and reassured about managing their child's chronic condition.

Example Sentences:

"El antibiótico que le estamos recetando se debe tomar dos veces al día, cada doce horas. Asegúrese de que termine todo el tratamiento, incluso si su hijo mejora antes."

(The antibiotic we are prescribing should be taken twice a day, every twelve hours. Make sure he finishes the entire treatment, even if he gets better before then.)

Examples of Conversations

Conversation 1: Doctor/Parent – Discussing a Vaccination

Spanish	Translation
Doctor: Hoy vamos a ponerle a su hijo la vacuna contra la varicela. Es una vacuna importante para prevenir esta enfermedad que puede ser grave en los niños	*Doctor*: Today we are going to give your child the chickenpox vaccine. It's an important vaccine to prevent this disease, which can be serious in children.
Paciente: ¿Es segura esta vacuna? ¿Puede tener efectos secundarios	*Patient*: Is this vaccine safe? Can it cause side effects?
Doctor: Sí, la vacuna es muy segura. Los efectos secundarios más comunes son fiebre leve o un poco de enrojecimiento en el lugar de la inyección. Estos síntomas suelen desaparecer en uno o dos días.	*Doctor*: Yes, the vaccine is very safe. The most common side effects are a mild fever or a little redness at the injection site. These symptoms usually go away in a day or two.
Paciente: ¿Cuándo necesitará su próxima vacuna?	*Patient*: When will he need his next vaccine?
Doctor: Después de esta, su hijo necesitará un refuerzo a los 4 o 6 años. Le daremos un calendario de vacunas para que pueda seguirlo.	*Doctor*: After this, your child will need a booster shot at 4 or 6 years old. We will give you a vaccination schedule so you can follow it.
Paciente: Gracias por explicarlo. Me preocupa que pueda tener fiebre después.	*Patient:* Thank you for explaining. I'm worried he might get a fever afterward.
Doctor: Es completamente normal tener fiebre leve. Si eso ocurre, puede darle paracetamol según la dosis recomendada para su edad y peso.	*Doctor:* It's completely normal to have a mild fever. If that happens, you can give him acetaminophen according to the recommended dosage for his age and weight.

Conversation 2: Doctor/Nurse – Preparing Medication Dosage Instructions

Spanish	Translation

Spanish	Translation
Doctor: María, por favor ayúdame a preparar la receta para el antibiótico de este niño. Necesita tomarlo dos veces al día, cada doce horas.	*Doctor:* María, please help me to prepare the prescription for this child's antibiotic. He needs to take it twice a day, every twelve hours.
Enfermera: De acuerdo, doctor. ¿Durante cuánto tiempo necesita el tratamiento?	*Nurse:* Alright, doctor. How long does he need the treatment for?
Doctor: Lo tomará por diez días. Asegúrate de explicarles a los padres que deben completar todo el tratamiento, incluso si el niño se siente mejor antes de que termine.	*Doctor:* He'll take it for ten days. Make sure to explain to the parents that they need to complete the entire treatment, even if the child feels better before finishing it.
Enfermera: Claro, doctor. También les mencionaré los posibles efectos secundarios como el malestar estomacal, y les diré que se pongan en contacto si ocurre algún problema.	*Nurse:* Of course, doctor. I'll also mention the possible side effects, like stomach upset, and I'll tell them to get in touch if there's any problem.
Doctor: Exactamente. Además, quiero que les demos una hoja de instrucciones con la dosis recomendada basada en el peso del niño.	*Doctor:* Exactly. Also, let's give them an instruction sheet with the recommended dosage based on the child's weight.
Enfermera: Lo haré. Voy a preparar todo para que puedan entender cómo darle el medicamento.	*Nurse:* I'll do that. I'll prepare everything so they can understand how to give the medication.

Conversation 3: Doctor/Nurse – Discussing Follow-Up for a Chronic Condition (Asthma)

Spanish	Translation
Doctor: Karen, este niño tiene asma y comenzará con un inhalador. Quiero que agendes una cita de seguimiento para dentro de un mes para evaluar cómo está respondiendo al tratamiento.	*Doctor:* Karen, this child has asthma and will start using an inhaler. I want you to schedule a follow-up appointment in a month to assess how he's responding to the treatment.
Enfermera: ¿Deberíamos darle también un plan de acción para el asma a los padres?	*Nurse:* Should we also give the parents an asthma action plan?
Doctor: Sí, eso es muy importante. Ellos deben saber qué hacer si el niño tiene una crisis de asma.	*Doctor:* Yes, that's very important. They need to know what to do if the child has an

Asegúrate de explicarles cómo usar el inhalador correctamente.	asthma attack. Make sure to explain how to use the inhaler correctly.
Enfermera: Voy a mostrarles el uso del inhalador con el espaciador para que lo entiendan bien. ¿Algo más que deba mencionar?	*Nurse:* I'll show them how to use the inhaler with the spacer so they fully understand it. Anything else I should mention?
Doctor: Recuerda decirles que es necesario evitar los desencadenantes del asma, como el polvo o el polen, y que el niño debe llevar el inhalador consigo en todo momento.	*Doctor:* Remember to tell them that it's necessary to avoid asthma triggers, like dust or pollen, and that the child should carry the inhaler with him at all times.
Enfermera: Lo haré. Además, me aseguraré de que sepan cuándo volver para el examen de control.	*Nurse:* I will. I'll also make sure they know when to come back for the follow-up check-up.

Key Takeaways

Pediatric care requires specialized vocabulary to address common symptoms and conditions in children.

This section emphasizes the importance of explaining both routine and complex pediatric conditions, such as respiratory infections, developmental issues, and chronic diseases, in a way that parents and caregivers can easily understand.

The book promotes competent care, enhancing trust and collaboration between providers and Spanish-speaking families through examples and vocabulary.

Exercises

Exercise 1

Match the English term to its Spanish translation.

1. Vaccines
2. Earache
3. Skin rash
4. Cough
5. Fever

Options:

a. Erupción cutánea
b. Tos
c. Dolor de oído
d. Fiebre
e. Vacunas

Exercise 2

Fill in the blanks with the correct Spanish term.

El niño tiene fiebre y una _____ en la piel.

Vamos a administrar _____ para prevenir enfermedades.

La _____ es un síntoma común en infecciones respiratorias.

Exercise 3

Write a conversation between a doctor and a parent discussing a child's vaccination schedule.

Exercise 4

Create a dialogue between a doctor and a nurse about a child's recent growth check-up.

Exercise 5

Translate the following sentences into Spanish:

1. The child has a skin rash and fever.
2. We will give him antibiotics for his ear infection.
3. The pediatric check-up is scheduled for next week.

Answer Key

Exercise 1

e - Vacunas

c - Dolor de oído

a - Erupción cutánea

b - Tos

d - Fiebre

Exercise 2

Erupción

Vacunas

Tos

Exercise 3

Spanish version: Doctor/Padre – Discutiendo el Calendario de Vacunación de un Niño

Doctor: Su hijo necesita recibir la vacuna contra el sarampión hoy, y luego tendrá un refuerzo a los 4 años. Es importante seguir el calendario de vacunas.

Padre: ¿Es segura esta vacuna? He escuchado algunos posibles efectos adversos.

Doctor: Sí, es muy segura. Los efectos secundarios son leves, como fiebre o enrojecimiento en el área de la inyección. Es esencial para protegerlo contra enfermedades graves.

English translation: Doctor/Parent – Discussing a Child's Vaccination Schedule

Doctor: Your child needs to receive the measles vaccine today, and then there will be a booster at 4 years old. It's important to follow the vaccination schedule.

Parent: Is this vaccine safe? I've heard some secondary effects.

Doctor: Yes, it's very safe. The side effects are mild, like fever or redness at the injection site. It's essential to protect him from serious diseases.

Exercise 4

Spanish version: Doctor/Enfermera – Discutiendo el Chequeo de Crecimiento Reciente de un Niño

Doctor: María, revisamos el crecimiento del niño hoy, y está un poco por debajo del promedio para su edad. Vamos a pedir análisis de sangre para verificar si hay algún problema nutricional.

Enfermera: De acuerdo, doctor. ¿También vamos a recomendar algún cambio en su dieta?

Doctor: Sí, les daremos a los padres algunas recomendaciones para mejorar su ingesta de proteínas y vitaminas. Programemos una cita de seguimiento en tres meses para ver el progreso.

English translation: Doctor/Nurse – Discussing a Child's Recent Growth Check-Up

Doctor: María, we checked the child's growth today, and he is a bit below average for his age. We're going to order blood tests to check for any nutritional issues.

Nurse: Alright, doctor. Are we also going to recommend any dietary changes?

Doctor: Yes, we'll give the parents some recommendations to improve his protein and vitamin intake. Let's schedule a follow-up appointment in three months to check on the progress.

Exercise 5

1. The child has a skin rash and fever.

El niño tiene una erupción cutánea y fiebre.

2. We will give him antibiotics for his ear infection.

Le daremos antibióticos para su infección de oído.

3. The pediatric check-up is scheduled for next week.

La consulta pediátrica está programada para la próxima semana.

Chapter II: Obstetrics & Gynecology

El problema del género es que prescribe cómo debemos ser, en vez de reconocer quienes somos.

Rosario Castellanos

Medical Terminology in Obstetrics & Gynecology

Gynecology refers to the branch of medicine that focuses on the health and diseases of the female reproductive system, encompassing the care of women from puberty through menopause and beyond. According to the American College of Obstetricians and Gynecologists (ACOG), "Gynecology deals with the diagnosis and treatment of disorders affecting the female reproductive organs, including hormonal disorders, menstruation, and fertility issues."

Understanding the unique physical and hormonal changes women experience at different life stages is the pillar of gynecological care. Also, obstetric care involves supporting a woman through her pregnancy, delivery, and recovery, ensuring careful monitoring and guidance during these critical periods.

This chapter goes through the fundamental and advanced terminology used in gynecology, covering common medical conditions, reproductive health, pregnancy, and menopause while highlighting doctor-patient interactions.

Basic Terminology in Gynecology

Gynecology and obstetrics require a comprehensive understanding of the female reproductive system, its anatomy, physiological processes, and related health conditions. This section will help you to learn and practice the vocabulary when discussing various topics such as menstruation, fertility, pregnancy, menopause, and gynecological disorders with your patients.

Medical terms in Spanish	Medical terms in English
Ginecología	Gynecology
Menstruación	Menstruation
Ovarios	Ovaries
Trompas de falopio	Fallopian Tubes
Útero	Uterus

Miometrio	Myometrium
Endometrio	Endometrium
Cérvix (Cuello Uterino)	Cervix (Cervical canal)
Vagina	Vagina
Labios mayores	Labia majora
Labios menores	Labia minora
Menopausia	Menopause
Clítoris	Clitoris
Vulva	Vulva
Fimbrias	Fimbriae
Folículos ováricos	Ovarian follicles
Monte de venus	Mons pubis
Fondo de útero	Uterine fundus
Saco de Douglas	Pouch of Douglas
Periné	Perineum
Himen	Hymen
Glándulas de Bartholin	Bartholin glands
Pared vaginal	Vaginal wall
Mesometrio	Mesometrium

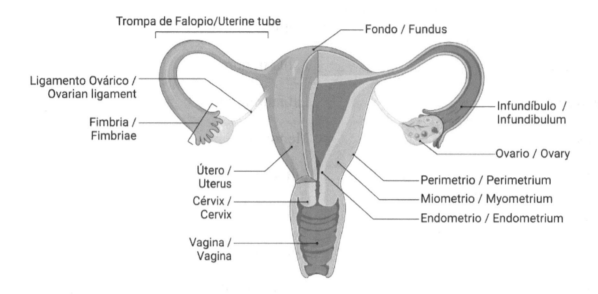

Aparato Reproductor Femenino / Female Reproductive System Anatomy

Trompa de Falopio/Uterine tube
Fondo / Fundus
Ligamento Ovárico /
Ovarian ligament
Fimbria /
Fimbriae
Útero /
Uterus
Cérvix /
Cervix
Vagina /
Vagina
Infundíbulo /
Infundibulum
Ovario / Ovary
Perimetrio / Perimetrium
Miometrio / Myometrium
Endometrio / Endometrium

Anatomy of the Female Reproductive System

Created with BioRender.com

Explanation:

Here, you will find the vocabulary needed when discussing topics such as the female reproductive system, menstruation, fertility, pregnancy, menopause, and gynecological disorders with their Spanish-speaking patients.

For example, a gynecologist might explain, "Vamos a realizar un ultrasonido transvaginal para examinar los ovarios y el útero," which means, "We are going to perform a transvaginal ultrasound to examine the ovaries and the uterus." Understanding and explaining anatomical structures such as los ovarios (ovaries), el útero (uterus), and las trompas de Falopio (fallopian tubes) is crucial when discussing fertility, pregnancy, or any gynecological concerns.

Similarly, terms like menopausia (menopause) and endometrio (endometrium) are important when explaining changes in a patient's reproductive health during different life stages. For instance, a doctor might say, "Durante la menopausia, el endometrio se adelgaza," which translates to, "During menopause, the endometrium thins."

Whether explaining the function of las glándulas de Bartholin (Bartholin glands) or discussing issues related to the cérvix (cervix), a solid command of this vocabulary is essential for ensuring patients feel informed and empowered to make decisions about their reproductive health.

Basic Terminology in Obstetrics

Obstetrics involves providing comprehensive care for women during pregnancy, labor, and postpartum. Knowing anatomical and procedural terms related to pregnancy and childbirth is key in this practice. This section provides a vocabulary that helps obstetricians ensure patients understand their medical conditions and the procedures associated with childbirth.

Medical terms in Spanish	Medical terms in English
Obstetricia	Obstetrics
Embarazo	Pregnancy
Primer trimestre	First trimester
Segundo trimestre	Second trimester
Tercer trimestre	Third trimester
Placenta	Placenta
Líquido amniótico	Amniotic fluid
Saco amniótico	Amniotic sac
Embrión	Embryo
Cordón umbilical	Umbilical cord
Dilatación cervical	Cervical dilation
Calostro	Colostrum
Fondo uterino	Uterine fundus
Ecografía obstétrica	Obstetric ultrasound
Posición fetal	Fetal position
Presentación cefálica	Cephalic presentation
Presentación podálica	Breech presentation
Contracciones uterinas	Uterine contractions

Explanation:

Common terms used, such as embarazo (pregnancy), dilatación cervical (cervical dilation), and contracciones uterinas (uterine contractions), are fundamental when discussing the different stages of labor and childbirth. A healthcare provider might explain to a patient, "La dilatación cervical debe alcanzar los 10 centímetros antes del parto" (Cervical dilation must reach 10 centimeters before delivery). Similarly, terms like placenta (placenta) and cordón umbilical (umbilical cord) are frequently mentioned when discussing the health and development of the fetus.

Understanding terms like posición fetal (fetal position) and presentación cefálica (cephalic presentation) is particularly important when discussing the baby's position during labor, as these factors play a critical role in determining the method of delivery, whether it be a natural vaginal delivery or a cesárea (cesarean section) if there are complications.

The vocabulary also extends to prenatal care, where terms such as ecografía obstétrica (obstetric ultrasound) and calostro (colostrum) are used to explain procedures and the production of the first breast milk, respectively. This terminology allows healthcare providers to guide patients through their pregnancy and postnatal care with confidence, ensuring that they fully understand the steps being taken to ensure both their health and the health of their baby.

Common Symptoms & Conditions in Gynecology

Gynecology involves addressing a wide range of common conditions, including menstrual irregularities, infections, and other reproductive health concerns. This section will give you vocabulary about symptoms that patients may experience;

Medical terms in Spanish	Medical terms in English
Dolor pélvico	Pelvic pain
Sangrado menstrual irregular	Irregular menstrual bleeding
Amenorrea	Amenorrhea
Dispareunia	Dyspareunia
Menorragia	Menorrhagia
Miomas	Fibroids
Quistes ováricos	Ovarian cysts
Prolapso uterino	Uterine prolapse

Endometriosis	Endometriosis
Infección vaginal	Vaginal infection
Flujo vaginal anormal	Abnormal vaginal discharge
Dismenorrea	Dysmenorrhea
Sangrado postmenopáusico	Postmenopausal bleeding
Mastalgia	Mastalgia
Prurito vaginal	Vaginal itching
Sequedad vaginal	Vaginal dryness
Sangrado intermenstrual	Intermenstrual bleeding
Síndrome de ovario poliquístico	Polycystic ovary syndrome

Explanation:

From menstrual irregularities to infections and from structural issues to hormonal imbalances, gynecologists must be able to explain these issues to their patients clearly.

For instance, symptoms like dolor pélvico (pelvic pain) or sangrado menstrual irregular (irregular menstrual bleeding) can be signs of various underlying conditions, including miomas (fibroids) or quistes ováricos (ovarian cysts). A thorough understanding of these terms enables gynecologists to explain why further diagnostic tests, such as ultrasounds or biopsies, may be necessary to investigate the cause of such symptoms. For example, a doctor might explain, "Es importante realizar una ecografía para examinar los miomas y determinar si son la causa de su dolor pélvico" (It's important to do an ultrasound to examine the fibroids and determine if they are causing your pelvic pain).

Furthermore, patients may present with concerns such as dispareunia (pain during intercourse), which could indicate conditions like endometriosis or prolapso uterino (uterine prolapse). For postmenopausal women, symptoms such as sequedad vaginal (vaginal dryness) or sangrado postmenopáusico (postmenopausal bleeding) are key indicators of changes in reproductive health, potentially signaling more serious conditions that need medical attention. Any healthcare provider in a Spanish-speaking situation should be able to count on someone able to discuss these issues compassionately, explaining the reasons behind treatments such as hormone replacement therapy or surgery.

In some cases, gynecologists may need to address concerns related to síndrome de ovario poliquístico (SOPQ) (polycystic ovary syndrome), a hormonal disorder that often leads to irregular periods, excess androgens, and ovarian cysts. Being able to discuss the symptoms of PCOS, including amenorrea (absence of menstruation) and hirsutismo (excess hair growth), is vital for guiding patients through lifestyle modifications or medical treatments that can improve their symptoms. Providing clear explanations about the importance of monitoring symptoms like menorragia (heavy menstrual bleeding) helps build trust and ensure patient cooperation in ongoing care.

Common Symptoms & Conditions in Obstetrics

This section introduces key terms that obstetricians often need to explain to their pregnant patients, covering the most common complications and symptoms that arise during pregnancy.

Medical terms in Spanish	Medical terms in English
Náuseas matutinas	Morning sickness
Preeclampsia	Preeclampsia
Placenta previa	Placenta previa
Diabetes gestacional	Gestational diabetes
Hipertensión gestacional	Gestational hypertension
Dolor abdominal	Abdominal pain
Sangrado vaginal	Vaginal bleeding
Rotura de membranas	Rupture of membranes
Contracciones	Contractions
Trabajo de parto prematuro	Preterm labor
Embarazo múltiple	Multiple pregnancy
Polihidramnio	Polyhydramnios
Oligohidramnios	Oligohydramnios
Incompetencia cervical	Cervical insufficiency
Placenta accreta	Placenta accreta
Síndrome de HELLP	HELLP syndrome
Hiperémesis gravídica	Hyperemesis gravidarum

Desprendimiento de placenta	Placental abruption
Embarazo ectópico	Ectopic pregnancy
Anemia durante el embarazo	Pregnancy-related anemia

Explanation:

Obstetricians should be prepared to effectively communicate the complexity of pregnancy-related issues. For example, náuseas matutinas (morning sickness) is one of the most common early pregnancy symptoms, and obstetricians need to explain why it occurs, reassuring patients that it is a normal part of pregnancy. A provider might say, "Las náuseas matutinas suelen ocurrir durante el primer trimestre y generalmente desaparecen en el segundo" (Morning sickness usually occurs during the first trimester and generally goes away in the second). Understanding and using terms like primer trimestre (first trimester) and segundo trimestre (second trimester) is fundamental to guiding patients through the stages of pregnancy.

More serious conditions, such as preeclampsia or hipertensión gestacional (gestational hypertension), require careful explanation, as they can have significant implications for both the mother and baby. Obstetricians must explain the importance of regular blood pressure monitoring, as well as the signs of potential complications. For instance, they might say, "Es fundamental que controlamos su presión arterial debido al riesgo de preeclampsia, una condición que puede afectar tanto a la madre como al bebé" (It is crucial that we monitor your blood pressure due to the risk of preeclampsia, a condition that can affect both the mother and the baby).

In later stages of pregnancy, terms such as contracciones (contractions) and ruptura de membranas (rupture of membranes) become critical in explaining the onset of labor. Being able to describe these processes in detail helps patients feel more prepared for labor and delivery. Obstetricians also should explain the implications of presentación cefálica (cephalic presentation) or presentación podálica (breech presentation), as these fetal positions may determine whether a natural vaginal delivery or cesárea (cesarean section) will be necessary. For example, "Si el bebé no se coloca en la posición cefálica antes del parto, es posible que necesitemos programar una cesárea" (If the baby does not move into a cephalic position before delivery, we may need to schedule a cesarean section).

Conditions like placenta previa (placenta previa) or desprendimiento de placenta (placental abruption) are also critical to discuss in clear, understandable terms, as these conditions can lead to emergency situations that require immediate intervention. Explaining the risks associated with these conditions ensures that patients are fully aware of potential complications and the steps that may need to be taken to ensure their safety and that of their baby.

Explaining Treatment Plans in Gynecology

In gynecology, healthcare providers must communicate a broad range of treatment options to patients, ranging from medications to manage infections or hormonal imbalances to more complex surgical interventions for structural issues or cancer treatments. When the communication channel is clear, patients will be able to fully understand their diagnosis, the proposed treatment options, and how these treatments will improve their condition.

Medical terms in Spanish	Medical terms in English
Tratamiento hormonal	Hormonal treatment
Píldora anticonceptiva	Birth control pill
Dispositivo intrauterino (DIU)	Intrauterine device (IUD)
Cirugía laparoscópica	Laparoscopic surgery
Histerectomía	Hysterectomy
Terapia de reemplazo hormonal	Hormone replacement therapy
Biopsia	Biopsy
Crioterapia	Cryotherapy
Ablación endometrial	Endometrial ablation
Ligadura de trompas	Tubal ligation
Colposcopia	Colposcopy
Examen pélvico	Pelvic exam
Conización cervical	Cervical conization
Láser CO_2	CO_2 laser therapy

Explanation:

Gynecology treatment plans vary depending on the patient's specific condition. For instance, tratamiento hormonal (hormonal treatment) is often prescribed for conditions like menopause, where the doctor may explain, "El tratamiento hormonal puede ayudar a regular sus niveles hormonales y aliviar los síntomas de la menopausia" (Hormonal treatment can help regulate your hormone levels and alleviate menopausal symptoms).

For birth control, options such as the píldora anticonceptiva (birth control pill) or dispositivo intrauterino (DIU) (intrauterine device) are commonly discussed, with the healthcare provider explaining the pros and cons of each method. It is important to explain the long-term and short-term benefits as well as possible side effects.

Surgical interventions like cirugía laparoscópica (laparoscopic surgery) are necessary for removing conditions such as ovarian cysts or fibroids, while a more invasive procedure, like a histerectomía (hysterectomy), may be required in severe cases of uterine conditions. Explaining surgical risks and the recovery process is crucial to prepare patients for what to expect. Additionally, for treating infections, tratamiento antibiótico (antibiotic treatment) can be necessary, and ensuring patients understand the importance of completing their prescribed medication is vital to avoiding complications.

In some cases, doctors may suggest procedures like biopsia (biopsy) or colposcopia (colposcopy) for further investigation into abnormal findings in the cervix or uterus.

Explaining Treatment Plans in Obstetrics

Clear communication about treatment plans in obstetrics involves explaining routine prenatal care, interventions during labor and delivery, and postpartum recovery processes. Each treatment plan must be tailored to the patient's individual needs, and patients should fully understand the significance of each step in their care.

Medical terms in Spanish	Medical terms in English
Control prenatal	Prenatal care
Monitorización fetal	Fetal monitoring
Inducción del parto	Labor induction
Cesárea	Cesarean section
Atención postparto	Postpartum care
Episiotomía	Episiotomy
Lactancia	Breastfeeding
Anestesia epidural	Epidural anesthesia
Amniocentesis	Amniocentesis
Ruptura artificial de membranas	Artificial rupture of membranes
Oxitocina	Oxytocin
Parto vaginal asistido	Assisted vaginal delivery
Succión fetal	Fetal vacuum extraction

Puerperio	Puerperium

Explanation:

Providers can emphasize the importance of regular check-ups to monitor both maternal and fetal health, saying things like, "El control prenatal nos permite vigilar la salud del bebé y detectar cualquier complicación a tiempo" (Prenatal care allows us to monitor the baby's health and detect any complications early). This routine care includes monitorización fetal (fetal monitoring), where the healthcare provider ensures the baby's heartbeat and movements are normal.

As labor approaches, the discussion may shift to options such as inducción del parto (labor induction), particularly if the pregnancy goes past the due date or if complications arise. It's important for healthcare providers to explain why labor induction might be recommended and how medications like oxitocina (oxytocin) are used to stimulate contractions.

For some patients, a cesárea (cesarean section) may be required, especially if there are complications such as fetal distress or failure to progress in labor. The doctor will need to explain the procedure and recovery process, as well as the differences between a parto vaginal asistido (assisted vaginal delivery) and a succión fetal (fetal vacuum extraction), which may be necessary if the baby is in a difficult position or labor is prolonged.

After delivery, atención postparto (postpartum care) is important to ensure the health of both mother and baby. This care includes managing issues like lactancia (breastfeeding) and the healing of any episiotomía (episiotomy) wounds. The patient must also understand the importance of anestesia epidural (epidural anesthesia) if pain relief during labor is desired, as well as any potential side effects or risks.

Throughout the pregnancy and delivery, procedures such as amniocentesis (amniocentesis) may be offered to diagnose genetic conditions, while vaccines like vacuna Tdap (Tdap vaccine) are given to protect both mother and baby from infections such as tetanus, diphtheria, and whooping cough. Clear communication regarding these treatments ensures that the patient understands their necessity and feels comfortable with the care provided.

Examples of Conversations

Conversation 1: Doctor/Patient – Discussing Hormonal Treatment

Spanish	Translation
Doctor: Vamos a iniciar un tratamiento hormonal para aliviar sus síntomas de la menopausia.	*Doctor*: We are going to start hormonal treatment to relieve your menopause symptoms.
Paciente: ¿Cuáles son los posibles efectos secundarios?	*Patient*: What are the possible side effects?

Spanish	Translation
Doctor: Los efectos secundarios comunes incluyen náuseas leves, dolor de cabeza y cambios en el estado de ánimo.	*Doctor*: Common side effects include mild nausea, headache, and mood changes.
Paciente: ¿Cuánto tiempo tendré que seguir con este tratamiento?	*Patient*: How long will I need to follow this treatment?
Doctor: Esto dependerá de cómo responda su cuerpo. Lo evaluaremos en su próxima consulta dentro de tres meses.	*Doctor*: This will depend on how your body responds. We'll evaluate it at your next appointment in three months.

Conversation 2: Doctor/Nurse – Discussing Gynecological Surgery (Hysterectomy)

Spanish	Translation
Doctor: Rocío, esta paciente requiere una histerectomía debido a sus síntomas persistentes de miomas y sangrado abundante. Su calidad de vida está afectada y ha probado varios tratamientos hormonales sin éxito.	*Doctor:* Rocío, this patient requires a hysterectomy due to her persistent symptoms of fibroids and heavy bleeding. Her quality of life is affected, and she has tried various hormonal treatments without success.
Enfermera: Entendido, doctor. ¿Ha hablado con la paciente sobre la posibilidad de una histerectomía y las implicaciones para su fertilidad?	*Nurse:* Understood, doctor. Have you discussed the possibility of a hysterectomy and the implications for her fertility?
Doctor: Sí, lo hemos discutido, y fue un tema sensible, ya que ella tiene 40 años y todavía esperaba tener más hijos. Sin embargo, debido a los riesgos y el dolor constante, ha decidido seguir adelante con la cirugía.	*Doctor:* Yes, we have discussed it, and it was a sensitive topic because she is 40 and was still hoping to have more children. However, due to the risks and constant pain, she has decided to proceed with the surgery.
Enfermera: ¿Qué tipo de apoyo adicional necesitará después de la cirugía, considerando su situación familiar?	*Nurse:* What kind of additional support will she need after surgery, considering her family situation?
Doctor: Debemos asegurarnos de que reciba orientación sobre el reposo necesario y el cuidado postoperatorio en casa. También quiero recomendarle que busque apoyo emocional, ya que perder la capacidad de tener hijos puede ser difícil para algunas pacientes en nuestra comunidad.	*Doctor:* We need to ensure she receives guidance on necessary rest and postoperative care at home. I also want to recommend she seek emotional support, as losing the ability to have children can be difficult for some patients in our community.

Enfermera: Claro, doctor. También preparé un plan de recuperación detallado para que su familia lo siga en casa.	*Nurse:* Of course, doctor. I'll also prepare a detailed recovery plan for her family to follow at home.

Conversation 3: Doctor/Nurse – Managing Gestational Diabetes in a Pregnant Patient

Spanish	Translation
Doctor: Karen, esta paciente está en su tercer trimestre y ha sido diagnosticada con diabetes gestacional. Necesitamos ajustar su dieta y enseñarle a controlar sus niveles de glucosa para evitar complicaciones durante el parto.	*Doctor*: Karen, this patient is in her third trimester and has been diagnosed with gestational diabetes. We need to adjust her diet and teach her how to control her glucose levels to avoid complications during delivery.
Enfermera: ¿Le sugerimos una consulta con la nutricionista para ayudarla a adaptar su dieta?	*Nurse:* Should we suggest a consultation with the nutritionist to help her adjust her diet?
Doctor: Sí, sería útil. Necesitamos explicarle cómo hacer cambios en su alimentación sin abandonar completamente sus comidas tradicionales.	*Doctor:* Yes, that would be helpful. We need to explain how to make dietary changes without completely abandoning her traditional foods.
Enfermera: También le mostraré cómo monitorear sus niveles de glucosa y le hablaré de la posibilidad de usar insulina si es necesario.	*Nurse:* I'll also show her how to monitor her glucose levels and talk to her about possibly using insulin if needed.
Doctor: Perfecto. Además, explícale el riesgo de macrosomía si no controlamos bien su diabetes, y que en algunos casos podríamos inducir el parto para evitar complicaciones.	*Doctor:* Perfect. Also, explain the risk of macrosomia if her diabetes isn't well-controlled, and that we may induce labor to avoid complications in some cases.
Enfermera: Lo haré. También le proporcionaré recursos en español para que pueda entender mejor cómo manejar su diabetes gestacional.	*Nurse:* I will. I'll also provide her with Spanish-language resources to help her better understand how to manage her gestational diabetes.

Key Takeaways

In gynecology, treatment plans vary widely, including medication, hormonal therapies, and surgical interventions.

Gynecological care often requires explaining the purpose and process of surgical procedures, such as a hysterectomy or laparoscopic surgery, in accessible language so that patients feel informed and comfortable with their healthcare decisions.

Exercises

Exercise 1

Match the English term to its Spanish translation.

1. Hysterectomy
2. Birth control pill
3. Laparoscopic surgery
4. Intrauterine device
5. Hormonal treatment

Options:

a. Cirugía laparoscópica
b. Tratamiento hormonal
c. Píldora anticonceptiva
d. Histerectomía
e. Dispositivo intrauterino

Exercise 2

Fill in the blanks with the correct Spanish term.

1. El paciente necesita una _____ para remover los miomas.

2. El doctor recomendó un _____ para tratar los síntomas de la menopausia.

3. Vamos a implantar un _____ como método anticonceptivo.

Exercise 3

Write a conversation between a doctor and a patient discussing a birth control method.

Exercise 4

Create a dialogue between a doctor and a nurse about a follow-up after a gynecological surgery.

Exercise 5

Translate the following sentences into Spanish

1. The patient needs an ultrasound to examine her ovaries.
2. We will recommend hormone replacement therapy to manage her symptoms.
3. After the surgery, she will need a follow-up in two weeks.

Answer Key

Exercise 1

Match the English term to its Spanish translation:

English	Spanish
Hysterectomy	Histerectomía
Birth control pill	Píldora anticonceptiva
Laparoscopic surgery	Cirugía laparoscópica
Intrauterine device	Dispositivo intrauterino
Hormonal Treatment	Tratamiento hormonal

Exercise 2

1. Histerectomía
2. Tratamiento hormonal
3. Dispositivo intrauterino

Exercise 3

Spanish conversation example:

Doctor: ¿Ha considerado usar la píldora anticonceptiva como método de control natal?

Paciente: ¿Cuáles son los efectos secundarios más comunes?

Doctor: Los efectos secundarios incluyen cambios en el estado de ánimo y dolores de cabeza, pero muchas pacientes lo toleran bien.

Exercise 4

Spanish dialogue example:

Doctor: Monica, asegúrate de que el paciente reciba instrucciones claras para el seguimiento después de su cirugía laparoscópica.

Nurse: Claro, doctor. ¿Cuándo debe regresar para su consulta de control?

Doctor: En dos semanas para evaluar la recuperación.

Exercise 5

1. La paciente necesita una ecografía para examinar sus ovarios.
2. Recomendaremos terapia de reemplazo hormonal para manejar sus síntomas.

3. Después de la cirugía, necesitará una consulta de seguimiento en dos semanas.

Chapter III: Oncology

Nos hemos olvidado que curar el cáncer comienza con prevenirlo.

David Agus

Medical Terminology in Oncology

According to the American Cancer Society, Oncology is the study of cancer. The word comes from the Greek word for tumor or mass. It encompasses medical oncology (the treatment of cancer with drugs), radiation oncology (the treatment of cancer with radiation), and surgical oncology (the treatment of cancer through surgery). Oncology deals with a wide variety of cancers affecting different organs and tissues, each requiring specialized treatments and approaches.

Cancer treatment requires both a deep understanding of the disease and a compassionate approach to patients and their families. Oncologists must be skilled in not only addressing physical symptoms but also managing the emotional and psychological effects of a cancer diagnosis. This chapter will help you learn Spanish medical terms related to oncology, including types of cancer, treatment options, and common symptoms.

Basic Terminology in Oncology

Patients with cancer and their families often need clear explanations of complex medical terms, particularly when discussing the diagnosis, prognosis, and treatment options. This section introduces concepts for oncologists in their practice.

Medical terms in Spanish	Medical terms in English
Oncología	Oncology
Cáncer	Cancer
Tumor maligno	Malignant tumor
Carcinoma	Carcinoma
Leucemia	Leukemia
Linfoma	Lymphoma
Sarcoma	Sarcoma

Adenocarcinoma	Adenocarcinoma
Mieloma	Myeloma
Neoplasia	Neoplasia
Oncogénesis	Oncogenesis
Carcinogénesis	Carcinogenesis
Metástasis	Metastasis
Estadio del cancer	Cancer stage
Oncólogo	Oncologist
Patología	Pathology
Histología	Histology
Biopsia	Biopsy
Citogénetica	Cytogenetics
Mutación genética	Genetic mutation
Oncología molecular	Molecular oncology
Biología tumoral	Tumor biology
Estroma	Stroma
Células madre cancerosas	Cancer stem cells
Infiltración tumoral	Tumoral infiltration
Proliferación celular	Cell proliferation
Angiogénesis	Angiogenesis
Gen supresor de tumores	Tumor suppressor gene
Proto-oncogenes	Proto-oncogenes
Invasión celular	Cell invasion

Apoptosis	Apoptosis
Respuesta inmunitaria	Immune response
Marcador genético	Genetic marker
Diferenciación celular	Cell differentiation
Microambiente tumoral	Tumor microenvironment
Estudio inmunohistoquímico	Immunohistochemical study
Genoma tumoral	Tumor genome
Carcinoma ductal	Ductal carcinoma
Carcinoma lobulillar	Lobular carcinoma
Mutación de línea germinal	Germline mutation

Explanation:

Discussing terms like metástasis (metastasis), carcinogénesis (carcinogenesis), and biopsia (biopsy) with oncological patients helps to explain the nature of cancer development, how it spreads, and how it is diagnosed. For example, oncologists may explain, "El carcinoma ductal es un tipo de cáncer de mama que se origina en los conductos mamarios," meaning, "Ductal carcinoma is a type of breast cancer that originates in the mammary ducts."

Understanding the molecular and cellular processes involved in cancer is essential when explaining oncogénesis (oncogenesis), angiogénesis (angiogenesis), or apoptosis (apoptosis). Such terms allow oncologists to give patients and families a clear understanding of how cancer develops and behaves at the biological level.

In addition to understanding cancer progression and biology, oncologists often discuss the estadio del cáncer (cancer stage) with patients, which refers to the extent to which the cancer has spread in the body. Terms like infiltración tumoral (tumoral infiltration) and invasión celular (cell invasion) help describe how cancer cells move from their point of origin to other tissues. Similarly, the microambiente tumoral (tumor microenvironment) plays a significant role in cancer growth and metastasis, as it encompasses the surrounding cells, blood vessels, and molecules that interact with the tumor.

Common Symptoms & Conditions in Oncology

Oncology patients often present with symptoms that can be indicative of cancer progression, side effects from treatments, or general health conditions exacerbated by the disease. These symptoms can vary greatly depending on the type of cancer, the stage at diagnosis, and individual patient factors.

Oncologists must be skilled in recognizing and explaining these symptoms to patients and their families in a way that promotes understanding and effective management of the disease.

Here, you can find key terminology related to signs and symptoms that are commonly observed in cancer patients.

Medical terms in Spanish	Medical terms in English
Fatiga	Fatigue
Pérdida de peso inexplicable	Unexplained weight loss
Alopecia	Hair loss
Anemia	Anemia
Inmunosupresión	Immunosuppression
Hemorragia	Bleeding
Linfadenopatía	Lymphadenopathy
Hiperplasia	Hyperplasia
Disfagia	Dysphagia
Ascitis	Ascites
Ictericia	Jaundice
Disnea	Shortness of breath
Hemoptisis	Hemoptysis
Caquexia	Cachexia
Hipoxia	Hypoxia
Debilidad muscular	Muscle weakness
Hematoma	Hematoma
Cefalea	Headache
Parestesias	Paresthesias

Trombosis	Thrombosis
Erupción cutánea	Skin rash
Estreñimiento	Constipation
Diarrea	Diarrhea
Palpitaciones	Palpitations
Confusión	Confusion
Visión borrosa	Blurred vision
Derrame pleural	Pleural effusion

Explanation:

Symptoms such as fatiga (fatigue), pérdida de peso inexplicable (unexplained weight loss), and dolor crónico (chronic pain) with patients often indicate the body's reaction to cancer or its treatments, such as chemotherapy or radiation therapy. For instance, an oncologist might explain, "La fatiga es un efecto común de la quimioterapia, y aunque es intensa, suele mejorar después de que termine el tratamiento," meaning, "Fatigue is a common side effect of chemotherapy, and while it is intense, it usually improves after treatment ends."

Other symptoms, like linfadenopatía (lymphadenopathy) and hemoptisis (coughing up blood), can signal more serious developments in the disease, and clear communication about these signs is critical for early intervention. Oncologists must also explain how certain symptoms, such as disnea (shortness of breath) or ascitis (fluid buildup in the abdomen), relate to the patient's specific type of cancer or its spread.

For example, a patient with lung cancer may present with disnea and derrames pleurales (pleural effusions), which an oncologist could explain as, "El cáncer está causando acumulación de líquido en los pulmones, lo que hace difícil respirar. Vamos a extraer el líquido y ajustar el tratamiento." ("The cancer is causing a fluid buildup in the lungs, making it difficult to breathe. We will drain the fluid and adjust the treatment.")

Symptoms such as alopecia (hair loss) and anemia (anemia) are common effects of chemotherapy or radiation, and patients often have concerns about these changes. Oncology professionals must be prepared to discuss these symptoms compassionately, providing both medical explanations and emotional support.

Explaining Treatment Plans in Oncology

Oncology treatment plans are often complex and multifaceted, involving surgery, chemotherapy, radiation therapy, immunotherapy, and other emerging treatments such as targeted therapies. The goal is to tailor the treatment plan to the type and stage of cancer, the patient's overall health, and their response to therapy. Oncologists must be able to clearly explain the steps involved in treatment, potential side effects, and the expected outcomes to help patients and their families make informed decisions.

In this section, we will introduce key terminology related to explaining treatment plans in oncology.

Medical terms in Spanish	Medical terms in English
Plan de tratamiento	Treatment plan
Cirugía	Surgery
Quimioterapia	Chemotherapy
Radioterapia	Radiotherapy
Inmunoterapia	Immunotherapy
Terapia dirigida	Targeted therapy
Terapia hormonal	Hormonal therapy
Terapia de mantenimiento	Maintenance therapy
Cirugía curativa	Curative surgery
Cirugía paliativa	Palliative surgery
Seguimiento	Follow-up
Evaluación de la respuesta	Response evaluation
Protocolo de tratamiento	Treatment protocol
Terapia adjuvante	Adjuvant therapy
Terapia neoadjuvante	Neoadjuvant therapy
Medicamento antineoplásico	Antineoplastic drug
Reducción tumoral	Tumor reduction
Remisión	Remission

Cura	Cure
Paliación	Palliation
Recaída	Relapse
Mejoría	Improvement
Ensayo clínico	Clinical trial
Pronóstico	Prognosis
Terapia de soporte	Supportive therapy
Equipo multidisciplinario	Multidisciplinary team
Atención integral	Comprehensive care
Gestión del dolor	Pain management

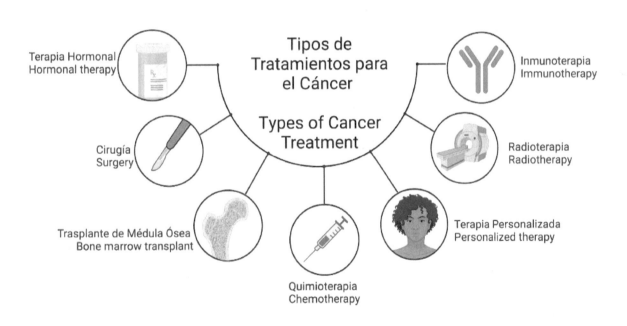

Types of cancer treatments

Explanation:

Oncologists often need to describe different treatment modalities like quimioterapia (chemotherapy), radioterapia (radiation therapy), and inmunoterapia (immunotherapy), depending on the type and stage of cancer. For instance, an oncologist might say, "Vamos a comenzar con la quimioterapia para reducir el tamaño del tumor antes de realizar la cirugía," which translates to, "We are going to start with chemotherapy to reduce the size of the tumor before performing surgery."

In addition to explaining the main treatment, it is important to discuss efectos secundarios (side effects), such as fatigue or nausea, so patients know what to expect. For example, "Este tratamiento puede causar náuseas y fatiga, pero le daremos medicamentos para manejar estos efectos secundarios" means, "This treatment may cause nausea and fatigue, but we will give you medications to manage these side effects."

Terapia adyuvante (adjuvant therapy) and terapia neoadyuvante (neoadjuvant therapy) are common strategies used to enhance the primary treatment. An oncologist might explain, "La terapia adyuvante después de la cirugía ayudará a destruir cualquier célula cancerosa restante," meaning, "Adjuvant therapy after surgery will help destroy any remaining cancer cells."

Moreover, communicating the goals of the treatment plan, whether the aim is curación (cure), paliación (palliation), or remisión (remission), is key in practice. For instance, in cases of advanced cancer where cure is not possible, the focus may shift toward paliación (palliation) to manage symptoms and improve the patient's calidad de vida (quality of life).

Finally, oncologists must emphasize the importance of seguimiento (follow-up) and monitoreo (monitoring) to track the patient's response to treatment and make any necessary adjustments.

Examples of Conversations

Conversation 1: Doctor/Patient Conversation - Discussing a Treatment Plan

Spanish	Translation
Doctor: Vamos a comenzar con un plan de tratamiento que incluye quimioterapia y radioterapia. El objetivo es reducir el tamaño del tumor antes de considerar la cirugía.	*Doctor*: We will start with a treatment plan that includes chemotherapy and radiotherapy. The goal is to reduce the size of the tumor before considering surgery.
Paciente: ¿Y qué efectos secundarios debo esperar?	*Patient*: And what side effects should I expect?

Doctor: Puede experimentar fatiga, náuseas y pérdida de cabello, pero estos efectos suelen ser manejables con medicamentos. También es importante hacer un seguimiento regular para evaluar cómo responde su cuerpo al tratamiento.	*Doctor*: You may experience fatigue, nausea, and hair loss, but these effects are usually manageable with medications. It's also important to have regular follow-up appointments to evaluate how your body is responding to the treatment.
Paciente: ¿Cuánto tiempo durará el tratamiento?	*Patient*: How long will the treatment last?
Doctor: Depende de cómo responda al tratamiento, pero planeamos evaluar su progreso después de tres meses y ajustar el protocolo según sea necesario.	*Doctor*: It depends on how you respond to the treatment, but we plan to evaluate your progress after three months and adjust the protocol as needed.

Conversation 2: Doctor/Nurse Conversation - Preparing for Chemotherapy

Spanish	Translation
Doctor: Ernesto, necesitamos preparar la quimioterapia para el paciente en la sala 2. Vamos a comenzar con un protocolo de tratamiento estándar.	*Doctor:* Ernesto, we need to prepare the chemotherapy for the patient in room 2. We will start with a standard treatment protocol.
Enfermero: De acuerdo, doctor. ¿Hay algo en particular que deba tener en cuenta para este paciente?	*Nurse:* Understood, doctor. Is there anything specific I should keep in mind for this patient?
Doctor: Sí, el paciente tiene antecedentes de inmunosupresión, así que monitorea de cerca cualquier signo de infección. Además, asegúrate de que se administren los medicamentos para controlar las náuseas antes de la sesión.	*Doctor:* Yes, the patient has a history of immunosuppression, so monitor closely for any signs of infection. Also, make sure the medications for nausea control are administered before the session.
Enfermero: Entendido. También informaré al paciente sobre los efectos secundarios y me aseguraré de que sepa cómo manejar los síntomas en casa.	*Nurse:* Got it. I will also inform the patient about the side effects and make sure they know how to manage symptoms at home.

Conversation 3: Nurse/Patient Conversation - Explaining Symptom Management

Spanish	Translation
Enfermera: Vamos a comenzar con la quimioterapia hoy. Es posible que sienta fatiga y náuseas después de la sesión.	*Nurse*: We will start with chemotherapy today. You may feel fatigue and nausea after the session.
Paciente: ¿Hay algo que pueda hacer para controlar esos síntomas?	*Patient:* Is there anything I can do to manage those symptoms?
Enfermera: Sí, le vamos a dar medicamentos para las náuseas. También le recomiendo descansar lo suficiente y mantenerse hidratado. Si experimenta debilidad extrema o algún otro síntoma, avísenos de inmediato.	*Nurse:* Yes, we will give you medications for nausea. I also recommend getting plenty of rest and staying hydrated. If you experience extreme weakness or any other symptoms, let us know immediately.
Paciente: ¿Puedo seguir con mi dieta normal?	*Patient:* Can I continue with my normal diet?
Enfermera: Sí, pero si nota que algunos alimentos le provocan malestar, trate de evitarlos. Si tiene problemas para comer, podemos hablar con un nutriólogo para ayudarle a adaptar su dieta.	*Nurse:* Yes, but if you notice that certain foods upset your stomach, try to avoid them. If you have trouble eating, we can talk to a nutritionist to help you adjust your diet.

Key Takeaways

Spanish-speaking healthcare professionals need to familiarize themselves with the specialized vocabulary to accurately convey information about different cancers, treatment modalities like chemotherapy, radiotherapy, and immunotherapy, as well as the psychological and physical impact on patients. Mastering terms like "metástasis" (metastasis), "quimioterapia" (chemotherapy), and "prognóstico" (prognosis) allows for better patient care and informed decision-making.

Exercises

Exercise 1

Write the Spanish translation of the following medical terms:

1. Metastasis
2. Chemotherapy
3. Tumor
4. Biopsy
5. Remission

Exercise 2

Fill in the blanks:

1. La _____ es el tratamiento de elección para reducir el tamaño de un tumor antes de la cirugía.
2. El oncólogo detectó la _____ del cáncer en el paciente.
3. El proceso de _____ describe cómo el cáncer se disemina a otras partes del cuerpo.
4. El médico solicitó una _____ para confirmar el diagnóstico de cáncer.
5. Después del tratamiento, el paciente entró en _____ completa.

Exercise 3

Write a brief conversation in Spanish between a doctor and a patient discussing the side effects of chemotherapy. Include at least 3 oncology-related terms in your dialogue.

Exercise 4

Translate the following sentences into English:

1. El cáncer de pulmón es una de las principales causas de muerte en el mundo.
2. La quimioterapia puede causar fatiga y náuseas intensas.
3. El médico explicó que la biopsia es necesaria para confirmar el tipo de cáncer.
4. Después de varias sesiones de radioterapia, el tumor se redujo considerablemente.
5. La metástasis a los huesos es una complicación grave del cáncer de mama.

Exercise 5

Translate the following sentences into Spanish:

1. The patient entered remission after completing the treatment.
2. Chemotherapy can weaken the immune system and cause hair loss.
3. The oncologist recommended an immunotherapy plan to enhance the body's response to cancer.
4. A biopsy was performed to obtain a tissue sample for diagnosis.

5. The tumor had metastasized to other organs.

Answer Key

Exercise 1

English	Spanish
Metastasis	Metástasis
Chemotherapy	Quimioterapia
Tumor	Tumor
Biopsy	Biopsia
Remission	Remisión

Exercise 2

1. La quimioterapia es el tratamiento de elección para reducir el tamaño de un tumor antes de la cirugía.
2. El oncólogo detectó la metástasis del cáncer en el paciente.
3. El proceso de carcinogénesis describe cómo el cáncer se disemina a otras partes del cuerpo.
4. El médico solicitó una biopsia para confirmar el diagnóstico de cáncer.
5. Después del tratamiento, el paciente entró en remisión completa.

Exercise 3 (Example dialogue)

Spanish version

- Doctor: Vamos a comenzar la quimioterapia. Es posible que experimente fatiga, pérdida de cabello, y náuseas.

- Paciente: ¿Cuánto tiempo durarán estos efectos secundarios?

- Doctor: Generalmente desaparecen después de las primeras semanas, pero le daremos medicamentos para ayudar a manejarlos.

English version

- Doctor: We will start chemotherapy. You may experience fatigue, hair loss, and nausea.

- Patient: How long will these side effects last?

- Doctor: They usually go away after the first few weeks, but we will provide medication to help manage them.

Exercise 4

1. Lung cancer is one of the leading causes of death worldwide.
2. Chemotherapy can cause intense fatigue and nausea.
3. The doctor explained that a biopsy is necessary to confirm the type of cancer.
4. After several sessions of radiotherapy, the tumor shrank significantly.
5. Metastasis to the bones is a serious complication of breast cancer.

Exercise 5

1. El paciente entró en remisión después de completar el tratamiento.
2. La quimioterapia puede debilitar el sistema inmunológico y causar pérdida de cabello.
3. El oncólogo recomendó un plan de inmunoterapia para mejorar la respuesta del cuerpo al cáncer.
4. Se realizó una biopsia para obtener una muestra de tejido para el diagnóstico.
5. El tumor había hecho metástasis a otros órganos.

BOOK 5

Clinical Conversations: Mastering Complex Medical Dialogues in Spanish

Advanced Communication Strategies
for Healthcare Professionals

Explore to Win

Book 5 Description

Managing healthcare for patients with multiple chronic illnesses can often feel like piecing together a complicated puzzle. "Managing Patients with Multiple Comorbidities" offers an invaluable resource for healthcare professionals, specifically crafted to tackle the unique challenges faced by this patient demographic, particularly within Spanish-speaking communities.

Beginning with a rich glossary of vital medical terms in both Spanish and English, the chapter empowers providers to facilitate clear dialogue with their patients. You will find expert insights into how to navigate the challenges of polypharmacy, with practical examples illustrating the importance of monitoring medication interactions to mitigate risks.

The chapter also emphasizes the significance of gathering comprehensive patient histories—personal and familial—to tailor treatment plans effectively. Understanding psychological factors and social determinants of health is crucial for anticipating complications and fostering adherence to treatment regimens.

Moreover, real-life dialogue examples, such as a doctor's interaction with a patient who is hesitant about medication side effects or a healthcare team discussing a patient's multifaceted care plan, enrich the reader's understanding. This hands-on approach ensures that healthcare providers can confidently address cultural nuances and leverage family support systems in their care strategies.

"Managing Patients with Multiple Comorbidities" serves as a critical guide for healthcare practitioners dedicated to improving patient outcomes through informed, culturally competent care. Equipped with the right tools and knowledge, providers can not only manage complex medical needs but also support their patients in navigating their healthcare journeys with confidence.

Chapter I: Managing Patients with Multiple Comorbidities

Hacen más por la medicina quienes buscan que quienes concluyen.

Ángeles Mastretta

Medical Terminology for Comorbidities

Patients with multiple comorbidities often present a unique challenge to healthcare providers due to the complexity of their medical needs. These patients frequently suffer from overlapping chronic conditions, such as diabetes, hypertension, chronic kidney disease, and heart failure. Properly managing these conditions involves coordinating care among various specialists, carefully monitoring medication interactions, and ensuring that the patient adheres to their treatment plan. This chapter provides the terminology, dialogue examples, and strategies necessary to navigate these complexities in Spanish-speaking populations.

Medical Terminology for Managing Comorbidities

Medical terms in Spanish	Medical terms in English
Motivo de consulta	Reason for consultation
Historia patológica personal	Personal pathological history
Historia patológica familiar	Family pathological history
Medicación actual	Current medication
Reacciones adversas a medicamentos (RAM)	Adverse drug reaction (ADR)
Antecedentes quirúrgicos	Surgical history
Comorbilidades	Comorbidities
Consumo de sustancia	Substance abuse
Cronología de los síntomas	Chronology of symptoms
Factores exacerbantes	Exacerbating factors

Factores atenuantes	Alleviating factors
Actividades de la vida diaria (AVD)	Activities of daily living (ADL)
Estado funcional	Functional status
Afectación psicoemocional	Psycho-emotional status
Polifarmacia	Polypharmacy
Interacción medicamentosa	Drug interaction
Adherencia al tratamiento	Treatment adherence
Insuficiencia renal	Renal insufficiency
Hepatopatía crónica	Chronic liver disease
Monitoreo terapéutico	Therapeutic monitoring
Ajuste de dosis	Dose adjustment
Efectos adversos	Adverse effects
Consulta multidisciplinaria	Multidisciplinary consultation
Aterosclerosis	Atherosclerosis
Dislipidemia	Dyslipidemia
Insuficiencia cardíaca congestiva	Congestive heart failure
Diuréticos	Diuretics
Diálisis peritoneal	Peritoneal dialysis
Nefropatía diabética	Diabetic nephropathy
Insulina de acción prolongada	Long-acting insulin
Glucosa en sangre	Blood glucose
Hipoglucemia	Hypoglycemia
Hiperglucemia	Hyperglycemia

Spanish	English
Control de peso	Weight control
Fatiga crónica	Chronic fatigue
Complicaciones metabólicas	Metabolic complications
Dieta hiposódica	Low-sodium diet
Terapia combinada	Combination therapy
Reducción del colesterol	Cholesterol reduction
Terapia anticoagulante	Anticoagulant therapy
Glucosa en ayunas	Fasting glucose
Control de lípidos	Lipid control
Hipertensión no controlada	Uncontrolled hypertension
Enfermedad vascular periférica	Peripheral vascular disease
Cardiopatía isquémica	Ischemic heart disease
Endocrinopatías	Endocrinopathies
Hemoglobina glicosilada	Glycated hemoglobin (HbA1c)
Insulina de acción rápida	Rapid-acting insulin
Insulina de acción intermedia	Intermediate-acting insulin
Insulina de acción prolongada	Long-acting insulin
Antihipertensivos	Antihypertensives
Prevención de complicaciones	Prevention of complications
Antiarrítmicos	Antiarrhythmics
Estatinas	Statins

Explanation:

Managing patients with multiple comorbidities requires clear and precise communication between healthcare providers and patients to ensure proper treatment, minimize risks, and optimize care.

These terms allow professionals to discuss everything from the patient's medical history to specific treatment adjustments, enabling a structured and effective approach in complex scenarios.

In this context, terms related to medical history are very relevant, as patients with multiple comorbidities often have extensive personal and family histories of illnesses. Concepts like "Historia patológica personal" (Personal pathological history) and "Historia patológica familiar" (Family pathological history) help gather valuable information that can influence the treatment plan. A thorough understanding of the patient's background is necessary to anticipate complications and determine the right course of action, especially when several conditions interact.

Equally important is the medication management aspect, reflected in terms like "Medicación actual" (Current medication), "Polifarmacia" (Polypharmacy), and "Interacción medicamentosa" (Drug interaction). These patients are often on numerous medications, which increases the risk of interactions and adverse effects. Accurately discussing their current regimen and being aware of potential drug interactions is crucial to avoid harmful complications. Healthcare providers need to carefully adjust dosages and manage side effects, making precise terminology essential for patient safety and treatment efficacy.

In addition to medication, this vocabulary supports conversations around treatment adherence and therapeutic monitoring. Terms like "Adherencia al tratamiento" (Treatment adherence) and "Monitoreo terapéutico" (Therapeutic monitoring) are vital for ensuring that the patient is following their treatment plan and that their response to therapies is being tracked. Patients with comorbidities are at higher risk for complications if they don't adhere to their prescribed treatments, so using clear language helps reinforce the importance of regular monitoring and adherence.

Finally, the multidisciplinary nature of care for patients with comorbidities is reflected in terms such as "Consulta multidisciplinaria" (Multidisciplinary consultation). These patients often require input from different specialists, including cardiologists, endocrinologists, nephrologists, and more.

Managing Comorbidities and Medication in Hispanic Communities

When dealing with patients with multiple comorbidities, you often encounter those who are prescribed multiple medications, sometimes with different routes of administration, such as oral pills, injections, or topical applications. Ensuring patients understand how and when to take their medications is a fundamental factor for successful treatment. In some cases, the risk of drug interactions may be high, and explaining this to the patient can help avoid complications.

For example, a patient may be hesitant to use certain medications due to traditional beliefs or fear of side effects. In these cases, healthcare providers must be equipped to address these concerns while respecting cultural values.

This becomes particularly important in Hispanic communities where chronic diseases like diabetes, hypertension, and cardiovascular disease are very prevalent. It is very common that for patients managing such conditions and taking multiple medications, the situation becomes overwhelming. Misunderstanding instructions or missing doses due to confusion can lead to serious complications.

Therefore, professionals must prioritize clear communication and consider using visual aids, written instructions, or family members to reinforce medication plans.

Moreover, there is a great deal of diversity within Hispanic cultures, and healthcare providers must recognize that care coordination strategies need to be adapted accordingly. For example, in Mexican or Central American cultures, reliance on traditional medicine, such as herbal treatments or consultations with community healers, is still common. A patient with multiple comorbidities might mix herbal remedies with prescribed medications, which can lead to dangerous interactions. For instance, if a patient is taking a diuretic for hypertension and also using herbal teas with diuretic effects, the combined impact could lead to severe dehydration or electrolyte imbalances. In such cases, the provider should acknowledge the patient's use of traditional remedies, showing respect for their cultural practices while educating them on potential risks.

Finally, Patients with multiple comorbidities need clear, understandable explanations about their medications. For example, a healthcare provider might break down a complex regimen into simple steps: "Take this pill with breakfast, this injection before lunch, and this one before bed." Using color-coded charts or pill organizers can also help patients keep track of their medications.

Examples of Conversations

Conversation 1: Doctor/Patient Conversation

Context: The patient is a 65-year-old woman named María, who has diabetes, hypertension, and chronic kidney disease. She is taking multiple medications, and during her consultation, the doctor notices she has been using herbal teas to manage her blood pressure in addition to her prescribed diuretic. The doctor needs to explain the risks of mixing medications and herbal remedies, ensure María understands how to properly take her medications, and discuss strategies for managing her conditions.

Spanish	Translation
Doctor: Buenos días, María. ¿Cómo se ha sentido últimamente con sus medicamentos?	*Doctor*: Good morning, María. How have you been feeling lately with your medications?
Paciente: Doctor, me he sentido bien, pero a veces siento mareos. También, he estado tomando té de hierbas para bajar la presión.	*Patient*: Doctor, I've been feeling fine, but sometimes I feel dizzy. Also, I've been drinking herbal tea to lower my blood pressure.
Doctor: Entiendo. Es importante que hablemos de eso. Usted ya está tomando un diurético para la presión alta, y mezclarlo con el té de hierbas puede ser peligroso. Puede causar deshidratación o	*Doctor*: I understand. It's important we discuss that. You are already taking a diuretic for high blood pressure, and mixing it with herbal tea can be dangerous. It can cause

alterar el equilibrio de los electrolitos en su cuerpo.	dehydration or disrupt your body's electrolyte balance.
Paciente: No sabía que podía ser peligroso. Solo lo tomo porque mi hermana dice que es natural y ayuda.	*Patient*: I didn't know it could be dangerous. I only take it because my sister says it's natural and helps.
Doctor: Lo comprendo. Muchas personas creen que lo natural es mejor, pero en este caso, combinar el té con su diurético puede tener efectos negativos. Le sugiero que deje de tomar el té de hierbas y que sigamos solo con los medicamentos que le recetamos.	*Doctor*: I understand. Many people believe that natural remedies are better, but in this case, combining the tea with your diuretic can have negative effects. I suggest you stop taking herbal tea and stick to the medications we prescribed.
Paciente: De acuerdo, doctor. ¿Qué debo hacer para evitar los mareos?	*Patient:* Okay, doctor. What should I do to avoid the dizziness?
Doctor: Los mareos pueden ser un efecto secundario de los medicamentos. ¿Está tomando sus medicamentos a la misma hora todos los días y con suficiente agua?	*Doctor:* Dizziness can be a side effect of the medications. Are you taking your medications at the same time every day and with enough water?
Paciente: A veces se me olvida tomar algunos.	*Patient:* Sometimes I forget to take some of them.
Doctor: Es muy importante que tome todos los medicamentos según lo indicado. Le voy a dar una tabla con los horarios para que los siga, y puede usar un organizador de pastillas para que no lo olvide.	*Doctor:* It's very important that you take all of your medications as prescribed. I'm going to give you a chart with the schedules to follow, and you can use a pill organizer to help you remember.
Paciente: Así lo hago entonces, ¿y si me confundo?	*Patient:* I will do it like that then, what if I get confused?
Doctor: Recuerde que también puede pedir ayuda a su familia si necesita apoyo con los horarios. Además, es crucial que venga a sus citas regularmente para que podamos monitorear su progreso y ajustar el tratamiento si es necesario.	*Doctor:* Perfect. Remember that you can also ask your family for help with the schedules if you need support. It's also crucial that you come to your regular appointments so we can monitor your progress and adjust the treatment if necessary.
Paciente: Lo haré, muchas gracias.	*Paciente:* I will, thank you so much.

Conversation 2: Nurse/ Doctor

The nurse is updating the doctor about María's condition and medication adherence. They discuss adjustments to her medication regimen, potential drug interactions, and María's cultural practices of using herbal remedies.

Spanish	Translation
Enfermera: Doctor, he revisado el historial de María y parece que no está siguiendo completamente su régimen de medicamentos. Además, me mencionó que está tomando té de hierbas para la presión alta.	*Nurse:* Doctor, I've reviewed María's medical history, and it seems she isn't fully following her medication regimen. She also mentioned that she's taking herbal tea for high blood pressure.
Doctor: Eso es preocupante. Ella ya está tomando un diurético, ¿verdad? Mezclar eso con remedios herbales podría ser riesgoso.	*Doctor:* That's concerning. She's already on a diuretic, right? Mixing that with herbal remedies could be risky.
Enfermera: Correcto, está tomando furosemida. Me preocupa que pueda deshidratarse o que sus electrolitos se desequilibren.	*Nurse:* Yes, she's taking furosemide. I'm worried she might get dehydrated or that her electrolytes might become unbalanced.
Doctor: Definitivamente. Vamos a ajustar su tratamiento y educarla sobre los riesgos de mezclar remedios herbales con medicamentos. También deberíamos monitorear su función renal con más frecuencia.	*Doctor:* Definitely. We'll need to adjust her treatment and educate her on the risks of mixing herbal remedies with medications. We should also monitor her kidney function more closely.
Enfermera: De acuerdo. También he notado que tiene dificultades para recordar tomar sus medicamentos. ¿Le parece que hablemos con su familia para que la ayuden a seguir el plan?	*Nurse:* Agreed. I've also noticed she's having trouble remembering to take her medications. Should we talk to her family to help her stay on track?
Doctor: Sí, es una buena idea. Involucremos a su familia en las instrucciones y asegurémonos de que entiendan la importancia de la adherencia. También podemos ofrecerle un organizador de pastillas.	*Doctor:* Yes, that's a good idea. Let's involve her family in the instructions and make sure they understand the importance of adherence. We can also offer her a pill organizer.
Enfermera: Haré eso. ¿Le parece que ajustemos la dosis de su diurético o esperemos a los resultados del próximo análisis de sangre?	*Nurse:* I'll do that. Should we adjust her diuretic dosage or wait for the next blood test results?

Doctor: Vamos a esperar a los resultados, pero monitoreemos de cerca su presión y signos de deshidratación.	*Doctor:* Let's wait for the results, but let's closely monitor her blood pressure and signs of dehydration.

Key Takeaways

Managing patients with multiple comorbidities requires a comprehensive approach involving coordination among healthcare providers and specialists to address complex medication regimens, manage drug interactions, and ensure treatment adherence. Cultural sensitivity is critical, especially in Hispanic communities, where patients may use herbal remedies alongside prescribed medications. Clear communication and precise medical terminology help prevent complications, while visual aids and family involvement can improve medication adherence. Finally, a multidisciplinary approach, including input from various specialists, ensures holistic care for those living with multiple conditions.

Exercises

Exercise 1

Match the English term to its Spanish translation.

1. Comorbidities
2. Polypharmacy
3. Renal insufficiency
4. Adverse drug reaction
5. Treatment adherence

Options:

a) Adherencia al tratamiento
b) Insuficiencia renal
c) Polifarmacia
d) Comorbilidades
e) Reacciones adversas a medicamentos (RAM)

Exercise 2

Fill in the blanks with the correct Spanish term from the word bank below.

Word Bank:

Medicación actual

Factores exacerbantes

Interacción medicamentosa

Historia patológica familiar

Monitoreo terapéutico

1. La paciente presenta una interacción entre dos de sus medicamentos, lo que puede causar efectos secundarios graves. Esto es un ejemplo de una _____.
2. Durante la consulta, es importante preguntar sobre la _____ para identificar posibles enfermedades hereditarias.
3. La _____ se debe hacer regularmente para verificar que los niveles de glucosa y lípidos estén bajo control.
4. Se observan _____, como el estrés, que empeoran los síntomas de la hipertensión.
5. Revisar la _____ del paciente ayuda a conocer los medicamentos que está tomando actualmente.

Exercise 3

Write a dialogue between a doctor and the caregiver of a patient with a complex chronic condition, such as diabetes and hypertension. The conversation should focus on the patient's treatment plan, including medication management and monitoring. Use at least three terms from the medical terminology i

Exercise 4

Create a conversation between a geriatrician and a medical assistant about a patient's recent check-up. The conversation should focus on the patient's glucose control, blood pressure, and treatment adjustments. Use at least three terms from the medical terminology.

Exercise 5

Translate the following sentences into Spanish.

1. The patient has uncontrolled hypertension and needs an adjustment in medication.
2. Monitoring blood glucose is essential for patients with diabetes.
3. Adverse drug reactions can be dangerous if not monitored properly.
4. Family history is important to identify potential comorbidities.
5. A multidisciplinary consultation will help manage the patient's comorbid conditions.

Answer Key

Exercise 1

1. d - Comorbilidades
2. c - Polifarmacia
3. b - Insuficiencia renal
4. e - Reacciones adversas a medicamentos (RAM)
5. a - Adherencia al tratamiento

Exercise 2

1. Interacción medicamentosa
2. Historia patológica familiar
3. Monitoreo terapéutico
4. Factores exacerbantes
5. Medicación actual

Exercise 3

Spanish version: Doctor/Cuidador del paciente –

Doctor: Buenas tardes. Quisiera hablar sobre el manejo de la diabetes y la hipertensión de su esposo. ¿Cómo ha estado con los medicamentos?

Cuidador: Ha estado bien, pero a veces se olvida de tomar la insulina a la hora correcta.

Doctor: Es muy importante que siga el horario de la insulina, especialmente porque también está tomando antihipertensivos. La interacción entre los medicamentos puede ser riesgosa si no se toman como se indica.

Cuidador: Entiendo. ¿Podríamos usar algún tipo de recordatorio o tabla para ayudarlo a recordar?

Doctor: Sí, le voy a proporcionar una tabla con los horarios y también puede usar un organizador de pastillas. Además, sería bueno que monitoreen su glucosa en sangre regularmente para evitar hipoglucemias.

Cuidador: De acuerdo. Lo ayudaremos a seguir el plan de tratamiento.

English translation: Doctor/Caregiver of the patient

Doctor: Good afternoon. I'd like to discuss managing your husband's diabetes and hypertension. How has he been with his medications?

Caregiver: He's been okay, but sometimes he forgets to take his insulin on time.

Doctor: It's very important that he follows the insulin schedule, especially because he's also taking antihypertensives. The interaction between these medications can be risky if not taken as directed.

Caregiver: I understand. Could we use some kind of reminder or chart to help him remember?

Doctor: Yes, I will provide a chart with the medication schedules, and you can also use a pill organizer. Additionally, it's crucial to monitor his blood glucose regularly to prevent hypoglycemia.

Caregiver: Got it. We'll make sure he follows the treatment plan.

Exercise 4

Spanish version: Geriatra/Asistente médico

Geriatra: Buenos días, ¿ya revisó los resultados de la paciente?

Asistente médico: Sí, doctor. Los niveles de glucosa en sangre están controlados, pero la presión arterial sigue alta.

Geriatra: Vamos a ajustar su tratamiento antihipertensivo. También hay que asegurarnos de que está siguiendo su dieta hiposódica.

Asistente médico: De acuerdo, hablaré con su familia para reforzar las indicaciones sobre la dieta. ¿Quiere que monitoreemos su función renal más seguido?

Geriatra: Sí, es mejor hacerlo cada tres meses, considerando su historial de insuficiencia renal.

English translation: Geriatrician/ Medical assistant

Geriatrician: Good morning, have you reviewed the patient's results?

Medical Assistant: Yes, doctor. Her blood glucose levels are controlled, but her blood pressure is still high.

Geriatrician: Let's adjust her antihypertensive treatment. We also need to make sure she's following her low-sodium diet.

Medical Assistant: Agreed, I'll speak with her family to reinforce the dietary guidelines. Do you want us to monitor her kidney function more frequently?

Geriatrician: Yes, let's do it every three months, considering her history of renal insufficiency.

Exercise 5

1. La paciente tiene hipertensión no controlada y necesita un ajuste en la medicación.
2. Monitorear la glucosa en sangre es esencial para los pacientes con diabetes.
3. Las reacciones adversas a medicamentos pueden ser peligrosas si no se monitorean adecuadamente.
4. La historia patológica familiar es importante para identificar posibles comorbilidades.
5. Una consulta multidisciplinaria ayudará a manejar las comorbilidades del paciente.

Chapter II: Delivering Bad News and Palliative Care Discussions

Donde quiera que se ama el arte de la medicina se ama también a la humanidad

Platon

In healthcare, few conversations are as emotionally charged and complex as delivering bad news or discussing palliative care options. This chapter is designed to help healthcare professionals master the nuanced communication skills needed to navigate these challenging conversations with Spanish-speaking patients and their families. Through a culturally sensitive lens, you will explore strategies for conveying difficult information in a compassionate, respectful, and ethically sound manner while incorporating specialized Spanish medical terminology essential for these discussions.

Delivering bad news in healthcare is not a one-size-fits-all approach, particularly in Hispanic communities, where cultural and familial dynamics play an integral role in patient care. For many Hispanic families, decisions about end-of-life care or serious diagnoses are made collectively, and the role of family in patient care is highly valued. A key focus of this chapter is to equip healthcare providers with the skills to recognize these cultural distinctions and adapt their communication styles to honor the unique beliefs, customs, and emotional needs of Hispanic patients and their families.

Considering the cultural context in many Hispanic cultures, discussions around death, terminal illness, and palliative care may be avoided or considered taboo. Some families may not want to openly discuss a terminal diagnosis with the patient, preferring to shield them from the reality of their condition. This cultural preference can sometimes conflict with the medical practice of full disclosure. This chapter provides you with tools to approach such delicate situations with cultural sensitivity, finding a balance between providing necessary information and respecting the patient's and family's values.

To assist in these challenging conversations, we will introduce the SPIKES protocol—a structured approach for delivering bad news in a way that is empathetic and respectful. SPIKES stands for:

S - Setting up the interview (Preparar el entorno): Ensure that you have a private and comfortable setting for the conversation to minimize distractions and foster open dialogue.

Spanish: Asegúrese de tener un entorno privado y cómodo para la conversación, lo que ayuda a minimizar distracciones y fomenta un diálogo abierto.

P - Assessing the patient's Knowledge (Evaluar el conocimiento del paciente): Gauge what the patient already knows or suspects about their condition to tailor your message appropriately.

Spanish: Evalúe lo que el paciente ya sabe o sospecha sobre su condición para adaptar su mensaje adecuadamente.

I - Obtaining the patient's Invitation (Obtener la invitación del paciente): Ask the patient if they wish to know the details about their diagnosis. Some may prefer to avoid complete information.

Spanish: Pregunte al paciente si desea conocer los detalles sobre su diagnóstico. Algunos pueden preferir evitar información completa.

K - Giving Knowledge (Dar la información): Deliver the news clearly and directly using simple, straightforward language, avoiding medical jargon while being honest about the situation.

Spanish: Dé las malas noticias de manera clara y directa utilizando un lenguaje simple y directo, evitando la jerga médica y siendo honesto sobre la situación.

E - Addressing Emotions with Empathic Response (Abordar las emociones con una respuesta empática): Acknowledge and validate the emotional response of the patient and/or their family, providing support and allowing them to express their feelings.

Spanish: Reconozca y valide la respuesta emocional del paciente y/o su familia, brindando apoyo y permitiéndoles expresar sus sentimientos.

S - Formulating a Strategy and Summary (Formular una estrategia y resumen): Discuss the next steps in their care plan and summarize the key points, ensuring the patient and family feel supported and informed.

Spanish: Discuta los próximos pasos en su plan de atención y resuma los puntos clave, asegurándose de que el paciente y la familia se sientan apoyados e informados.

This framework not only helps facilitate difficult discussions but also emphasizes the importance of understanding and incorporating the family's role, spirituality, and holistic well-being in the patient's care.

In addition to cultural nuances, this chapter will guide you through how to explain palliative care concepts in a way that acknowledges the importance of family, spirituality, and holistic well-being.

Basic Terminology in Palliative Care

The following table lists key palliative care terms in Spanish and English, covering important topics like terminal illness, pain management, and emotional support to help communicate effectively about end-of-life care.

Medical terms in Spanish	Medical terms in English
Enfermedad terminal	Terminal illness
Cuidados paliativos	Palliative care
Calidad de vida	Quality of life
Manejo del dolor	Pain management

Sedación paliativa	Palliative sedation
Soporte emocional	Emotional support
Duelo	Grief
Ética médica	Medical ethics
Comunicación compasiva	Compassionate communication
Alivio del dolor	Pain relief
Cuidado en el hogar	Home care
Decisiones informadas	Informed decisions
Tratamiento paliativo	Palliative treatment
Limitación del tratamiento	Treatment limitation
Pronóstico reservado	Guarded prognosis
Asistencia espiritual	Spiritual assistance
Apoyo psicológico	Psychological support
Soporte familiar	Family support
Autonomía del paciente	Patient autonomy
Crisis emocional	Emotional crisis
Fase terminal	Terminal phase
Prolongación de vida	Life extension
Deterioro cognitivo	Cognitive decline
Cuidados continuos	Continuous care
Insuficiencia respiratoria	Respiratory failure
Apoyo social	Social support
Alivio sintomático	Symptom relief

Cuidado compasivo	Compassionate care
Cuidados integrales	Holistic care
Sedación consciente	Conscious sedation

Discussing palliative care and end-of-life decisions often involves more than just the patient. Family plays a central role in decision-making, and cultural values surrounding life, death, and healthcare are deeply rooted. This makes it important for healthcare providers to not only use accurate medical terminology but also to understand the broader cultural context when engaging with patients and their families.

For example, terms like soporte familiar (family support) and asistencia espiritual (spiritual assistance) are of particular importance. In many Hispanic cultures, emotional and spiritual well-being are considered just as vital as physical health. Patients may rely heavily on their family's support to navigate difficult health decisions, and they may turn to religious or spiritual leaders for guidance. Therefore, using terms like soporte emocional (emotional support) and apoyo espiritual (spiritual support) can help healthcare professionals acknowledge these important elements of care, ensuring that patients feel understood and respected.

Clear communication is also essential when discussing complex medical topics such as voluntades anticipadas (advance directives) or decisiones sobre el final de la vida (end-of-life decisions). These conversations can be emotionally charged and may require extra care and empathy. Healthcare professionals should ensure that both the patient and their family fully understand the implications of these decisions and are given ample time to reflect on their choices. It is important to be aware that in some Hispanic cultures, openly discussing death or terminal illness may be seen as inappropriate or even harmful, making terms like fases terminales (terminal phases) and prolongación de vida (life extension) potentially sensitive topics.

Furthermore, when explaining concepts like manejo del dolor (pain management) or sedación paliativa (palliative sedation), healthcare providers must approach these conversations with cultural awareness. Some patients or families may express concerns about treatments that alter consciousness or might have misconceptions about pain management interventions. Using culturally sensitive language and offering thorough explanations of the benefits of treatments like sedación consciente (conscious sedation) or alivio sintomático (symptom relief) can help bridge this gap, fostering trust and cooperation.

Finally, given the significance of family involvement in decision-making, it's vital to engage the family in discussions about planificación avanzada (advance planning) and retirada del tratamiento (treatment withdrawal). Involving family members ensures that the patient's wishes are carried out while respecting the cultural value placed on collective decision-making. By using terms like evaluación funcional (functional assessment) and cuidados continuos (continuous care).

Examples of Conversations

Conversation 1: Doctor/Patient and Family – Discussing End-of-Life Decisions with a Patient and Family

A doctor is meeting with a terminally ill patient, Ana, and her family to discuss her options for end-of-life care. The doctor needs to explain the concept of advance directives, the importance of family support, and the option of palliative sedation to manage Ana's pain and improve her quality of life. The family is worried about how to make these difficult decisions and wants to ensure they honor Ana's wishes.

Spanish	Translation
Doctor: Buenas tardes, Ana. Hoy quiero hablar sobre sus cuidados a largo plazo, dado que su enfermedad es terminal. Es importante que discutamos las voluntades anticipadas, lo que significa tomar decisiones sobre su tratamiento futuro y manejo del dolor.	*Doctor*: Good afternoon, Ana. Today, I'd like to talk about your long-term care, given that your illness is terminal. It's important that we discuss advance directives, which means making decisions about your future treatment and pain management.
Ana: Sí, doctor. Quiero saber cómo puedo estar más cómoda en estos momentos.	Ana: Yes, doctor. I want to know how I can be more comfortable during this time.
Doctor: Podemos enfocarnos en mejorar su calidad de vida con cuidados paliativos. También hay opciones como la sedación paliativa para ayudarle a controlar el dolor y otros síntomas. Esta opción le permitirá descansar sin sufrimiento.	*Doctor*: We can focus on improving your quality of life with palliative care. There are also options like palliative sedation to help you manage pain and other symptoms. This option will allow you to rest without suffering.
Hija de Ana: ¿La sedación paliativa significa que ella estará dormida todo el tiempo?	*Ana's daughter*: Does palliative sedation mean that she'll be asleep all the time?
Doctor: No necesariamente. La sedación consciente le permitirá estar más cómoda sin perder completamente la consciencia. Queremos asegurarnos de que su madre esté libre de dolor pero todavía pueda estar con ustedes	*Doctor*: Not necessarily. Conscious sedation will allow her to be more comfortable without losing complete consciousness. We want to make sure your mother is pain-free but still able to be with you.
Hija de Ana: Entiendo. Queremos que esté cómoda, pero también que pueda disfrutar el tiempo que le queda con nosotros. ¿Cómo podemos ayudar?	*Ana's daughter*: I understand. We want her to be comfortable, but we also want her to enjoy the time she has left with us. How can we help?

Spanish	Translation
Doctor: El apoyo familiar es muy importante en este proceso. Ustedes pueden ayudar a Ana a tomar decisiones sobre su tratamiento y acompañarla emocionalmente. Las voluntades anticipadas le permitirán expresar sus deseos y planificar cómo quiere ser cuidada en sus últimos días.	*Doctor:* Family support is very important in this process. You can help Ana make decisions about her treatment and provide emotional support. Advance directives will allow her to express her wishes and plan how she wants to be cared for in her final days.
Ana: Me gustaría tomar decisiones con mi familia. Quiero asegurarme de que mis últimos momentos sean tranquilos.	*Ana:* I'd like to make decisions with my family. I want to make sure my last moments are peaceful.
Doctor: Por supuesto, Ana. Juntos, podemos hacer un plan que respete sus deseos y le proporcione el soporte emocional que necesita en este tiempo.	*Doctor:* Absolutely, Ana. Together, we can make a plan that respects your wishes and provides the emotional support you need during this time.

Conversation 2: Nurse/Patient and Family – Discussing Hospice Care with a Family

A nurse is meeting with the family of Carlos, a patient with advanced lung disease, to explain the transition to hospice care. Carlos has been experiencing severe respiratory distress, and his family is unsure about the next steps. The nurse needs to explain the goals of hospice care, the importance of comfort care, and how the family can participate in the decision-making process.

Spanish	Translation
Enfermera: Buenas tardes, familia. Quisiera hablar con ustedes sobre el próximo paso en el cuidado de Carlos. Su condición ha avanzado, y ahora recomendamos los cuidados de hospicio para mejorar su calidad de vida.	*Nurse:* Good afternoon, family. I'd like to talk with you about the next step in Carlos' care. His condition has progressed, and we now recommend hospice care to improve his quality of life.
Esposa de Carlos: ¿Qué significa exactamente los cuidados de hospicio? No queremos que sufra.	*Carlo's wife:* What exactly does hospice care mean? We don't want him to suffer.
Enfermera: Los cuidados de hospicio se enfocan en el alivio sintomático y el soporte emocional para Carlos. No estamos buscando curar su enfermedad, sino asegurar que esté lo más cómodo posible.	*Nurse:* Hospice care focuses on symptom relief and emotional support for Carlos. We're not aiming to cure his illness but rather to ensure that he's as comfortable as possible.

Hija de Carlos: ¿Eso significa que dejaremos de darle tratamiento?	*Carlos' wife:* Does that mean we'll stop giving him treatment?
Enfermera: No necesariamente. Continuaremos proporcionando tratamientos que le den comodidad, como el manejo del dolor y la asistencia respiratoria, pero evitaremos tratamientos que podrían prolongar su sufrimiento. Nuestro objetivo es mejorar su bienestar y reducir el sufrimiento.	*Nurse:* Not exactly. We'll continue providing treatments that bring him comfort, such as pain management and assisted breathing, but we will avoid treatments that might prolong his suffering. Our goal is to improve his well-being and reduce his suffering.
Esposa de Carlos: Queremos lo mejor para él. ¿Cómo podemos ayudar?	*Carlos' wife:* We want what's best for him. How can we help?
Enfermera: Su soporte familiar es clave. Ustedes pueden ayudarlo tomando decisiones juntos, brindándole compañía, y asegurando que sus deseos sean respetados. También, podemos hablar sobre su planificación avanzada para asegurarnos de que las próximas decisiones se alineen con lo que él quiere.	*Nurse:* Your family support is crucial. You can help by making decisions together, being there for him, and ensuring that his wishes are respected. We can also discuss his advance planning to make sure the next steps align with what he wants.
Hija de Carlos: Eso nos tranquiliza. Queremos estar involucrados en su cuidado y asegurarnos de que no sufra más.	*Carlos' daughter:* That's reassuring. We want to be involved in his care and make sure he doesn't suffer anymore.
Enfermera: Eso es exactamente lo que los cuidados de hospicio buscan. Estaremos aquí para guiarlos en cada paso y asegurarnos de que Carlos reciba el mejor cuidado posible.	*Nurse:* That's exactly what hospice care is about. We'll be here to guide you through every step and ensure that Carlos gets the best care possible.

Key Takeaways

In Hispanic healthcare settings, conversations about death, terminal illness, and palliative care often involve the entire family and require sensitivity to cultural values around collective decision-making and spirituality. Family support plays a critical role in these discussions, and healthcare professionals must engage with the patient's family, respecting their cultural preference for shared decision-making. It is essential to balance full medical disclosure with compassionate communication, especially in cultures where discussing death may be seen as taboo or distressing. Terms like "palliative sedation" and "advance directives" must be explained in a culturally appropriate manner, focusing on comfort and quality of life while addressing any concerns about the interventions. The SPIKES protocol provides a structured framework for delivering bad news that is adaptable to cultural sensitivities, ensuring patients and families feel emotionally supported and fully informed about their options.

Exercises

Exercise 1

Match the English term to its Spanish translation.

1. Terminal illness
2. Palliative care
3. Quality of life
4. Pain management
5. Advance directives

Options:

a) Cuidados paliativos
b) Voluntades anticipadas
c) Calidad de vida
d) Manejo del dolor
e) Enfermedad terminal

Exercise 2

Fill in the blanks with the correct Spanish term.

1. El paciente está en la _____ y necesita un plan de cuidados paliativos. (Fase terminal)
2. Es importante asegurar el _____ del paciente durante el tratamiento. (Bienestar)
3. La familia proporcionó un fuerte _____ durante la conversación sobre cuidados de hospicio. (Soporte familiar)
4. El médico habló sobre los beneficios de la _____ para manejar el dolor del paciente. (Sedación paliativa)
5. Discutimos las _____ para asegurar que se respeten los deseos del paciente. (Voluntades anticipadas)

Exercise 3

Write a conversation between a doctor and a patient discussing palliative care options.

Prompt:

Write a short dialogue (5-6 lines) between a doctor and a patient where the doctor explains the options for palliative care, focusing on pain management and emotional support.

Exercise 4

Create a dialogue between a nurse and a doctor discussing a patient's palliative care plan.

Prompt:

Write a conversation between a nurse and a doctor discussing a patient's progress and the implementation of palliative care, focusing on pain relief and patient autonomy.

Exercise 5

Translate the following sentences into Spanish.

1. The patient has a terminal illness and will receive palliative care.
2. Family support is crucial during end-of-life discussions.
3. We will use pain management techniques to improve the patient's quality of life.
4. Advance directives allow the patient to express their wishes.
5. Compassionate communication is important when delivering bad news.

Answer Key

Exercise 1

Match the English term to its Spanish translation:

1. e) Enfermedad terminal
2. a) Cuidados paliativos
3. c) Calidad de vida
4. d) Manejo del dolor
5. b) Voluntades anticipadas

Exercise 2

Fill in the blanks with the correct Spanish term.

1. Fase terminal
2. Bienestar
3. Soporte familiar
4. Sedación paliativa
5. Voluntades anticipadas

Exercise 3

Write a conversation between a doctor and a patient discussing palliative care options.

Spanish conversation example:

Doctor: Ana, quiero hablar sobre sus opciones de cuidados paliativos para ayudarla a manejar su dolor.

Ana: ¿Eso significa que ya no hay tratamiento para mi enfermedad?

Doctor: No, los cuidados paliativos no son para curar, sino para mejorar su calidad de vida y asegurarnos de que esté cómoda.

Ana: ¿Incluirá apoyo para mi familia también?

Doctor: Sí, su familia recibirá soporte emocional y trabajaremos juntos para respetar sus deseos.

English conversation example:

Doctor: Ana, I want to talk about your palliative care options to help you manage your pain.

Ana: Does that mean there's no longer any treatment for my illness?

Doctor: No, palliative care is not for curing, but for improving your quality of life and making sure you're comfortable.

Ana: Will it also include support for my family?

Doctor: Yes, your family will receive emotional support, and we will work together to respect your wishes.

Exercise 4

Create a dialogue between a nurse and a doctor discussing a patient's palliative care plan.

Enfermera: Doctor, he revisado el plan de tratamiento para Carlos. Creo que deberíamos considerar la sedación paliativa.

Doctor: Estoy de acuerdo, está sufriendo mucho y necesita alivio del dolor.

Enfermera: ¿Le parece bien si hablo con su familia sobre las voluntades anticipadas de Carlos?

Doctor: Sí, es importante que se respete su autonomía y que su familia esté involucrada en las decisiones.

English translation:

Nurse: Doctor, I've reviewed Carlos' treatment plan. I think we should consider palliative sedation.

Doctor: I agree, he is suffering a lot and needs pain relief.

Nurse: Do you think it's okay if I talk to his family about Carlos' advance directives?

Doctor: Yes, it's important to respect his autonomy and involve his family in the decisions.

Exercise 5

Translate the following sentences into Spanish.

1. El paciente tiene una enfermedad terminal y recibirá cuidados paliativos.
2. El soporte familiar es crucial durante las discusiones sobre el final de la vida.
3. Usaremos técnicas de manejo del dolor para mejorar la calidad de vida del paciente.
4. Las voluntades anticipadas permiten al paciente expresar sus deseos.
5. La comunicación compasiva es importante al dar malas noticias.

Chapter III: Respectful Communication with Socioeconomically Disadvantaged Patients

El médico competente, antes de dar una medicina a su paciente, se familiariza no sólo con la enfermedad que desea curar, sino también con los hábitos y la constitución del enfermo.

Marco Tulio

If you want to learn how healthcare professionals can build effective, compassionate communication with socioeconomically disadvantaged Hispanic patients, this chapter is for you. Many patients face financial hardships, limited health literacy, and significant barriers to care that affect their health outcomes. This chapter focuses on providing healthcare providers with the tools to recognize and address these challenges while maintaining respect and empathy. It emphasizes the importance of understanding social determinants of health, such as education, income, and access to resources that play a major role in a patient's ability to navigate the healthcare system. This chapter goes beyond general advice by offering medical terminology in both Spanish and English, practical strategies, and dialogue examples to create a culturally appropriate communication framework.

Understanding the intersection of socioeconomic status and healthcare in Hispanic cultures is crucial. Patients may face unique obstacles such as transportation limitations, language barriers, and concerns about immigration status, which complicate their access to healthcare services. Healthcare providers must be able to offer solutions like financial aid programs, community health clinics, and flexible scheduling while avoiding assumptions and cultural stereotypes. In this chapter, we provide step-by-step strategies for discussing cost-effective treatment options, addressing concerns about the affordability of medications, and referring patients to community resources. These strategies are paired with dialogue examples that reflect real-world scenarios in Hispanic healthcare, making this chapter an indispensable resource for professionals working with underserved populations.

A key focus of this chapter is on cultural humility and clear communication, ensuring that healthcare providers can convey complex medical information in plain language that patients from all educational backgrounds can understand. Special attention is given to the use of respectful language, avoiding medical jargon, and checking for understanding in each conversation.

Understanding the Social Determinants of Health

The social determinants of health are the non-medical factors that influence health outcomes. They are the conditions in which people are born, grow, live, work, and age, including factors like socioeconomic status, education, neighborhood, employment, and social support networks. Recognizing how these determinants affect patient health is crucial for healthcare providers aiming to deliver holistic and patient-centered care.

Medical terms in Spanish	Medical terms in English
Determinantes sociales de la salud	Social determinants of health
Pobreza	Poverty
Educación	Education
Entorno social	Social environment
Vulnerabilidad	Vulnerability
Equidad en salud	Health equity
Barreras de acceso	Access barriers
Estigma	Stigma
Alfabetización en salud	Health literacy
Recursos comunitarios	Community resources
Asistencia financiera	Financial assistance
Desigualdades en salud	Health disparities
Empleo	Employment
Vivienda adecuada	Adequate housing
Seguridad alimentaria	Food security
Acceso a la atención médica	Access to medical care
Apoyo social	Social support
Exclusión social	Social exclusion
Determinantes económicos	Economic determinants
Riesgos ambientales	Environmental risks
Nivel socioeconómico	Socioeconomic status

Condiciones laborales	Working conditions
Acceso a la educación	Access to education
Política sanitaria	Health policy
Justicia social	Social justice
Tarifas de escala móvil	Sliding scale fees

Relevance and Usage in Healthcare:

Understanding and using this vocabulary will allow you to discuss complex social factors that impact patient health. For example, discussing "barreras de acceso" (access barriers) enables providers to identify obstacles a patient may face in obtaining care. Talking about "alfabetización en salud" (health literacy) helps assess a patient's understanding of medical information, which is particularly important in Hispanic communities where language barriers may exist. Recognizing "desigualdades en salud" (health disparities) and striving for "equidad en salud" (health equity) ensures that providers are committed to offering fair and just care to all patients, regardless of their socioeconomic status.

By using the appropriate terminology, you can engage in meaningful conversations that acknowledge the patient's context, thereby fostering trust and improving health outcomes.

Connecting Patients with Resources and Financial Assistance

Many Hispanic patients may not be aware of available services due to language barriers or lack of information. By providing guidance and support, healthcare providers can help patients overcome obstacles related to cost, transportation, and access to care.

Understanding Hispanic communities' socio-economic challenges allows healthcare professionals to offer tailored solutions. This may include referring patients to low-cost clinics, assisting with enrollment in government programs, or connecting them with social workers who can provide additional support.

Medical terms in Spanish	Medical terms in English
Recursos comunitarios	Community resources
Asistencia financiera	Financial assistance
Trabajador social	Social worker
Centro de salud	Health center
Programas de asistencia para medicamentos	Medication assistance programs

Servicios de transporte	Transportation services
Programas gubernamentales	Government programs
Seguro médico	Medical insurance
Ayuda económica	Economic aid
Organizaciones sin fines de lucro	Non-profit organizations
Subsidios	Subsidies
Programas comunitarios	Community programs
Atención médica gratuita	Free medical care
Programas de descuento	Discount programs
Recursos locales	Local resources
Asistencia legal	Legal assistance
Programas de apoyo	Support programs
Servicios de consejería	Counseling services
Línea de ayuda	Helpline
Beneficios públicos	Public benefits
Vivienda asequible	Affordable housing
Educación para la salud	Health education
Programas de nutrición	Nutrition programs

Relevance and Usage in Healthcare

With the above vocabulary, you can start to communicate options and resources to patients in need. For example, discussing "programas gubernamentales" (government programs) or "programas de asistencia para medicamentos" (medication assistance programs) can help patients access necessary treatments they might otherwise forgo due to cost.

Referring patients to a "trabajador social" (social worker) or "administrador de casos" (case manager) can provide them with comprehensive support beyond medical care, addressing issues like housing, legal assistance, or food insecurity. Understanding terms like "tarifas de escala móvil" (sliding scale fees) allows providers to explain payment options that align with the patient's financial situation.

In Hispanic communities, where family and community play significant roles, connecting patients with "programas comunitarios" (community programs) and "organizaciones sin fines de lucro" (non-profit organizations) can be particularly effective. These resources not only provide practical assistance but also reinforce social support networks that are integral to patient well-being.

Examples of Conversations

Conversation 1: Doctor/Patient Conversation - Addressing Financial Concerns

Context:

Mr. López is a 55-year-old patient diagnosed with hypertension. He works a low-wage job without health insurance and struggles to afford his medications. During his follow-up appointment, he expresses concern about the cost of his prescribed medication. The doctor aims to address his financial concerns while ensuring he receives the necessary treatment.

Spanish	Translation
Doctor: Buenas tardes, señor López. ¿Cómo se ha sentido desde nuestra última visita?	*Doctor*: Good afternoon, Mr. López. How have you been feeling since our last visit?
Paciente: Bueno, Doctor, para ser honesto, estoy un poco preocupado.	*Patient*: Well, Doctor, to be honest, I'm a bit worried.
Doctor: Siento escuchar eso. ¿Qué le preocupa?	*Doctor*: I'm sorry to hear that. What's concerning you?
Paciente: El medicamento que me recetó está ayudando, pero es caro. No tengo seguro y no estoy seguro de poder seguir pagándolo.	*Patient*: The medication you prescribed is helping, but it's expensive. I don't have insurance, and I'm not sure I can keep paying for it.
Doctor: Entiendo que las preocupaciones financieras pueden ser estresantes. Veamos cómo podemos hacer esto más manejable para usted.	*Doctor*: I understand how financial concerns can be stressful. Let's see how we can make this more manageable for you.
Paciente: Eso sería útil. Realmente quiero mantener mi presión arterial bajo control.	*Patient:* That would be helpful. I really want to keep my blood pressure under control.
Doctor: Absolutamente. Hay algunas opciones que podemos considerar. Primero, podemos cambiar a	*Doctor:* Absolutely. There are a few options we can consider. First, we can switch to a

Spanish	Translation
una versión genérica del medicamento, que es mucho más asequible.	generic version of the medication, which is much more affordable.
Paciente: No sabía que había una opción genérica. ¿Funcionará igual?	*Patient:* I didn't know there was a generic option. Will it work the same?
Doctor: Sí, el medicamento genérico tiene los mismos ingredientes activos y es igual de efectivo. Además, podemos buscar programas de asistencia para medicamentos que ayudan a cubrir costos para pacientes sin seguro.	*Doctor:* Yes, the generic medication has the same active ingredients and is just as effective. Additionally, we can look into medication assistance programs that help cover costs for patients without insurance.
Paciente: Eso suena prometedor. ¿Cómo solicito esos programas?	*Patient:* That sounds promising. How do I apply for those programs?
Doctor: Puedo referir a nuestra trabajadora social, la señora García. Ella se especializa en conectar a los pacientes con recursos comunitarios y asistencia financiera.	*Doctor:* I can refer you to our social worker, Ms. García. She specializes in connecting patients with community resources and financial assistance.
Paciente: Le agradezco eso. Ha sido difícil tratar de manejar todo por mi cuenta.	*Patient:* I appreciate that. It's been tough trying to manage everything on my own.
Doctor: No está solo, señor López. Estamos aquí para apoyarlo.	*Doctor:* You're not alone, Mr. López. We're here to support you.
Paciente: Gracias, Doctor. Esto me hace sentir mucho mejor acerca de continuar mi tratamiento.	*Patient:* Thank you, Doctor. This makes me feel much better about continuing my treatment.

Conversation 2: Doctor/Nurse Conversation – Overcoming Access Barriers

Ms. Pérez is a 60-year-old patient with diabetes who has missed several appointments. The healthcare team discovers that she lacks reliable transportation and feels embarrassed to ask for help. The doctor and nurse discuss strategies to assist her in overcoming this barrier to ensure she receives consistent care.

Spanish	Translation
Doctor: Enfermera Sánchez, he notado que la señora Pérez no ha asistido a sus citas	*Doctor:* Nurse Sánchez, I've noticed that Ms. Pérez hasn't been attending her appointments

regularmente. ¿Tenemos alguna actualización sobre su situación?	regularly. Do we have any updates on her situation?
Enfermera: Sí, Doctor. Me comuniqué con ella, y mencionó que ya no tiene coche. Ha estado dependiendo de amigos, pero no siempre es posible.	*Nurse:* Yes, Doctor. I reached out to her, and she mentioned that she doesn't have a car anymore. She's been relying on friends, but it's not always possible.
Doctor: Ya veo. El transporte puede ser una barrera significativa. ¿Mencionó alguna otra preocupación?	*Doctor:* I see. Transportation can be a significant barrier. Did she mention any other concerns?
Enfermera: Parecía reacia a pedir ayuda. Creo que le preocupa ser una carga.	*Nurse:* She seemed hesitant to ask for help. I think she's worried about being a burden.
Doctor: Es importante que sepa que estamos aquí para apoyarla. Exploremos algunas opciones para ayudar con sus necesidades de transporte.	*Doctor:* It's important that she knows we're here to support her. Let's explore some options to assist with her transportation needs.
Enfermera: Hay servicios de transporte comunitario disponibles para citas médicas. Ofrecen viajes de bajo costo o incluso gratuitos para personas mayores.	*Nurse:* There are community transportation services available for medical appointments. They offer low-cost or even free rides for seniors.
Doctor: Es una gran idea. ¿Podría proporcionarle esa información y ayudarla a programar estos servicios?	*Doctor:* That's a great idea. Could you provide her with that information and assist her in scheduling these services?
Enfermera: Por supuesto. La llamaré y la guiaré a través del proceso.	*Nurse:* Absolutely. I'll give her a call and walk her through the process.
Doctor: Además, consideremos programar sus citas en momentos que sean más convenientes para ella, quizás cuando los servicios de transporte estén más disponibles.	*Doctor:* Also, let's consider setting up her appointments at times that are most convenient for her, perhaps when transportation services are readily available.
Enfermera: Buen punto. También discutiré opciones de programación con ella. Gracias doctor.	*Nurse:* Good point. I'll discuss scheduling options with her as well. Thank you Doctor.

Key Takeaways

This chapter emphasizes that understanding social determinants of health—such as education, income, and access to resources—is essential for delivering holistic, patient-centered care. By recognizing challenges like financial hardships, limited health literacy, transportation barriers, language differences, and immigration concerns, doctors, nurses, or social workers can tailor their approach to meet the unique needs of each patient.

Moreover, the chapter underscores the necessity of cultural humility and clear communication. It advises healthcare providers to convey complex medical information in clear and accessible Spanish language, adapted to the patient's understanding level. By using respectful language, avoiding medical jargon, and actively checking for understanding, providers can build trust and improve health outcomes. This chapter also offers strategies for connecting patients with financial aid programs, community health clinics, and other resources, enabling them to overcome barriers to care.

Exercises

Exercise 1

Translate the following medical terms from English to Spanish:

1. Health disparities
2. Access barriers
3. Social determinants of health
4. Vulnerability
5. Health literacy
6. Financial assistance
7. Community resources
8. Social support
9. Economic aid
10. Food security

Exercise 2

Fill in the blanks:

1. Fill in the blanks with the appropriate term from the vocabulary list provided:
2. _____ es fundamental para entender las necesidades de los pacientes y evitar malentendidos. (Cultural humility)
3. Muchos pacientes enfrentan _____ que les impiden acceder a servicios médicos. (Access barriers)
4. La _____ ayuda a los pacientes a comprender mejor sus diagnósticos y tratamientos. (Health literacy)
5. Es importante proporcionar _____ a los pacientes que no pueden pagar sus medicamentos. (Financial assistance)
6. Los _____ pueden ofrecer apoyo adicional y recursos comunitarios. (Social workers)

Exercise 3

Write a brief conversation in Spanish:

Scenario: A patient is worried about the cost of their medication. Write a brief conversation in Spanish between a doctor and this patient, using at least five vocabulary words from the chapter's medical terminology list.

Exercise 4

Translate the following sentences into English:

1. La alfabetización en salud es esencial para que los pacientes entiendan sus opciones de tratamiento.
2. Existen programas de asistencia financiera para ayudar a quienes no pueden pagar sus facturas médicas.
3. Las barreras de acceso pueden incluir problemas de transporte y falta de seguro médico.
4. Los determinantes sociales de la salud afectan el bienestar general del paciente.

Exercise 5

Translate the following sentences into Spanish:

1. Cultural humility allows healthcare providers to connect better with their patients.
2. We should avoid medical jargon when communicating with patients.
3. Social workers can help patients find community resources.
4. Health equity is a goal we should strive for in all healthcare settings.

Answer Key

Exercise 1

Match the English term to its Spanish translation:

1. Health disparities - Desigualdades en salud
2. Access barriers - Barreras de acceso
3. Social determinants of health - Determinantes sociales de la salud
4. Vulnerability - Vulnerabilidad
5. Health literacy - Alfabetización en salud
6. Financial assistance - Asistencia financiera
7. Community resources - Recursos comunitarios
8. Social support - Apoyo social
9. Economic aid - Ayuda económica
10. Food security - Seguridad alimentaria

Exercise 2

Fill in the blanks:

1. La Humildad cultural es fundamental para entender las necesidades de los pacientes y evitar malentendidos.
2. Muchos pacientes enfrentan barreras de acceso que les impiden acceder a servicios médicos.
3. La alfabetización en salud ayuda a los pacientes a comprender mejor sus diagnósticos y tratamientos.
4. Es importante proporcionar asistencia financiera a los pacientes que no pueden pagar sus medicamentos.
5. Los trabajadores sociales pueden ofrecer apoyo adicional y recursos comunitarios.

Exercise 3

Write a brief conversation in Spanish:

Spanish version

Doctor: Buenas tardes, señor Gómez. ¿Cómo se siente hoy?

Paciente: Doctor, estoy preocupado por el costo de mis medicamentos.

Doctor: Entiendo su preocupación. Podemos buscar programas de asistencia financiera para ayudarle.

Paciente: ¿Qué tipo de recursos comunitarios están disponibles?

Doctor: Hay varias organizaciones sin fines de lucro y programas gubernamentales que ofrecen ayuda. También puedo referirlo a nuestro trabajador social.

Paciente: Eso sería muy útil. Muchas gracias por su ayuda.

(Vocabulary used: programas de asistencia financiera, recursos comunitarios, organizaciones sin fines de lucro, programas gubernamentales, trabajador social)

English version:

Doctor: Good afternoon, Mr. Gómez. How are you feeling today?

Patient: Doctor, I'm worried about the cost of my medications.

Doctor: I understand your concern. We can look for financial assistance programs to help you.

Patient: What kind of community resources are available?

Doctor: There are several non-profit organizations and government programs that offer help. I can also refer you to our social worker.

Patient: That would be very helpful. Thank you very much for your assistance.

Exercise 4

Translate the following sentences into English:

1. Health literacy is essential for patients to understand their treatment options.
2. There are financial assistance programs to help those who cannot pay their medical bills.
3. Access barriers can include transportation issues and lack of medical insurance.
4. Social determinants of health affect the patient's overall well-being.

Exercise 5

Translate the following sentences into Spanish:

1. La humildad cultural permite a los proveedores de salud conectarse mejor con sus pacientes.
2. Debemos evitar la jerga médica al comunicarnos con los pacientes.
3. Los trabajadores sociales pueden ayudar a los pacientes a encontrar recursos comunitarios.
4. La equidad en salud es una meta por la que debemos esforzarnos en todos los entornos de atención médica.

BOOK 6

Patient Care in Spanish: Focused Practice for High-Impact Scenarios

Navigating Ethical Decision-Making in Critical and Mental Health Settings

Explore to Win

Book 6 Description

This book confronts the pressing issues of healthcare disparities faced by Hispanic patients, particularly in intensive care and mental health settings. Here, we make a comprehensive analysis of the factors contributing to healthcare inequality and offer actionable strategies to enhance care for this vulnerable demographic.

In Chapter I, "Intensive Care Unit (ICU) Interactions," the book examines the alarming discrepancies in ICU outcomes for Hispanic patients. It highlights how language barriers, cultural differences, and socioeconomic factors lead to increased mortality rates and complications such as ventilator-associated pneumonia and delirium. Readers will find evidence-based recommendations for improving communication and fostering culturally competent care, including practical terminology in both Spanish and English that healthcare providers can use to explain complex procedures like intubation and sedation effectively.

Chapter II, "Mental Health Crisis Intervention," shows the unique mental health challenges faced by the Hispanic community, exploring the impact of chronic stressors stemming from immigration, discrimination, and socioeconomic hardship. The chapter outlines culturally specific approaches to mental health care, emphasizing the importance of understanding the immigrant experience. It offers guidance on how healthcare can bridge communication gaps and give effective support through therapy that respects cultural values, integrating family involvement to enhance patient recovery.

The concluding Chapter III, "Navigating Consent and Ethical Dilemmas," tackles the intricate balance of bioethics and patient rights within the context of Hispanic healthcare. It discusses the importance of informed consent, respecting patient autonomy, and the collective family decision-making process prevalent in many Hispanic communities.

With practical tools, real-world examples, and a strong focus on cultural empathy, "Navigating Healthcare Equity" is a useful educational tool for healthcare providers aiming to improve the quality of care for Hispanic patients. This book not only highlights the disparities in healthcare delivery but also empowers doctors, nurses, and other providers with the knowledge and skills to create a more equitable and compassionate healthcare environment.

Chapter I: Intensive Care Unit (ICU) Interactions

La muerte sólo tiene importancia en la medida que nos hace reflexionar sobre el valor de la vida.

André Malraux

Healthcare inequality continues to impact outcomes for minority groups in the ICU, and Hispanic patients are especially vulnerable. Studies have revealed that Hispanic patients face higher mortality rates and poorer outcomes due to a range of factors, including socioeconomic disparities, language barriers, and outdated clinical practices. For instance, during the COVID-19 pandemic, Hispanic patients were more likely to receive sedative medications, such as benzodiazepines, which are associated with higher risks of complications like ventilator-associated pneumonia and delirium. These disparities have underscored the need for improved communication and culturally competent care.

Why is this important? Research has shown that communication barriers in the ICU can lead to a threefold increase in adverse events, with patients who cannot effectively communicate at a 26% greater risk of multiple complications. Language barriers can lead to miscommunication regarding patient needs, increased use of sedation, and a failure to adequately assess conditions like delirium. These issues are further exacerbated by the lack of accessible communication tools for non-English-speaking patients, making it harder for healthcare providers to understand and address their concerns. Hispanic patients, for instance, are half as likely to receive necessary delirium assessments compared to their non-Hispanic counterparts, increasing their risk for long-term cognitive and psychological issues post-ICU.

The choice to apply Do Not Resuscitate (DNR) orders within the Hispanic community is often shaped by deeply rooted cultural beliefs and family structures. Many Hispanic families may express hesitation around DNR orders due to cultural values that prioritize familial decision-making and life-preserving beliefs. Sensitivity and open discussion around these beliefs are crucial. Thus, healthcare providers must engage in meaningful, empathetic discussions about what DNR entails, clarifying the medical rationale behind it and the importance of aligning with the patient's wishes.

In the Hispanic healthcare setting, you should also evaluate the patient's decision-making capacity and proactively educate family members about the significance of honoring the patient's autonomy. Providing straightforward explanations alongside compassionate support can help clarify misconceptions about DNR, emphasizing that opting for palliative care or a DNR order is not a sign of defeat but a recognition of the patient's dignity and a commitment to their quality of life.

Medical Terminology in Critical Care Settings

This table presents a comprehensive list of critical care medical terms in both Spanish and English. Refer to this resource to familiarize yourself with essential terminology in critical care scenarios.

Medical terms in Spanish	Medical terms in English
Ventilación mecánica	Mechanical ventilation
Sedoanalgesia	Sedoanalgesia
Monitoreo hemodinámico	Hemodynamic monitoring
Fallo multiorgánico	Multiple organ failure
Intubación	Intubation
Extubación	Extubation
Monitor de signos vitales	Vital signs monitor
Paro cardiorrespiratorio	Cardiac arrest
Reanimación cardiopulmonar (RCP)	Cardiopulmonary Resuscitation (CPR)
Oxigenoterapia	Oxygen therapy
Sonda nasogástrica	Nasogastric tube
Electrocardiograma (ECG)	Electrocardiogram (ECG)
Insuficiencia respiratoria	Respiratory failure
Choque séptico	Septic shock
Sedación	Sedation
Escala de coma de Glasgow	Glasgow coma scale
Hemorragia	Hemorrhage
Traumatismo craneoencefálico	Traumatic brain injury
Control de líquidos	Fluid management

Gasometría	Gasometry
Anestesia general	General anesthesia
Rehabilitación	Rehabilitation
Lavado broncoalveolar	Bronchoalveolar lavage
Ventilación no invasiva	Non-invasive ventilation
Complicaciones postoperatorias	Post-operative complications
Monitorización continua	Continuous monitoring
Asistencia ventilatoria	Ventilatory assistance

Explanation:

ICU-related medical terminology can often be unfamiliar or overwhelming for families who may not have extensive experience with advanced medical care. Terms like ventilación mecánica (mechanical ventilation) or intubación (intubation) might need additional explanation beyond their direct meaning. In many Hispanic families, decisions about medical interventions are made collectively, involving multiple family members. This dynamic can require healthcare providers to explain procedures more than once, using language that is both accessible and culturally appropriate.

Moreover, words like choque séptico (septic shock) and fallo multiorgánico (multiple organ failure) can carry a heavy emotional weight. In some cases, families may be less familiar with the outcomes associated with these conditions, and there may be a need to explain them in a way that acknowledges the gravity of the situation while offering clarity. Hispanic families often place great value on hope and persistence in medical care, which can influence their decisions about treatment options like cuidados paliativos (palliative care) or the continuation of aggressive treatment.

Remember, some terms, such as rehabilitación (rehabilitation) and control de líquidos (fluid management), may not immediately resonate with families in terms of their long-term importance for recovery. Healthcare providers should take time to break down these concepts and explain how they fit into the broader scope of patient care within their team and patients. This approach not only helps families understand the immediate needs of the patient but also prepares them for potential ongoing care after the ICU.

Examples of Conversations

Conversation 1: Doctor/Family – Explaining the Need for Intubation to a Patient's Family

One of the most challenging conversations in the ICU involves explaining the need for intubation, especially when communicating with families who may not be familiar with the procedure or its purpose. In Hispanic settings, where family involvement in decision-making is often significant, it is essential to explain not only the procedure but also the implications and what the family should expect afterward.

Spanish	Translation
Doctor: Buenas tardes, soy el Dr. Pérez. Estoy aquí para hablar con ustedes sobre la situación de su familiar, el Sr. Gómez. Su respiración ha empeorado significativamente, y hemos determinado que lo mejor para su bienestar es intubarlo para ayudarle a respirar mejor.	*Doctor*: Good afternoon, I'm Dr. Pérez. I'm here to talk to you about your relative, Mr. Gómez. His breathing has worsened significantly, and we've determined that the best course of action is to intubate him to help him breathe better.
Familiar: ¿Qué significa exactamente intubar? ¿Es peligroso?	*Family member*: What exactly does intubation mean? Is it dangerous?
Doctor: Entiendo su preocupación. Permítanme explicarles. La intubación es el proceso de insertar un tubo a través de la boca hacia la tráquea para que una máquina, llamada ventilador, pueda ayudarle a respirar. Es un procedimiento común en la UCI cuando los pacientes tienen dificultades para respirar por sí mismos. Aunque cualquier intervención tiene riesgos, este procedimiento es seguro y necesario en este caso. Lo más importante es que le permitirá estabilizarse mientras tratamos la causa de su insuficiencia respiratoria.	*Doctor*: I understand your concern. Let me explain. Intubation involves placing a tube through the mouth and into the trachea, allowing a machine, called a ventilator, to assist with breathing. This is a common procedure in the ICU when patients struggle to breathe on their own. While any procedure carries some risks, this one is safe and necessary in this case. The most important thing is that it will help him stabilize while we treat the cause of his respiratory failure.
Familiar: ¿Y cuánto tiempo estará con el ventilador? ¿Es algo permanente?	*Family member:* And how long will he be on the ventilator? Is it something permanent?
Doctor: La duración depende de cómo responda al tratamiento. Nuestro objetivo es mantenerlo en el	*Doctor*: The duration depends on how he responds to treatment. Our goal is to keep

ventilador solo el tiempo necesario, hasta que pueda respirar por sí mismo. Evaluaremos su progreso todos los días. Si su condición mejora, retiraremos el tubo tan pronto como sea seguro. No es un proceso permanente, y siempre buscamos extubarlo lo más pronto posible.

him on the ventilator only as long as necessary, until he can breathe on his own. We will assess his progress daily. If his condition improves, we will remove the tube as soon as it is safe to do so. It is not a permanent process, and we always aim to extubate as soon as possible.

Familiar: ¿Qué tan sedado estará? ¿Estará consciente o podrá sentir dolor?

Family member: How sedated will he be? Will he be conscious or feel pain?

Doctor: Estará bajo sedación, lo que significa que estará dormido y no sentirá dolor durante el proceso de intubación ni mientras esté en el ventilador. Utilizamos sedantes para mantenerlo cómodo y relajado, ya que la intubación puede ser incómoda si está despierto. Monitorearemos cuidadosamente los niveles de sedación para asegurarnos de que no sienta dolor ni ansiedad durante este tiempo.

Doctor: He will be sedated, meaning he will be asleep and won't feel pain during the intubation process or while he's on the ventilator. We use sedatives to keep him comfortable and relaxed, as being awake with intubation can be uncomfortable. We will closely monitor the sedation levels to ensure he doesn't feel pain or anxiety during this time.

Familiar: ¿Y cuáles son los riesgos de esto? Estoy preocupada de que algo salga mal.

Family member: And what are the risks of this? I'm worried something could go wrong.

Doctor: Entiendo completamente su preocupación, y es normal sentirse así. Siempre hay riesgos en cualquier procedimiento médico. En este caso, los principales riesgos son infecciones o complicaciones pulmonares, pero tomamos muchas precauciones para minimizar estos riesgos. El equipo médico monitoreará de cerca cada aspecto de su condición, y en la mayoría de los casos, los pacientes responden bien. La intubación en realidad puede salvarle la vida al permitir que reciba el oxígeno que necesita.

Doctor: I completely understand your concern, and it's normal to feel this way. There are always risks with any medical procedure. In this case, the primary risks are infections or lung complications, but we take many precautions to minimize these risks. The medical team will monitor every aspect of his condition closely, and in most cases, patients respond well. Intubation can save his life by allowing him to receive the oxygen he needs.

Familiar: ¿Y después qué? ¿Qué pasará después de que lo intuben?

Family member: And what happens after? What will happen after he's intubated?

Doctor: Después de la intubación, lo mantendremos sedado para que esté cómodo mientras esté conectado al ventilador. Monitorearemos sus signos

Doctor: After the intubation, we'll keep him sedated to ensure he's comfortable while on the ventilator. We will constantly monitor

Spanish	Translation
vitales constantemente y ajustaremos el tratamiento según su respuesta. El equipo de enfermería y los médicos estarán aquí las 24 horas para asegurarnos de que reciba la mejor atención posible. Si todo sale bien y su condición mejora, el próximo paso será retirar el tubo y ayudarlo a respirar por sí mismo nuevamente.	his vital signs and adjust treatment as needed based on his response. The nursing team and doctors will be here 24/7 to ensure he receives the best care possible. If everything goes well and his condition improves, the next step will be to remove the tube and help him breathe on his own again.

Conversation 2: Doctor/Nurse – Discussing Prognosis and Potential Outcomes

When a patient's condition is critical, families often seek clarity about their loved one's prognosis and what to expect in the coming days. These discussions require a sensitive yet informative approach, providing families with honest information while also offering support.

Spanish	Translation
Doctor: Hola, Ana. ¿Cómo está el paciente hoy?	*Doctor:* Hello, Ana. How is the patient today?
Enfermera: El paciente ha mostrado signos de fallo multiorgánico, y su pronóstico es reservado. A pesar del tratamiento, no hemos visto mejoría significativa. Deberíamos hablar con la familia sobre las posibles opciones que tenemos.	*Nurse:* The patient has shown signs of multiple organ failure, and his prognosis is guarded. Despite the treatment, we haven't seen significant improvement. We should talk to the family about the possible options we have.
Doctor: De acuerdo. Es fundamental que los familiares entiendan la gravedad de la situación, pero también que sepan que estamos haciendo todo lo posible para estabilizarlo. Sabemos que estas conversaciones son difíciles, y tenemos que abordar el tema con mucha empatía. ¿La familia ya ha sido informada sobre su estado crítico?	*Doctor:* Agreed. It's essential that the family understands the severity of the situation, but also that they know we are doing everything possible to stabilize him. We know these conversations are difficult, and we need to approach them with empathy. Has the family already been informed about his critical condition?
Enfermera: Sí, les mencioné que estamos en un momento delicado, pero no les he dado detalles sobre el fallo multiorgánico. Están muy preocupados y quieren saber qué sigue.	*Nurse:* Yes, I mentioned that we are in a delicate moment, but I haven't gone into details about the multiple organ failure. They are very worried and want to know what comes next.

Doctor: Está bien. Vamos a darles una explicación clara, pero no abrumadora. Hablemos primero de los pasos que estamos tomando ahora, como el monitoreo constante y los tratamientos que estamos aplicando para darle la mejor oportunidad. Luego, si están preparados, podemos discutir las opciones a largo plazo, como la posibilidad de cuidados paliativos, si la condición no mejora.

Doctor: That's fine. Let's give them a clear but not overwhelming explanation. We'll first talk about the steps we are currently taking, like continuous monitoring and the treatments we are using to give him the best chance. Then, if they are ready, we can discuss long-term options, such as the possibility of palliative care if the condition doesn't improve.

Key Takeaways

Effective Communication is Essential: ICU interactions require clear, compassionate, and precise communication. This is particularly important when discussing invasive procedures or difficult prognosis scenarios.

Empathy is Crucial: Always approach family members with empathy and respect, understanding the emotional weight these conversations hold.

Clarity About Procedures: Ensure families understand the reasoning behind decisions like intubation or DNR orders. Clarity can reduce anxiety and build trust between healthcare providers and families.

Respecting Ethical Decisions: Handling DNR (do-not-resuscitate) orders requires extreme sensitivity. Families should feel supported and reassured that their loved one will still receive the best care, even if life-saving measures are not employed.

Familiarity with Medical Terminology: Understanding and properly using specialized ICU terms is key for effective communication with both the medical team and the patient's family.

Exercises

Exercise 1

Match the English term to its Spanish translation.

1. Mechanical ventilation
2. Multiple organ failure
3. Sedoanalgesia
4. Hemodynamic monitoring

Options:

a) Monitoreo hemodinámico
b) Fallo multiorgánico
c) Ventilación mecánica
d) Sedoanalgesia

Exercise 2

Fill in the blanks with the correct Spanish term from the word bank below.

Word Bank:

Ventilación mecánica

Sedoanalgesia

Fallo multiorgánico

Monitoreo hemodinámico

1. Cuando un paciente no puede respirar por sí mismo, a menudo se requiere _____ para asegurar la oxigenación adecuada.
2. La _____ se utiliza para administrar medicamentos que mantienen al paciente cómodo durante procedimientos invasivos.
3. En el caso de _____, es esencial un monitoreo constante de la función de los órganos.
4. El _____ permite a los médicos evaluar la presión arterial y el flujo sanguíneo del paciente en tiempo real.

Exercise 3

In pairs, role-play a scenario in the ICU where one person acts as the doctor explaining the need for intubation, and the other acts as a family member. Use at least three medical terms from the terminology list.

Exercise 4

Discuss a hypothetical situation where a patient's DNR order is not honored. What actions should be taken? Consider how to communicate this situation to the family effectively.

Exercise 5

Reflect on your communication style when interacting with patients and families in critical situations. Write down at least three ways you can improve your communication in the ICU setting.

Answer Key

Exercise 1

Match the English term to its Spanish translation.

1. c) Ventilación mecánica
2. b) Fallo multiorgánico
3. d) Sedoanalgesia
4. a) Monitoreo hemodinámico

Exercise 2

Fill in the blanks with the correct Spanish term.

1. Ventilación mecánica
2. Sedoanalgesia
3. Fallo multiorgánico
4. Monitoreo hemodinámico

Exercise 3

Example Response for Role-Playing Scenario:

Spanish version:

Doctor: "La situación del paciente ha empeorado, y recomendamos la ventilación mecánica para mantener sus niveles de oxígeno."

Familiar: "¿Qué riesgos existen con este procedimiento?"

Doctor: "Existen algunos riesgos, como infección, pero el monitoreo hemodinámico constante ayudará a detectar cualquier problema de inmediato."

Familiar: "Entiendo. Hagan lo que sea necesario."

English translation:

Doctor: "The patient's condition has worsened, and we recommend mechanical ventilation to maintain their oxygen levels."

Family Member: "What risks are there with this procedure?"

Doctor: "There are some risks, such as infection, but constant hemodynamic monitoring will help detect any problems immediately."

Family Member: "I understand. Do whatever is necessary."

Exercise 4

Response Example: If a DNR order is not honored, immediate steps should be taken to inform the family of the situation. An apology should be given, and healthcare staff should review their processes to ensure this does not happen again. Open, transparent communication with the family is essential to maintain trust.

Exercise 5

Reflection:

1. I can focus on using simpler language when explaining complex procedures.
2. I will ensure I ask families if they have any questions more frequently during discussions.
3. I will work on being more empathetic and patient when discussing difficult prognoses.

Chapter II: Mental Health Crisis Intervention

La salud mental no es un destino, sino un proceso. Se trata de cómo conduces, no de adónde vas.

Noam Shpancer

Understanding Mental Health Care Needs for Hispanic Americans

The Hispanic community is characterized by a shared cultural heritage, with the Spanish language and various traditions serving as common threads that connect individuals, regardless of their roots in Africa, Asia, Europe, or the Americas. The immigrant experience, which many within the community have faced, further bonds this diverse population. This diversity brings a wealth of cultural richness but also results in varied experiences of migration, socioeconomic conditions, and integration into American society. These varied migration experiences shape the mental health landscape for Hispanic Americans, as each group brings its unique history of trauma, displacement, and adaptation to life. Central Americans, for instance, may have higher rates of post-traumatic stress disorder (PTSD) due to exposure to war and political violence in their countries of origin. Meanwhile, second-generation Hispanic Americans, particularly those with parents who are undocumented, may face chronic stress related to family separation and the fear of deportation, contributing to anxiety and depression.

Additionally, the cultural stigma surrounding mental illness and language barriers further limit access to care. Approximately 40% of Hispanics report limited English proficiency, complicating communication with providers and often leading to misdiagnosis.

Moreover, the "immigrant paradox" highlights that first-generation Hispanic immigrants generally have lower rates of mental disorders compared to later generations. This resilience is attributed to strong cultural ties and community support. However, acculturation increases exposure to stressors like discrimination, which heightens mental health risks for subsequent generations.

Economic barriers, such as high rates of poverty and limited health insurance, exacerbate these challenges, leading many Hispanics to rely on general healthcare rather than specialized mental health services. There is also a significant shortage of bilingual, culturally competent therapists, further limiting access.

Addressing these mental health needs requires culturally aware, empathetic, and accessible care that respects the diverse experiences of Hispanic Americans. This chapter aims to equip healthcare providers with the tools needed to support Hispanic patients in crisis, emphasizing the importance of integrating cultural understanding into mental health care.

Medical Terminology in Mental Health Crisis Intervention

Understanding specific mental health terms is crucial for effectively communicating with Spanish-speaking patients during a crisis. The following vocabulary includes key terms related to mental health, from symptoms to treatment approaches, allowing providers to convey information accurately and compassionately.

Medical terms in Spanish	Medical terms in English
Trastorno de ansiedad	Anxiety disorder
Depresión mayor	Major depression
Esquizofrenia	Schizophrenia
Intento de suicidio	Suicide attempt
Psicosis aguda	Acute psychosis
Trastorno de estrés postraumático (TEPT)	Post-traumatic stress disorder (PTSD)
Terapia cognitivo-conductual	Cognitive-behavioral therapy
Hospitalización involuntaria	Involuntary hospitalization
Evaluación de salud mental	Mental health assessment
Intervención en crisis	Crisis intervention
Despersonalización	Depersonalization
Bipolaridad	Bipolar disorder
Ansiedad generalizada	Generalized anxiety
Trastorno de pánico	Panic disorder
Abuso de sustancia	Substance abuse
Desórdenes del estado de ánimo	Mood disorders
Psicoterapia	Psychotherapy
Medicación antipsicótica	Antipsychotic medication

Consulta psiquiátrica	Psychiatric consultation
Terapia de grupo	Group therapy
Terapia familiar	Family therapy
Trastorno de personalidad	Personality disorder
Alucinaciones	Hallucinations
Delirios	Delusions
Insomnio	Insomnia
Trastorno obsesivo-compulsivo (TOC)	Obsessive-compulsive disorder (OCD)
Autolesiones	Self-harm
Anhedonia	Anhedonia
Ideación suicida	Suicidal ideation
Aislamiento social	Social isolation
Terapia de exposición	Exposure therapy
Crisis nerviosa	Nervous breakdown
Manejo del estrés	Stress management
Conducta agresiva	Aggressive behavior
Trastorno de adaptación	Adjustment disorder
Ingresar a un centro psiquiátrico	Admission to a psychiatric facility
Terapia ocupacional	Occupational therapy
Apoyo psicosocial	Psychosocial support

Explanation:

These terms allow clinicians to explain diagnoses, treatments, and symptoms in ways that are both medically accurate and culturally sensitive. For example, psicosis aguda (acute psychosis) or trastorno de estrés postraumático (post-traumatic stress disorder) help to clarify complex conditions in terms that patients and their families can grasp without feeling overwhelmed by medical jargon.

Additionally, other terms, like nervios (nerves), carry unique cultural meanings that might not have a direct medical equivalent in English. Recognizing such expressions helps providers to connect with patients' lived experiences, acknowledging the ways in which mental distress is discussed within their cultural context. This approach fosters a deeper rapport, allowing patients to express their concerns more openly and making them feel seen as whole individuals, not just as a set of symptoms.

Examples of Conversations

Conversation 1: Doctor/Patient – Addressing Acute Psychosis

The conversation takes place between a doctor and a patient who has been experiencing symptoms of acute psychosis. She describes hearing voices and feeling intense fear, which is impacting her daily life and sleep patterns. The doctor explains the nature of her symptoms, emphasizing the need for a combination of cognitive-behavioral therapy and antipsychotic medication. He reassures her that the treatment will be carefully monitored to ensure her safety and support a steady recovery.

Spanish	Translation
Doctor: Hola, Marta, soy el Dr. Ramírez. He revisado tu caso y entiendo que últimamente has estado experimentando episodios de psicosis aguda. Esto significa que a veces puedes sentirte desconectada de la realidad, como si escucharas o vieras cosas que los demás no perciben. ¿Podrías contarme un poco más sobre lo que has estado sintiendo?	*Doctor*: Hello, Marta, I'm Dr. Ramirez. I've reviewed your case and understand that you've been experiencing episodes of acute psychosis. This means that sometimes you might feel disconnected from reality, as if you're hearing or seeing things that others don't perceive. Can you tell me a bit more about what you've been feeling?
Paciente: Doctor, es como si alguien me hablara cuando estoy sola, y a veces siento un miedo intenso, como si estuviera en peligro. No puedo dormir, y cuando trato, tengo pesadillas que me hacen despertar sudando.	*Patient*: Doctor, it feels like someone is talking to me when I'm alone, and sometimes I feel an intense fear, like I'm in danger. I can't sleep, and when I try, I have nightmares that make me wake up sweating.
Doctor: Entiendo. Esa sensación de miedo puede ser parte del trastorno de ansiedad que mencionaste antes, pero los síntomas auditivos que describes son característicos de la psicosis aguda. Voy a recomendar una combinación de terapia cognitivo-conductual para ayudarte a gestionar esos pensamientos y algunos	*Doctor*: I understand. That feeling of fear might be part of the anxiety disorder you mentioned earlier, but the auditory symptoms you describe are characteristic of acute psychosis. I'm going to recommend a combination of cognitive-behavioral therapy to help you manage those thoughts and some antipsychotic medications that will help

medicamentos antipsicóticos que te ayudarán a reducir las alucinaciones. ¿Qué te parece?	reduce the hallucinations. How does that sound to you?
Paciente: Suena bien, doctor, pero me preocupa tomar medicamentos. ¿Voy a tener que tomarlos por mucho tiempo?	*Patient*: That sounds good, doctor, but I'm worried about taking medication. Will I have to be on medication for a long time?
Doctor: No necesariamente. Nuestro objetivo es estabilizarte primero y luego, con la ayuda de la terapia, ir ajustando la medicación según tu progreso. Siempre monitorearemos los efectos secundarios y ajustaremos la dosis para que te sientas lo mejor posible. Lo más importante es que estés segura y estable, y que puedas retomar una vida tranquila.	*Doctor*: Not necessarily. Our goal is to stabilize you first and then, with the help of therapy, gradually adjust the medication according to your progress. We'll always monitor for side effects and adjust the dose to ensure you feel as good as possible. The most important thing is that you stay safe and stable, and that you can return to a more peaceful life.

Conversation 2: Nurse/ Patient – Discussing Involuntary Hospitalization for a Suicide Attempt

This scenario involves a conversation between a nurse and the mother of a young man named Alejandro, who has been admitted to the hospital following a suicide attempt. Due to the severity of his mental state, the healthcare team has decided that involuntary hospitalization is necessary to protect Alejandro from self-harm. The nurse explains to Alejandro's mother why this measure is in place, the nature of the care he will receive during his stay, and how family involvement, including her support during family therapy sessions, is crucial for his recovery. The nurse provides reassurance while emphasizing the importance of professional supervision to stabilize Alejandro's condition.

Spanish	Translation
Enfermera: Buenas tardes, Sra. Gómez. Lamentablemente, su hijo, Alejandro, ha sido ingresado después de un intento suicida. Debido a la gravedad de la situación y su estado de riesgo inminente, los médicos han decidido que necesita una hospitalización involuntaria para garantizar su seguridad.	*Nurse:* Good afternoon, Mrs. Gomez. Unfortunately, your son, Alejandro, has been admitted after a suicide attempt. Due to the severity of the situation and his state of imminent risk, the doctors have decided that he needs involuntary hospitalization to ensure his safety.
Familiar: No entiendo, ¿qué significa exactamente eso? ¿Por cuánto tiempo lo van a tener ahí? Él solo necesita un poco de descanso, y yo puedo cuidarlo en casa.	*Family member:* I don't understand, what exactly does that mean? How long will they keep him there? He just needs some rest, and I can take care of him at home.

Enfermera: Comprendo que esto es difícil de aceptar. La hospitalización involuntaria se utiliza cuando una persona, como Alejandro, está en riesgo de hacerse daño a sí mismo o a otros. Aquí en el hospital, recibirá supervisión continua, terapia de emergencia, y apoyo de un equipo especializado en salud mental para ayudarlo a estabilizarse. Este tipo de ingreso generalmente dura entre 72 horas a una semana, dependiendo de su progreso.

Nurse: I understand that this is difficult to accept. Involuntary hospitalization is used when a person, like Alejandro, is at risk of harming themselves or others. Here at the hospital, he will receive continuous supervision, emergency therapy, and support from a specialized mental health team to help stabilize him. This type of admission typically lasts between 72 hours to a week, depending on his progress.

Familiar: Entiendo que quieren ayudarlo, pero estoy preocupada. Alejandro nunca ha estado en una situación así antes. ¿Cómo puedo ayudarlo yo mientras está aquí?

Family member: I understand that you want to help him, but I'm worried. Alejandro has never been in a situation like this before. How can I help him while he's here?

Enfermera: Usted puede ser una parte fundamental de su recuperación. Puede visitarlo y estar presente durante las sesiones de terapia familiar, donde hablaremos de cómo apoyar a Alejandro una vez que sea dado de alta. Es importante que él sepa que cuenta con su apoyo y que no está solo en este proceso. Además, podemos brindarle recursos sobre cómo manejar el trastorno de depresión mayor que ha estado enfrentando.

Nurse: You can be a crucial part of his recovery. You can visit him and be present during family therapy sessions, where we will discuss how to support Alejandro once he is discharged. It's important for him to know that he has your support and that he is not alone in this process. Additionally, we can provide you with resources on how to manage the major depressive disorder he has been facing.

Familiar: Gracias, eso me da un poco de esperanza. Solo quiero lo mejor para él y que se recupere pronto.

Family member: Thank you, that gives me some hope. I just want the best for him and for him to recover soon.

Nurse: Lo entiendo perfectamente, Sra. Gómez. Y estamos aquí para asegurar que Alejandro reciba el mejor cuidado posible. Juntos, trabajaremos para que él salga de esta situación más fuerte y con las herramientas necesarias para seguir adelante.

Nurse: I completely understand, Mrs. Gomez. We are here to ensure that Alejandro receives the best care possible. Together, we will work to ensure he comes out of this situation stronger and with the tools he needs to move forward.

Key Takeaways

A patient's cultural background can shape their perception of mental illness, their willingness to seek help, and their response to treatments. Terms like "nervios" and "susto" might carry specific meanings and require sensitivity to their cultural context during interventions.

First-generation Hispanic immigrants often have lower rates of mental disorders, benefiting from strong cultural ties and community support. However, as they acculturate, they face increased stressors, such as discrimination and economic challenges, which can elevate mental health risks in later generations.

Many Hispanic Americans experience barriers to mental health care, such as language difficulties and economic limitations, leading to underutilization of specialized services. Addressing these barriers requires a focus on increasing access to bilingual, culturally competent care to ensure effective communication and trust between providers and patients.

Intervening during a mental health crisis requires a careful balance of empathy, clear communication, and appropriate use of medical interventions, such as cognitive-behavioral therapy or antipsychotic medication.

Building trust with Hispanic patients often involves addressing the stigma surrounding mental illness in their community.

Exercises

Exercise 1

Match the English term to its Spanish translation.

1. Anxiety disorder
2. Suicide attempt
3. Cognitive-behavioral therapy
4. Acute psychosis
5. Post-traumatic stress disorder

Spanish Translations:

a) Psicosis aguda
b) Trastorno de ansiedad
c) Intento de suicidio
d) Terapia cognitivo-conductual
e) Trastorno de estrés postraumático (TEPT)

Exercise 2

Fill in the blanks with the correct Spanish term.

1. El paciente fue hospitalizado debido a una crisis de _____. (acute psychosis)
2. La _____ ayuda a los pacientes a cambiar patrones de pensamiento negativos. (cognitive-behavioral therapy)
3. Después de su _____, la familia del paciente recibió apoyo psicosocial. (suicide attempt)
4. La evaluación reveló un diagnóstico de _____. (generalized anxiety)
5. El diagnóstico de _____ es común en pacientes que han experimentado eventos traumáticos. (post-traumatic stress disorder)

Exercise 3

Write a short conversation where a doctor explains to a patient that they have been diagnosed with major depression and suggests a treatment plan.

Exercise 4

Write a dialogue where a nurse explains to a patient's family member why involuntary hospitalization is necessary after a severe mental health crisis.

Exercise 5

Translate the following sentences into Spanish

1. The patient was diagnosed with schizophrenia and needs antipsychotic medication.
2. Cognitive-behavioral therapy can help manage anxiety disorders.
3. Involuntary hospitalization is necessary for his safety after the suicide attempt.
4. The psychiatrist will conduct a mental health assessment tomorrow.

5. Family therapy sessions can support the recovery process.

Answer Key

Exercise 1

Match the English term to its Spanish translation.

1. b. Anxiety disorder - Trastorno de ansiedad
2. c. Suicide attempt - Intento de suicidio
3. d. Cognitive-behavioral therapy - Terapia cognitivo-conductual
4. a. Acute psychosis - Psicosis aguda
5. e. Post-traumatic stress disorder - Trastorno de estrés postraumático (TEPT)

Exercise 2

Fill in the blanks with the correct Spanish term.

1. El paciente fue hospitalizado debido a una crisis de psicosis aguda.
2. La terapia cognitivo-conductual ayuda a los pacientes a cambiar patrones de pensamiento negativos.
3. Después de su intento de suicidio, la familia del paciente recibió apoyo psicosocial.
4. La evaluación reveló un diagnóstico de ansiedad generalizada.
5. El diagnóstico de trastorno de estrés postraumático (TEPT) es común en pacientes que han experimentado eventos traumáticos.

Exercise 3

Short conversation:

Spanish version:

Doctor: Hola, Carlos. Después de revisar los resultados de tu evaluación, hemos determinado que estás enfrentando un caso de depresión mayor. Esto significa que los sentimientos de tristeza y desesperanza que has tenido son más intensos de lo que pensábamos.

Paciente: ¿Eso significa que necesitaré tomar medicamentos, doctor?

Doctor: Posiblemente, sí. Vamos a empezar con una combinación de terapia cognitivo-conductual para ayudarte a cambiar algunos de esos pensamientos negativos, y si es necesario, añadiremos un antidepresivo. Lo importante es que no tienes que pasar por esto solo; estamos aquí para apoyarte.

Paciente: Gracias, doctor. Estoy dispuesto a intentarlo.

English version

Doctor: Hello, Carlos. After reviewing the results of your evaluation, we have determined that you are facing a case of major depression. This means that the feelings of sadness and hopelessness you have been experiencing are more intense than we initially thought.

Patient: Does that mean I will need to take medication, doctor?

Doctor: Possibly, yes. We'll start with a combination of cognitive-behavioral therapy to help you change some of those negative thoughts, and if necessary, we will add an antidepressant. The important thing is that you don't have to go through this alone; we are here to support you.

Patient: Thank you, doctor. I am willing to try it.

Exercise 4

Spanish dialogue example:

Enfermera: Buenas tardes, Sra. Torres. Debido a la severidad del estado de su hija, hemos decidido proceder con una hospitalización involuntaria para garantizar su seguridad.

Familiar: ¿Hospitalización involuntaria? ¿Es realmente necesario? Pensé que solo necesitaba descansar en casa.

Enfermera: Entiendo su preocupación. Sin embargo, en estos momentos, existe un riesgo de autolesiones, y creemos que la mejor manera de estabilizarla es mantenerla bajo supervisión médica constante por algunos días. Esto nos permitirá brindarle el apoyo y la atención que necesita.

Familiar: Si es lo mejor para ella, lo entiendo. Solo quiero que esté bien.

English version:

Nurse: Good afternoon, Mrs. Torres. Due to the severity of your daughter's condition, we have decided to proceed with involuntary hospitalization to ensure her safety.

Family Member: Involuntary hospitalization? Is that really necessary? I thought she just needed to rest at home.

Nurse: I understand your concern. However, at this moment, there is a risk of self-harm, and we believe that the best way to stabilize her is to keep her under constant medical supervision for a few days. This will allow us to provide her with the support and care she needs.

Family Member: If it's the best for her, I understand. I just want her to be okay.

Exercise 5

Translate the following sentences into Spanish.

1. El paciente fue diagnosticado con esquizofrenia y necesita medicación antipsicótica.
2. La terapia cognitivo-conductual puede ayudar a manejar los trastornos de ansiedad.
3. La hospitalización involuntaria es necesaria para su seguridad después del intento de suicidio.
4. El psiquiatra realizará una evaluación de salud mental mañana.
5. Las sesiones de terapia familiar pueden apoyar el proceso de recuperación.

Chapter III: Navigating Consent and Ethical Dilemmas

Cura a veces, trata con frecuencia, consuela siempre

Hipócrates

Bridging Bioethics and Patient Rights in Hispanic Healthcare

The intersection between bioethics and human rights has become increasingly significant, particularly within Latin American contexts, where historical and socio-political experiences shape unique perspectives on patient care. These fields, although rooted in a shared post-World War II commitment to human dignity, have evolved differently in regions where collective memory of state violence, economic disparities, and cultural diversity deeply influences how care is understood and delivered.

In many Latin American and Hispanic communities, patient care extends beyond the individual, deeply intertwined with family dynamics and cultural norms. Concepts like informed consent, autonomy, and patient rights, which are fundamental to global bioethics, must be adapted to recognize the collective decision-making processes that characterize many Hispanic families. This perspective aligns with the broader Latin American approach to bioethics, which often emphasizes social justice, community well-being, and the importance of respecting cultural traditions.

As highlighted in the discourse on bioethics and human rights in Latin America, there is a need to integrate ethical principles with a sensitivity to the historical and cultural realities of the region. The Universal Declaration on Bioethics and Human Rights by UNESCO, while setting international standards, emphasizes the need for cultural contexts to be considered in the application of these norms. In practice, this means that healthcare providers must navigate the delicate balance between respecting cultural norms and upholding ethical obligations to ensure the patient's well-being and rights.

The Affordable Care Act (ACA) aimed to address some of these disparities, yet significant gaps remain, particularly for undocumented individuals and those with limited access to culturally competent care. For healthcare providers, this means that effective communication, trust-building, and a deep understanding of cultural values are essential for ensuring equitable care.

This chapter explores these complexities by offering practical tools and strategies for healthcare providers working with Hispanic patients. By addressing scenarios that involve informed consent, decision-making capacity, and ethical dilemmas in the context of cultural and family values, the goal is to empower professionals to provide care that respects both the rights of patients and their cultural identities.

Medical Terminology in Ethical Decision-Making

Understanding the vocabulary related to ethical decision-making is key for healthcare providers working with Hispanic patients, especially when navigating sensitive discussions around consent, patient autonomy, and medical ethics. The following table includes key terms frequently encountered in discussions of ethical dilemmas and patient rights in healthcare settings.

Medical terms in Spanish	Medical terms in English
Capacidad de decisión	Decision-making capacity
Autonomía del paciente	Patient autonomy
Dignidad humana	Human dignity
Ética médica	Medical ethics
Derechos del paciente	Patient rights
Beneficiencia	Beneficence
No maleficencia	Non-maleficence
Confidencialidad	Confidentiality
Justicia	Justice
Vulnerabilidad	Vulnerability
Equidad en la atención	Equity in care
Conflicto ético	Ethical conflict
Empoderamiento del paciente	Patient empowerment
Toma de decisiones compartida	Shared decision-making
Cuidados paliativos	Palliative care
Dilema ético	Ethical dilemma
Dilema profesional	Professional dilemma
Integridad profesional	Professional integrity

Respeto a la autonomía	Respect for autonomy
Derecho a rechazar tratamiento	Right to refuse treatment
Derecho a la privacidad	Right to privacy
Derecho a la información	Right to information
Intervención mínima	Minimal intervention
Consentimiento verbal	Verbal consent
Consentimiento escrito	Written consent
Valores culturales	Cultural values
Voluntad anticipada	Living Will

Explanation:

In practice, these terms serve as the foundation for meaningful conversations between healthcare providers, patients, and families, particularly when facing challenging decisions. For example, discussing consentimiento informado (informed consent) with a patient's family involves more than just explaining the procedure; it requires clarifying the patient's right to make decisions, acknowledging their cultural beliefs about autonomy, and ensuring they fully understand the implications. This is especially vital in cultures where family input is central to decision-making and where concepts like autonomía del paciente may be interpreted differently.

Moreover, terms like beneficencia (beneficence) and no maleficencia (non-maleficence) guide clinicians in balancing the benefits and risks of treatment options, helping families understand why a particular course of action is recommended. These discussions can become even more complex when addressing cuidados paliativos (palliative care), as patients and their families may have different expectations about the end-of-life care process. Using this vocabulary thoughtfully helps bridge cultural and emotional gaps, ensuring that patients' dignity and rights are respected throughout their care journey.

Examples of Conversations

Conversation 1: Doctor/Patient's Family Conversation - Discussing the Role of Family in Medical Decisions

Dr. Morales is speaking with the family of Mrs. García, a 75-year-old patient with advanced kidney failure. Mrs. García signed an informed consent form to decline dialysis, preferring palliative care over invasive treatments. However, her family believes that dialysis could prolong her life and is pressuring the doctor to continue with the treatment.

Spanish	Translation
Doctora: Buenas tardes, familia García. Sé que esta es una situación difícil para todos. La Sra. García ha firmado un consentimiento donde expresa que no desea continuar con la diálisis y prefiere recibir cuidados paliativos para mantener su comodidad y dignidad en esta etapa de su vida.	*Doctor*: Good afternoon, García family. I know this is a difficult situation for everyone. Mrs. García has signed a consent form expressing that she does not want to continue with dialysis and prefers to receive palliative care to maintain her comfort and dignity at this stage of her life.
Hija: Doctora, entendemos que mi madre firmó eso, pero creemos que no sabía lo que realmente implicaba. Nosotros queremos que ella siga luchando. ¿No puede ignorar ese consentimiento y seguir con la diálisis?	Daughter: Doctor, we understand that my mother signed that, but we believe she didn't really understand what it meant. We want her to keep fighting. Can't you ignore that consent and continue with the dialysis?
Doctora: Entiendo su preocupación, y es un tema muy delicado. Sin embargo, la Sra. García tomó esta decisión cuando aún tenía plena capacidad de decisión. Respetar su autonomía es fundamental, aunque a veces puede ser doloroso para los seres queridos. Ella quería evitar tratamientos que le causarán más dolor, y ahora mi responsabilidad ética es respetar su voluntad.	*Doctor*: I understand your concern, and this is a very sensitive issue. However, Mrs. García made this decision when she still had full decision-making capacity. Respecting her autonomy is fundamental, even though it may be painful for loved ones. She wanted to avoid treatments that would cause her more pain, and now my ethical responsibility is to respect her wishes.
Hija: Pero, doctora, si la diálisis le da más tiempo, ¿no sería mejor?	*Daughter*: But, doctor, if dialysis gives her more time, wouldn't that be better?
Doctora: La diálisis podría prolongar su vida, pero también podría generar un sufrimiento que ella misma eligió evitar. Como médica, debo asegurarme de que su madre reciba el tratamiento que respete su dignidad y deseos. Les propongo que hablemos de cómo podemos acompañarla en este proceso con los cuidados paliativos y asegurarnos de que esté rodeada de la familia que la ama.	*Doctor*: Dialysis could prolong her life, but it could also cause suffering that she chose to avoid. As a physician, I have to ensure that your mother receives care that respects her dignity and wishes. I suggest that we discuss how we can support her during this process with palliative care and ensure that she is surrounded by the family who loves her.

Hija: Gracias, doctora. Es difícil aceptarlo, pero entiendo que debemos respetar lo que mi madre decidió.	*Daughter:* Thank you, doctor. It's hard to accept, but I understand that we have to respect what my mother decided.

Conversation 2: Nurse/ Family Conversation – Nurse and Family Discussing End-of-Life Care

Nurse Rodríguez is speaking with the family of Mr. López, an 82-year-old patient with advanced lung cancer who has chosen to focus on palliative care rather than aggressive treatment. The patient's family, however, wants the medical team to continue with chemotherapy, believing it might extend his life. This situation creates a common ethical dilemma in Hispanic healthcare settings, where family wishes sometimes conflict with the patient's expressed desires.

Spanish	Translation
Enfermera: Buenas tardes, familia López. He venido a hablar con ustedes sobre la decisión de su padre de continuar sólo con cuidados paliativos. Él ha expresado claramente su deseo de no seguir con la quimioterapia, prefiriendo estar más cómodo en estos momentos.	*Nurse:* Good afternoon, López family. I've come to talk with you about your father's decision to focus solely on palliative care. He has clearly expressed his desire not to continue with chemotherapy, preferring to be more comfortable during this time.
Hijo: Pero, ¿no existe una posibilidad de que la quimioterapia le dé más tiempo de vida? Nosotros queremos hacer todo lo posible por él.	*Son:* But isn't there a chance that chemotherapy could give him more time? We want to do everything possible for him.
Enfermera: Entiendo su preocupación y el deseo de que él viva más tiempo. Es una situación difícil, y respeto profundamente lo que están sintiendo. Sin embargo, él ha tomado esta decisión basándose en su derecho a la autonomía y en la ética médica, que nos orienta a respetar las decisiones del paciente.	*Nurse:* I understand your concern and your desire for him to have more time. It's a difficult situation, and I deeply respect what you're feeling. However, he made this decision based on his right to autonomy, and medical ethics guide us to respect the patient's decisions.
Hijo: Pero no creemos que él esté pensando con claridad. Ha estado muy deprimido y cansado últimamente.	*Son:* But we don't think he's thinking clearly. He's been very depressed and tired lately.
Enfermera: Es cierto que la fatiga puede influir en su ánimo, pero como equipo médico, evaluamos su capacidad de decisión y confirmamos que comprende su situación. Parte	*Nurse:* It's true that fatigue can affect his mood, but as a medical team, we have assessed his decision-making capacity and confirmed that he understands his situation.

de nuestro papel es asegurar que se sienta escuchado y apoyado, especialmente en estos momentos tan delicados.	Part of our role is to ensure that he feels heard and supported, especially during such delicate moments.
Hijo: Entonces, ¿no hay nada más que podamos hacer? ¿Solo aceptar su decisión?	*Son:* So, is there nothing more we can do? Do we just have to accept his decision?
Enfermera: Pueden acompañarlo y apoyarlo durante este proceso. Su padre quiere sentirse en paz y rodeado de sus seres queridos sin el sufrimiento adicional de un tratamiento agresivo. Nuestra prioridad ahora es asegurar su comodidad y calidad de vida. La decisión final de rechazar el tratamiento está en sus manos, y nosotros estamos aquí para acompañarlos a todos en este proceso.	*Nurse:* You can be there for him and support him through this process. Your father wants to feel at peace and surrounded by his loved ones without the added suffering of aggressive treatment. Our priority now is to ensure his comfort and quality of life. The final decision to refuse treatment is in his hands, and we are here to support all of you through this process.
Hijo: Es difícil, pero si eso es lo que él quiere, supongo que debemos respetarlo. Solo queremos lo mejor para él.	*Son:* It's hard, but if that's what he wants, I guess we have to respect it. We just want what's best for him.
Enfermera: Y lo mejor para él es también respetar sus deseos. Recuerden que estamos aquí para ofrecer apoyo emocional a todos ustedes y a su padre durante esta etapa.	*Nurse:* And what's best for him is also respecting his wishes. Remember, we're here to offer emotional support to all of you and to your father during this time.

Key Takeaways

One of the central tenets of ethical decision-making in healthcare is respecting patient autonomy. This means acknowledging the patient's right to make informed decisions about their own care, even when those decisions may differ from the wishes of their family. This is particularly significant in Hispanic healthcare settings, where collective decision-making is often preferred.

Understanding cultural values, such as the importance of family involvement in care decisions, is crucial for healthcare providers working with Hispanic patients. Providers must navigate the delicate balance between respecting these cultural norms and upholding ethical responsibilities, such as honoring a patient's wishes when they conflict with the family's preferences.

Providers should be aware of the legal aspects surrounding consent, decision-making capacity, and patient rights, especially when patients choose to refuse treatment. Understanding these legal frameworks helps ensure that care is delivered ethically and that patients' rights are protected.

Exercises

Exercise 1

Match the English term to its Spanish translation.

1. Capacidad de decisión
2. Cuidados paliativos
3. Consentimiento informado
4. Derecho a rechazar tratamiento
5. Dignidad humana

Options:

a. Right to refuse treatment
b. Palliative care
c. Informed consent
d. Decision-making capacity
e. Human dignity

Exercise 2

Fill in the blanks.

1. La familia de la paciente pidió más información sobre el proceso de _____ (informed consent).

2. El _____ (right to refuse treatment) del paciente fue respetado por el equipo médico.

3. La _____ (decision-making capacity) de la Sra. Gómez fue evaluada antes de tomar la decisión final.

4. Durante la conversación, se enfatizó la importancia de la _____ (human dignity) de cada paciente.

5. El equipo médico propuso _____ (palliative care) para mejorar la calidad de vida del paciente..

Exercise 3

Write a dialogue where a nurse explains to a family why respecting the patient's right to refuse treatment is crucial, even if the family disagrees with the decision.

Exercise 4

Discuss a scenario where a patient's living will contradict the family's wishes. What steps should healthcare providers take to navigate this situation while respecting the patient's autonomy?

Exercise 5

Translate the following sentences into Spanish.

1. The patient has the right to choose palliative care instead of invasive treatment.
2. Decision-making capacity is essential to ensure the patient's wishes are respected.
3. The medical team explained the importance of informed consent to the family.
4. Human dignity should be considered in every aspect of patient care.
5. The patient's right to refuse treatment must be honored, even in difficult situations.

Answer Key

Exercise 1

Match the English term to its Spanish translation.

1. d. Capacidad de decisión - Decision-making capacity
2. b. Cuidados paliativos - Palliative care
3. c. Consentimiento informado - Informed consent
4. a. Derecho a rechazar tratamiento - Right to refuse treatment
5. e. Dignidad humana - Human dignity

Exercise 2

Fill in the blanks.

1. La familia de la paciente pidió más información sobre el proceso de consentimiento informado.
2. El derecho a rechazar tratamiento del paciente fue respetado por el equipo médico.
3. La capacidad de decisión de la Sra. Gómez fue evaluada antes de tomar la decisión final.
4. Durante la conversación, se enfatizó la importancia de la dignidad humana de cada paciente.
5. El equipo médico propuso cuidados paliativos para mejorar la calidad de vida del paciente.

Exercise 3

Example dialogue:

Spanish Version:

Enfermera: Buenas tardes, Sra. Ramos. Entiendo que esta situación es difícil para usted y su familia. Su padre firmó un consentimiento informado para no recibir tratamientos agresivos y enfocarse en los cuidados paliativos.

Sra. Ramos: Lo sé, pero siento que podríamos hacer algo más para prolongar su vida. ¿No podría reconsiderar su decisión?

Enfermera: Entiendo su preocupación, Sra. Ramos. Sin embargo, la autonomía del paciente es fundamental en estas situaciones. Su padre tomó esta decisión de forma consciente, considerando su calidad de vida. Los cuidados paliativos que hemos iniciado buscan garantizar su confort y dignidad durante este tiempo.

Sra. Ramos: Pero, ¿no estamos abandonando la lucha por su vida?

Enfermera: No se trata de abandonar, sino de respetar su dignidad humana y sus deseos de no someterse a tratamientos invasivos. Él prefirió pasar este tiempo sin dolor y cerca de su familia. Estamos aquí para brindarle el mejor cuidado posible de acuerdo a su voluntad.

Sra. Ramos: Gracias por su apoyo. Es difícil, pero quiero respetar lo que mi padre deseaba.

English Version:

Nurse: Good afternoon, Mrs. Ramos. I understand that this situation is difficult for you and your family. Your father signed an informed consent to not receive aggressive treatments and to focus on palliative care.

Mrs. Ramos: I know, but I feel like we could do more to prolong his life. Couldn't he reconsider his decision?

Nurse: I understand your concern, Mrs. Ramos. However, patient autonomy is fundamental in these situations. Your father made this decision consciously, considering his quality of life. The palliative care we have initiated aims to ensure his comfort and dignity during this time.

Mrs. Ramos: But aren't we giving up the fight for his life?

Nurse: It's not about giving up; it's about respecting his human dignity and his wishes not to undergo invasive treatments. He preferred to spend this time pain-free and close to his family. We are here to provide him with the best possible care according to his wishes.

Mrs. Ramos: Thank you for your support. It's difficult, but I want to respect what my father wanted.

Exercise 4

Discuss a scenario:

Spanish version:

Enfermera: Buenas tardes, Sr. Vargas. Su madre expresó en su voluntad anticipada que no deseaba ser alimentada por sonda en caso de llegar a esta etapa de su enfermedad.

Sr. Vargas: Sé que ella lo escribió, pero ahora verla tan débil me hace dudar. ¿Y si la alimentación por sonda le diera más tiempo?

Enfermera: Entiendo lo difícil que es esta situación para usted. Sin embargo, la voluntad anticipada de su madre es una expresión de su autonomía del paciente. Ella tomó esta decisión para evitar procedimientos que no mejoren su calidad de vida.

Sr. Vargas: Pero siento que si respeto esa decisión, la estoy dejando ir demasiado pronto.

Enfermera: Lo que usted está haciendo es respetar la dignidad humana de su madre, permitiéndole no recibir tratamientos que ella consideró innecesarios. Nuestro equipo se asegurará de que esté cómoda y que no sufra durante este tiempo. Estamos aquí para apoyar tanto a usted como a ella.

Sr. Vargas: Gracias por ayudarme a entenderlo mejor. Haré lo que ella quiso.

English Version:

Nurse: Good afternoon, Mr. Vargas. Your mother expressed in her living will that she did not want to be fed through a tube if she reached this stage of her illness.

Mr. Vargas: I know she wrote that, but seeing her so weak now makes me doubt. What if the feeding tube could give her more time?

Nurse: I understand how difficult this is for you. However, your mother's living will is an expression of her patient autonomy. She made this decision to avoid procedures that wouldn't improve her quality of life.

Mr. Vargas: But I feel like if I respect that decision, I'm letting her go too soon.

Nurse: What you are doing is respecting your mother's human dignity, allowing her not to undergo treatments she considered unnecessary. Our team will ensure she remains comfortable and does not suffer during this time. We are here to support both you and her.

Mr. Vargas: Thank you for helping me understand. I will honor her wishes.

Exercise 5

Translate the following sentences into Spanish.

1. El paciente tiene el derecho de elegir cuidados paliativos en lugar de un tratamiento invasivo.
2. La capacidad de decisión es esencial para asegurar que se respeten los deseos del paciente.
3. El equipo médico explicó la importancia del consentimiento informado a la familia.
4. La dignidad humana debe ser considerada en cada aspecto del cuidado del paciente.
5. El derecho del paciente a rechazar tratamiento debe ser respetado, incluso en situaciones difíciles.

BOOK 7

Comprehensive Medical Spanish Review: Integrated Learning and Application

Enhancing Patient Communication and Cultural Competence for Healthcare Professionals

Explore to Win

Book 7 Description

Welcome to the seventh and final volume of the "Medical Spanish for Healthcare Professionals" series: "Comprehensive Medical Spanish Review: Integrated Learning and Application." This book encapsulates the entire series, serving as both a culmination of your hard-earned skills and a springboard into the dynamic world of healthcare communication. As healthcare professionals, we recognize that language is more than mere words; it is a bridge to understanding, empathy, and effective care for our patients. With this volume, you are not just revisiting lessons but embarking on a holistic integration of language with cultural adeptness.

Throughout the previous six volumes, you have immersed yourself in the nuances of medical Spanish, from foundational vocabulary to specialized terminology and from cultural insights to complex clinical dialogs. Now, this book aims to weave these diverse strands into a robust framework that enhances every aspect of your interaction with Spanish-speaking patients. Here, the emphasis is on application—practicing and honing your skills through integrated exercises, real-world simulations, and reflective feedback.

Imagine walking into a clinic, fully prepared to navigate sensitive conversations about treatment options, confidently engage in nuanced discussions about cultural practices, and smoothly handle emergencies with the precision that only comes from practice and understanding. With each page, you will reinforce your proficiency, gaining confidence and fluency that will resonate with your patients, fostering trust and critical rapport. These competencies are especially vital in an age where linguistic barriers can impact patient outcomes and where cultural competence can profoundly enhance the patient experience.

More than a textbook, this volume is a companion in your journey to becoming a truly bilingual and culturally sensitive healthcare provider. Engage actively with the material, partake in simulations that mirror real-life complexities, and embrace feedback mechanisms designed to polish your skills. This is not merely the end of a series—it's the beginning of a new phase in your professional journey, where each interaction with a Spanish-speaking patient is an opportunity to apply your knowledge effectively and compassionately.

With passion and dedication, prepare to transform your practice and redefine patient care in today's multicultural world. Welcome to this pivotal phase of your journey—an opportunity to integrate, reflect, and excel in providing outstanding healthcare to Spanish-speaking communities.

Chapter I: Comprehensive Review

La primera riqueza es la salud

Ralph W. Emerson

Effective communication is the cornerstone of quality healthcare, particularly in increasingly diverse societies. The Medical Spanish series consists of seven comprehensive volumes designed to equip healthcare professionals with essential language skills to communicate effectively with Spanish-speaking patients. Each book builds on the previous one, progressively enhancing vocabulary, cultural competence, and practical communication skills needed in various medical settings. This structured approach ensures a thorough understanding of both medical terminology and the cultural context of patient care.

Overview of the Medical Spanish Series

BOOK 1: Introduction to Medical Spanish and Basics

Description:

Book 1 sets the stage for understanding medical Spanish by introducing the essential foundations. It opens with a compelling introduction detailing the numerous benefits of being bilingual in healthcare—enhancing patient trust, improving outcomes, and reducing the likelihood of errors related to misunderstandings.

Chapters Summary:

- Chapter I: Introduction

  Discusses the importance of bilingualism, offers an overview of the content and structure, and outlines the guidelines for learning medical Spanish, complete with a suggested study plan.

- Chapter II: Spanish Basics

  Covers the Spanish alphabet, phonetics, and basic phrases for greetings and introductions. It features common conversational phrases tailored for healthcare settings alongside practical notes to aid retention.

- Chapter III: Basic Medical Terminology

  Introduces foundational medical terms, providing pronunciation guides and spelling rules. This chapter features numerous examples of typical conversations between healthcare providers and patients to reinforce learning.

Integration Benefits:

Establishing a solid linguistic foundation in Book 1 provides learners with essential tools needed for conversations in subsequent books. A strong grasp of basic Spanish prepares healthcare professionals to engage confidently with patients from the outset.

BOOK 2: Spanish Medical Communication: Anatomy, Procedures, Prescription, and Emergencies

Description:

Building on the groundwork laid in Book 1, this volume dives deeper into specific medical vocabulary and communication strategies vital for daily practice. Each chapter is thematically organized around critical areas of medical communication.

Chapters Summary:

- Chapter I: Anatomy and Physiology

  Discusses basic anatomy and physiology terminology in Spanish, focusing on the parts of the body and their functions, reinforced through patient consultation conversations.

- Chapter II: Medical Procedures and Exams

  Covers vocabulary specific to medical procedures, including how to ask questions and give instructions to patients in Spanish.

- Chapter III: Prescription and Medication

  Teaches the terms necessary for discussing prescriptions, including how to inquire about allergies and explain medication dosages in Spanish.

- Chapter IV: Medical Emergencies

  Focuses on emergency vocabulary and phrases, preparing providers to give and receive information in crisis situations.

Integration Benefits:

This book helps healthcare providers acquire the necessary vocabulary to perform effectively in real clinical settings. By mastering specific terms and phrases relevant to anatomy, procedures, and emergencies, practitioners enhance their ability to interact clinically with patients and colleagues.

BOOK 3: Cultural Competence in Healthcare and Additional Practice

Description:

Understanding cultural nuances is essential for effective healthcare delivery, particularly in a multicultural environment. Book 3 emphasizes cultural competence alongside language skills.

Chapters Summary:

- Chapter I: Introduction

  Introduces the concept of cultural competence and its relevance in healthcare.

- Chapter II: Enhancing Cultural Competence in Healthcare

  Discusses cultural diversity, effective communication strategies for Spanish-speaking patients, and common patient responses.

- Chapter III: Cultural Concepts in Hispanic Healthcare

  Provides insights into building trust, exploring traditional healing practices, understanding common ailments, and the role of family in Hispanic healthcare settings.

- Chapter IV: Additional Practice Exercises

  Offers pronunciation practice, vocabulary exercises by specialty, role-playing scenarios, and cultural competence scenarios.

Integration Benefits:

By addressing cultural considerations and their impact on patient experiences, this book equips learners with the insights needed to deliver compassionate care. This knowledge significantly enhances trust and rapport with patients, aligning clinical practice with their cultural beliefs.

BOOK 4: Advanced Medical Spanish: Specialized Vocabulary for Healthcare Disciplines

Description:

Book 4 targets advanced learners working in specialized fields of healthcare, offering dedicated vocabulary related to pediatric, obstetric, gynecological, and oncological care.

Chapters Summary:

- Chapter I: Pediatrics

  Covers pediatric medical terminology, common symptoms, and example conversations pertinent to this age group.

- Chapter II: Obstetrics & Gynecology

  Focuses on terminology and conditions specific to women's health, including explaining treatment plans in both obstetrics and gynecology.

- Chapter III: Oncology
- Provides the necessary language to communicate effectively regarding oncology terminology, cancers, and treatment options.

Integration Benefits:

This book equips practitioners with specialized vocabulary essential for their fields, enhancing their competence when discussing diagnoses and treatment options with patients. Understanding this advanced terminology enables healthcare providers to improve patient educational efforts and optimize care delivery, ultimately leading to better health outcomes.

BOOK 5: Clinical Conversations: Mastering Complex Medical Dialogues in Spanish

Description:

As healthcare providers often encounter multi-faceted scenarios requiring nuanced communication, Book 5 focuses on mastering clinical conversations. This volume prepares readers to handle complex dialogues about patient management, emotional discussions, and multidisciplinary communication.

Chapters Summary:

- Chapter I: Managing Patients with Multiple Comorbidities

  Explores terminology specific to various chronic conditions and addresses communication strategies for effectively managing these patients through example dialogues.

- Chapter II: Delivering Bad News and Discussing Palliative Care

  Discusses techniques for delivering difficult news and engaging in compassionate discussions about palliative care, reinforcing the need for sensitivity in these conversations.

- Chapter III: Supporting Significant Lifestyle Changes

  Focuses on motivational interviewing and counseling strategies that encourage patients to adopt healthier lifestyles, illustrated through practical dialogue examples.

- Chapter IV: Enhancing Patient Engagement and Adherence

  Provides insights into strategies for improving patient engagement through clear communication, motivational techniques, and understanding patient motivations.

- Chapter V: Multidisciplinary Communication in Healthcare

  Highlights the importance of collaborative communication among healthcare professionals, utilizing example conversations that show interprofessional dialogue and coordination of care.

Integration Benefits:

By focusing on complex medical dialogues, Book 5 empowers healthcare providers to navigate sensitive conversations with confidence. It emphasizes the significance of empathy and active listening, vital skills for maintaining patient trust and fostering an environment conducive to open communication.

BOOK 6: Patient Care in Spanish: Focused Practice for High-Impact Scenarios

Description:

Book 6 is dedicated to high-impact medical situations, providing healthcare professionals with the necessary language skills and contextual knowledge to manage critical scenarios effectively.

Chapters Summary:

- Chapter I: Intensive Care Unit Interactions

  Explores the unique communication dynamics in critical care settings, addressing communication barriers and the impact of healthcare inequality on patient outcomes. Terminology and examples specific to ICU settings are included.

- Chapter II: Mental Health Crisis Intervention

  Addresses the specific needs of Hispanic Americans in mental health care. It discusses cultural considerations and effective communication strategies to support individuals in crisis.

- Chapter III: Navigating Consent and Ethical Dilemmas

  Covers key issues related to informed consent, medical ethics, and decision-making in sensitive situations, along with relevant vocabulary and illustrative conversations.

Integration Benefits:

Through focused practice in scenarios commonly encountered in critical care and mental health, Book 6 prepares learners to address urgent and sensitive patient needs effectively. The emphasis on the navigation of ethical dilemmas enhances the healthcare provider's capacity to uphold patient rights while delivering compassionate care.

BOOK 7: Comprehensive Medical Spanish Review: Integrated Learning and Application

Description:

The final volume in the series serves as a comprehensive review, synthesizing all learning from the previous books into a cohesive understanding of medical Spanish. This book is designed to reinforce language retention and application through integrated practice.

Chapters Summary:

- Chapter I: Comprehensive Review

  Recaps medical terminology, key concepts, and conversational patterns from earlier volumes, ensuring that learners can connect disparate pieces of knowledge.

- Chapter II: Integrated Practice

  Offers diverse exercises that encompass vocabulary, grammar, pronunciation, and cultural concepts, creating opportunities for active learning and real-world application.

- Chapter III: Simulated Scenarios

  Engages readers through role-playing exercises and real-life simulations that reflect actual patient-provider interactions, enhancing confidence in practical application.

- Chapter IV: Feedback and Improvement

  Provides tools for self-assessment and reflection, allowing learners to identify areas for continued growth and improvement in their language skills and cultural competency.

Integration Benefits:

By consolidating knowledge from all previous volumes, Book 7 ensures that healthcare professionals emerge with a comprehensive command of medical Spanish. The review of key concepts, combined with practical exercises, prepares them to engage effectively in a variety of clinical settings, enhancing their ability to provide high-quality, culturally sensitive care.

Interactive Recap of Advanced Medical Terminology

This recap covers the advanced vocabulary covered in Books 4, 5, and 6, focusing on Pediatrics, Obstetrics and Gynecology, Oncology, and the management of patients with multiple comorbidities, particularly within Intensive Care Units (ICU), crisis intervention in mental health, and navigating ethical dilemmas in patient care. Each chapter provided us with crucial vocabulary, practical scenarios, and insights into how cultural context influences patient interactions.

Book 4: Advanced Medical Spanish

Chapter I: Pediatrics

Key Vocabulary:

- Pediatría (Pediatrics): The branch of medicine dealing with the health and medical care of infants, children, and adolescents.
- Crecimiento (Growth): Refers to the physical changes and development during childhood.
- Desarrollo (Development): Encompasses cognitive and emotional growth, along with physical changes.
- Vacunas (Vaccines): Biological preparations administered to enhance immunity to particular infections.
- Consulta pediátrica (Pediatric consultation): The appointment where children receive medical assessments.

Example Interaction:

A pediatrician communicates with a parent about vaccinations:

Pediatrician: "Es importante que su hijo reciba todas sus vacunas para evitar enfermedades graves. ¿Ha leído el calendario de vacunación?"

Translation: "It's important for your child to receive all their vaccines to prevent serious illnesses. Have you read the vaccination schedule?"

Interactive Activity:

Discussion Prompts:

- What common fears do parents have regarding vaccinations?
- How would you reassure a parent who is hesitant about vaccine side effects?

Chapter II: Obstetrics & Gynecology

Key Vocabulary:

- Ginecología (Gynecology): The medical specialty dealing with the female reproductive system and its disorders.
- Embarazo (Pregnancy): The period during which a fetus develops inside a woman's womb.
- Menopausia (Menopause): The time in a woman's life when menstrual periods cease, often accompanied by various physical and emotional symptoms.
- Ecografía obstétrica (Obstetric ultrasound): An imaging technique used to monitor the embryo or fetus during pregnancy.
- Dilatación cervical (Cervical dilation): The process of the cervix opening during labor.

Example Interaction:

An obstetrician discussing care during pregnancy:

Obstetrician: "Durante su embarazo, es crítico realizar chequeos regulares. Esto nos ayudará a monitorear su salud y la del bebé."

Translation: "During your pregnancy, regular checkups are crucial. This will help us monitor your health and that of the baby."

Interactive Activity:

Reflection Questions:

How do you think cultural beliefs about pregnancy can influence a patient's treatment plan?

What steps can healthcare providers take to address fears about labor and delivery?

Chapter III: Oncology

Key Vocabulary:

- Cáncer (Cancer): A group of diseases characterized by uncontrolled cell growth.
- Biopsia (Biopsy): A procedure involving the extraction of tissue for diagnostic examination.
- Metástasis (Metastasis): The spread of cancer cells to distant parts of the body.
- Quimioterapia (Chemotherapy): A type of cancer treatment using drugs to kill cancer cells.

- Remisión (Remission): A period during which the signs and symptoms of cancer are reduced or disappear.

Example Interaction:

An oncologist explaining treatment to a patient:

Oncologist: "Vamos a iniciar quimioterapia, que puede tener efectos secundarios, pero es una parte importante de su tratamiento para reducir el tumor."

Translation: "We are going to start chemotherapy, which may have side effects, but it's an important part of your treatment to reduce the tumor."

Interactive Exercise:

Group Discussion:

How can healthcare professionals provide emotional support to patients diagnosed with cancer?

Discuss the role of family in the treatment decision-making process.

Book 5: Clinical Conversations: Mastering Complex Medical Dialogues in Spanish

Chapter I: Managing Patients with Multiple Comorbidities

Key Vocabulary:

- Comorbilidades (Comorbidities): The presence of two or more chronic diseases in a patient.
- Polifarmacia (Polypharmacy): The simultaneous use of multiple medications, which increases the risk of drug interactions.
- Adherencia al tratamiento (Treatment adherence): The extent to which patients follow prescribed treatment regimens.
- Interacción medicamentosa (Drug interaction): Refers to how different medications can affect each other's efficacy.
- Historia clínica (Medical history): Comprehensive documentation of the patient's health conditions and treatments.

Example Interaction:

Imagine a doctor discussing medication management with a patient who has multiple health issues:

Doctor: "Es crucial que sigas todas las indicaciones de tu tratamiento. ¿Cómo ha sido tu experiencia con los medicamentos?"

Translation: "It's crucial that you follow all the treatment instructions. How has your experience been with the medications?"

Interactive Activity:

Breakout Session:

Role-play a scenario where one participant is a physician managing a patient with diabetes and hypertension.

Discuss strategies to enhance medication adherence.

Questions for Reflection:

What challenges might Hispanic patients face regarding medication management?

How can you incorporate family support into treatment plans for these patients?

Chapter II: Mental Health Crisis Intervention

Key Vocabulary:

- Trastorno de ansiedad (Anxiety disorder): A mental health condition characterized by excessive worry and fear.
- Depresión mayor (Major depression): A more severe form of depression affecting daily functioning.
- Hospitalización involuntaria (Involuntary hospitalization): Admission to a facility for treatment against the patient's will, typically during a mental health crisis.
- Intervención en crisis (Crisis intervention): Immediate and short-term assistance provided during a mental health crisis.
- Terapia cognitivo-conductual (Cognitive-behavioral therapy): A common therapeutic approach that changes patterns of thinking or behavior.

Example Interaction:

A doctor is addressing a mental health crisis with a distressed patient:

Doctor: "Comprendo que te sientes abrumada. Los trastornos de ansiedad son comunes, y hay tratamientos que pueden ayudarte. ¿Te gustaría explorar algunas opciones de terapia?"

Translation: "I understand you feel overwhelmed. Anxiety disorders are common, and there are treatments that can help you. Would you like to explore some therapy options?"

Interactive Exercise:

Discussion Prompts:

How do cultural perceptions of mental health impact a patient's willingness to seek help?

Share strategies for building a supportive environment during mental health interventions.

Chapter III: Navigating Consent and Ethical Dilemmas

Key Vocabulary:

- Consentimiento informado (Informed consent): The process of getting permission from a patient before providing treatment, ensuring they understand the risks and benefits.
- Autonomía del paciente (Patient autonomy): The right of patients to make decisions about their medical care without their healthcare provider trying to influence the decision.

- Conflicto ético (Ethical conflict): Situations where ethical principles collide, often complicating decision-making.
- Toma de decisiones compartida (Shared decision-making): Collaborative process that involves patients and physicians working together to make decisions.
- Derecho a rechazar tratamiento (Right to refuse treatment): A patient's legal right to refuse any medical treatment or procedure.

Example Interaction:

A healthcare provider discusses end-of-life decisions with a patient's family:

Provider: "Es fundamental que respetemos los deseos de su padre, quien ha decidido rechazar el tratamiento agresivo. ¿Están de acuerdo en apoyar su elección de cuidados paliativos?"

Translation: "It is essential that we respect your father's wishes, who has chosen to refuse aggressive treatment. Do you agree to support his choice of palliative care?"

Book 6: Patient Care in Spanish

Chapter I: Intensive Care Unit (ICU) Interactions

Key Vocabulary:

- Ventilación mecánica (Mechanical ventilation): A life-support procedure when patients cannot breathe unaided.
- Sedoanalgesia (Sedoanalgesia): A process that involves using sedatives for pain management during procedures.
- Fallo multiorgánico (Multiple organ failure): A critical condition where two or more organ systems fail.
- Intubación (Intubation): The placement of a tube into the trachea to maintain an open airway.
- Reanimación cardiopulmonar (CPR): A life-saving technique used in emergencies when someone has stopped breathing, or their heart has stopped.

Example Interaction:

Imagine a doctor discussing intubation with a patient's family:

Doctor: "Están luchando para respirar, así que necesitamos intubarlo. Esto le ayudará a recibir el oxígeno necesario a través de un ventilador."

Translation: "He's struggling to breathe, so we need to intubate him. This will help him receive the necessary oxygen through a ventilator."

Interactive Exercise:

Role-Playing Scenario:

One participant acts as the physician explaining the need for a ventilator, while the other plays a worried family member.

Questions for Discussion:

How can providers reassure families regarding the necessity of invasive procedures?

What cultural beliefs might influence their understanding of these interventions?

Chapter II: Mental Health Crisis Intervention

Key Vocabulary:

- Trastorno de ansiedad (Anxiety disorder): A mental health condition characterized by excessive worry.

- Depresión mayor (Major depression): A severe form of depression affecting daily life.

- Psicosis aguda (Acute psychosis): A condition that may involve hallucinations and delusions.

- Intervención en crisis (Crisis intervention): Immediate support for individuals experiencing a mental health crisis.

- Terapia cognitivo-conductual (Cognitive-behavioral therapy): A common therapeutic technique used to treat various mental health disorders.

Example Interaction:

Picture a nurse discussing options with a family member of a patient in crisis:

Nurse: "Es fundamental que su hermano reciba terapia cognitivo-conductual en adición a los medicamentos. Esto le ayudará a cambiar pensamientos negativos."

Translation: "It's essential for your brother to receive cognitive-behavioral therapy in addition to medications. This will help him change negative thoughts."

Interactive Activity:

Group Discussion:

How do cultural perceptions of mental illness influence a patient's willingness to seek help?

Discuss methods for reducing the stigma surrounding mental health care within Hispanic communities.

Chapter III: Navigating Consent and Ethical Dilemmas

Key Vocabulary:

- Consentimiento informado (Informed consent): A process whereby a patient is informed about the risks and benefits of a treatment and provides their agreement.

- Autonomía del paciente (Patient autonomy): The right and ability of the patient to make decisions about their care.

- Conflicto ético (Ethical conflict): Situations where moral principles clash during medical decision-making.

- Derecho a rechazar tratamiento (Right to refuse treatment): Patients' legal right to decline medical procedures.

- Toma de decisiones compartida (Shared decision-making): Collaborative process allowing patients and healthcare providers to work together on treatment plans.

Example Interaction:

Imagine a physician speaking with a family about a patient's wishes regarding treatment:

Physician: "Su madre ha decidido que no desea recibir tratamiento agresivo. Es esencial respetar su autonomía y deseos."

Translation: "Your mother has decided that she does not wish to receive aggressive treatment. It is essential to respect her autonomy and wishes."

Interactive Exercise:

Scenario Discussion:

How can healthcare providers help families understand the importance of adhering to a patient's wishes in a living will, especially when those wishes conflict with family desires?

Discuss how cultural values influence perceptions around end-of-life care. What strategies can enhance respectful conversations?

Milestones of the Series

Beginning with foundational concepts in Book 1, the series progresses through essential medical terminology, specialized vocabulary, and complex clinical dialogues, culminating in a thorough review of skills acquired. Each milestone builds upon the previous one, ensuring that readers not only learn the language but also understand the cultural nuances critical to providing patient-centered care.

BOOK 1: Introduction to Medical Spanish and Basics

- Milestone 1: Understand the benefits of bilingualism in healthcare.
- Milestone 2: Familiarize yourself with basic Spanish vocabulary, including greetings and introductions.
- Milestone 3: Learn essential medical terminology and pronunciation rules.
- Milestone 4: Engage in practical conversations between healthcare providers and patients.

BOOK 2: Spanish Medical Communication: Anatomy, Procedures, Prescription, and Emergencies

- Milestone 5: Master anatomy and physiology terms in Spanish.
- Milestone 6: Communicate effectively regarding medical procedures and patient instructions.
- Milestone 7: Understand prescription terminology and explain medication dosages.
- Milestone 8: Respond appropriately in emergency medical scenarios.

BOOK 3: Cultural Competence in Healthcare and Additional Practice

- Milestone 9: Enhance understanding of cultural diversity in healthcare.
- Milestone 10: Apply effective communication strategies for Spanish-speaking patients.
- Milestone 11: Recognize and integrate traditional healing practices in patient care.
- Milestone 12: Engage in role-playing exercises for practical application of medical Spanish.

BOOK 4: Advanced Medical Spanish: Specialized Vocabulary for Healthcare Disciplines

- Milestone 13: Acquire specialized vocabulary in pediatrics, obstetrics, gynecology, and oncology.
- Milestone 14: Translate common symptoms and explain treatment plans in specialized fields.

BOOK 5: Clinical Conversations: Mastering Complex Medical Dialogues in Spanish

- Milestone 15: Develop terminology for managing patients with multiple comorbidities.
- Milestone 16: Learn effective communication strategies for delivering bad news and palliative care.
- Milestone 17: Enhance engagement and adherence to treatment through motivational interviewing.

BOOK 6: Patient Care in Spanish: Focused Practice for High-Impact Scenarios

- Milestone 18: Understand communication processes in ICU settings and mental health crisis intervention.
- Milestone 19: Navigate ethical dilemmas and informed consent with Spanish-speaking patients.

BOOK 7: Comprehensive Medical Spanish Review: Integrated Learning and Application

- Milestone 20: Review and integrate all learned material for comprehensive application in healthcare settings.
- Milestone 21: Prepare for real-world application and ongoing learning in medical Spanish.

This structured approach helps healthcare professionals build language skills progressively while emphasizing cultural competence and practical application.

Final thoughts on the importance of learning medical Spanish in healthcare

In today's world, it is essential for healthcare professionals to be able to communicate effectively with patients of diverse backgrounds. With the increasing number of Spanish-speaking patients in the United States, it is more important than ever for healthcare professionals to learn medical Spanish.

The benefits of being bilingual in this setting are numerous, including improving patient outcomes, reducing medical errors, and increasing patient satisfaction. Bilingual professionals can communicate directly with patients, provide more accurate diagnoses and treatment plans, and build trust and rapport with patients.

Learning medical Spanish is not only beneficial for Spanish-speaking patients, but it also provides healthcare professionals with a competitive advantage in the job market. Healthcare facilities are looking for bilingual professionals who can provide high-quality care to a diverse patient population.

Chapter II: Integrated Practice

Diez gramos de prevención equivalen a un kilogramo de curación

Lao Tse

Integrated practice in healthcare refers to the collaborative approach that combines various medical disciplines to ensure comprehensive patient care. For healthcare professionals working in Hispanic communities, integrating language skills, cultural awareness, and medical knowledge is vital to addressing patient needs effectively. This chapter will explore medical vocabulary related to integrated practice, role-playing exercises, and examples to enhance communication with Spanish-speaking patients.

Extended Exercises for Integrated Practice

Exercise 1: Vocabulary Match

Match the following medical terms in English with their corresponding Spanish translations.

1. Chronic illness	a) Recursos comunitarios
2. Pain management	b) Derechos del paciente
3. Health literacy	c) Alfabetización en salud
4. Community resources	d) Manejo del dolor
5. Patient rights	e) Enfermedad crónica

Exercise 2: Medical Terminology Fill-in-the-Blanks

Complete the sentences using the key vocabulary from the previous chapters.

1. La _____ es esencial para asegurarse de que los pacientes entiendan su diagnóstico y tratamiento. (Health literacy)

2. El médico debe obtener el _____ del paciente antes de realizar el procedimiento. (Informed consent)

3. Los _____ son esenciales para coordinar la atención de los pacientes con múltiples condiciones médicas. (Community resources)

4. La _____ implica actuar en el mejor interés del paciente, asegurando su bienestar. (Beneficence)

5. La _____ de los tratamientos está basada en el deseo y el entendimiento del paciente. (Autonomy)

Exercise 3: Scenario-Based Dialogues

Write a dialogue for the following scenario where a healthcare provider discusses medication adherence with a patient who has diabetes.

Scenario: A patient is having difficulties adhering to their medication regimen and expresses concerns about side effects.

Exercise 4: Role-Playing Practice

In pairs, role-play the following situation: A nurse explains the importance of regular follow-up appointments to a patient with hypertension.

- Key Terms to Use:
  - Monitoreo (Monitoring)
  - Efectos secundarios (Side effects)
  - Adherencia al tratamiento (Treatment adherence)

Exercise 5: Translation Exercise

Translate the following English sentences into Spanish.

1. "Ensure you take your medication with food to avoid an upset stomach."
2. "It is important to discuss all your symptoms openly with your doctor."
3. "We have various community programs available for financial assistance."
4. "Please bring your medication list to your next appointment."
5. "Patient education is a key component of effective treatment."

Exercise 6: Healthcare Scenario Responses

Respond to the following scenarios in Spanish using appropriate medical vocabulary.

1. A patient refuses a recommended blood transfusion due to cultural beliefs. Explain their rights and the importance of their decision.
2. A family member of a patient in the ICU expresses distress about their loved one's condition. Offer empathetic support and inform them about the care provided.

Exercise 7: Matching Vocabulary

Match the medical term on the left with its definition on the right.

1. Trastorno de ansiedad
2. Cuidados paliativos
3. Consentimiento informado
4. Dignidad humana
5. Conflicto ético

a) A state of apprehension or fear related to upcoming situations.
b) Care focused on providing relief from pain and other symptoms of serious illness.
c) A patient's right to understand risks before agreeing to treatment.
d) The inherent value of every individual that should be respected.
e) A situation in which two ethical principles clash during decision-making.

Exercise 8: Fill in the Blanks with Medical Terms

Complete the sentences with the right medical vocabulary from your studies:

1. Cuando un paciente decide no recibir tratamiento, estamos obligados a respetar su _____. (autonomía)
2. La _____ es el proceso que permite a los pacientes tomar decisiones informadas sobre su atención médica. (consentimiento informado)
3. La _____ es un principio clave en la ética médica que promueve el bienestar del paciente. (beneficencia)
4. En situaciones de _____, los proveedores de salud deben tomar decisiones difíciles. (conflicto ético)
5. Es fundamental mantener la _____ de los pacientes durante todo el proceso de atención médica. (dignidad)

Exercise 9: Understanding Cultural Sensitivity

Discuss the following question in groups:

- Question: How might cultural beliefs around health and illness influence a patient's decision-making? Provide an example.

Exercise 10: Constructing Conversations

Write a brief interaction between a healthcare provider and a patient regarding the following topics:

1. Discussing anxiety symptoms and treatment options.
2. Explaining the importance of follow-up appointments after a new diagnosis.

Exercise 11: Personal Reflection and Strategy Development

Write down three strategies you feel are important to improve your communication with Spanish-speaking patients in your practice. Consider both verbal and non-verbal communication.

Exercise 12: Real-Life Application – Case Study Analysis

Analyze the following case study and provide recommendations based on the principles discussed in this book:

Case Study:

A 70-year-old Hispanic man with chronic heart disease refuses to take prescribed medication due to his belief in traditional remedies. He expresses feeling that his symptoms are manageable and does not want to rely on pharmaceuticals. His family is concerned about his health but also respects his wishes.

Instructions:

- Analyze the case using principles of integrated practice and cultural sensitivity.
- Provide recommendations on how to approach this situation, considering the individual's beliefs, the importance of medication adherence, and the role of family support.

Answer Key

Exercise 1: Vocabulary Match

1. - e
2. - d
3. - c
4. - a
5. - b

Exercise 2: Medical Terminology Fill-in-the-Blanks

1. Alfabetización en salud
2. Consentimiento informado
3. Recursos comunitarios
4. Beneficencia
5. Autonomía

Exercise 3: Scenario-Based Dialogues

(Sample Dialogue):

Doctor: "Hola, Juan. ¿Has estado siguiendo tu plan de medicación para la diabetes?"

Juan: "Doctor, a veces me olvido de tomar la medicina y me preocupa si causaré efectos secundarios."

Doctor: "Es comprensible. ¿Qué tipo de efectos secundarios te preocupan?"

Juan: "He escuchado que algunos medicamentos pueden causar mareos y náuseas."

Doctor: "Hablemos sobre tus preocupaciones y veamos cómo podemos ayudarte a recordar tus medicamentos."

Exercise 4: Role-Playing Practice

(Sample Scenario):

Nurse: "Es muy importante que vengas a tus citas de seguimiento. Esto nos permite monitorear tu presión arterial y ajustar el tratamiento si es necesario."

Patient: "¿Y si me siento bien, por qué debería venir?"

Nurse: "Incluso si te sientes bien, algunas condiciones como la hipertensión pueden no mostrar síntomas. También discutiremos cualquier efecto secundario que puedas tener con tus medicamentos."

Exercise 5: Translation Exercise

1. "Asegúrate de tomar tu medicamento con comida para evitar molestias estomacales."
2. "Es importante discutir todos tus síntomas abiertamente con tu médico."
3. "Tenemos varios programas comunitarios disponibles para asistencia financiera."

4. "Por favor, trae tu lista de medicamentos a tu próxima cita."

5. "La educación del paciente es un componente clave de un tratamiento efectivo."

Exercise 6: Healthcare Scenario Responses

1. Doctor: "Entiendo que sus creencias son importantes. Usted tiene el derecho de rechazar cualquier tratamiento, y eso incluye la transfusión de sangre. Respetamos su decisión y estamos aquí para asegurarnos de que reciba otros cuidados que considere apropiados."

2. Doctor: "Entiendo lo difícil que debe ser esta situación para usted. Queremos que sepa que estamos haciendo todo lo posible para cuidar a su ser querido. En la UCI, tenemos un equipo especializado que está monitoreando constantemente su condición y ofreciendo el mejor tratamiento disponible. Si tiene alguna pregunta, por favor no dude en preguntar."

Exercise 7: Matching Vocabulary

1. - a
2. - b
3. - c
4. - d
5. - e

Exercise 8: Fill in the Blanks with Medical Terms

1. Autonomía

2. Consentimiento informado

3. Beneficencia

4. Conflicto ético

5. Dignidad

Exercise 9: Understanding Cultural Sensitivity

Sample Group Discussion Points:

- Cultural beliefs may cause patients to prefer traditional healing methods over modern medicine. For instance, a Hispanic patient may trust "curanderismo" (folk healing) that their family used instead of conventional treatments.

- Addressing these beliefs requires healthcare providers to communicate respectfully and acknowledge the validity of these traditions while offering evidence-based alternatives.

Exercise 10: Constructing Conversations

Sample Dialogue Exercise:

1. Doctor: "Hola, María. ¿Cómo has estado manejando tu ansiedad últimamente?"
   Translation: "Hello, María. How have you been managing your anxiety lately?"

2. Patient: "No estoy segura, me siento abrumada a menudo. ¿Qué puedo hacer?"
   Translation: "I'm not sure; I often feel overwhelmed. What can I do?"

3. Doctor: "Podemos considerar terapia cognitivo-conductual y revisar la posibilidad de medicamentos que ayuden a controlar tus síntomas."
   Translation: "We can consider cognitive-behavioral therapy and review the possibility of medications to help control your symptoms."

4. Doctor: "Es crucial que vengas a tus citas de seguimiento. Esto nos permitirá asegurarnos de que la ansiedad se esté manejando adecuadamente y ajustar el tratamiento si es necesario."
   Translation: "It's crucial to come to your follow-up appointments. This will allow us to ensure that the anxiety is being managed appropriately and adjust the treatment if necessary."

Exercise 11: Personal Reflection and Strategy Development

Sample Responses:

1. Use Clear, Simple Language: Avoid complicated medical jargon and opt for layman's terms to ensure understanding.

2. Encourage Family Participation: Involve family members in consultations to ensure that they understand the treatment plan and can support the patient afterward.

3. Utilize Visual Aids: Incorporate diagrams, charts, or models when explaining complex concepts to enhance comprehension.

Exercise 12: Real-Life Application – Case Study Analysis

Sample Recommendations for the Case Study:

1. Engagement and Respect:
   - Begin by acknowledging the patient's beliefs about traditional remedies. This shows respect for his cultural practices and creates an open dialogue.
   - Example statement: "Entiendo que prefieres usar remedios tradicionales y que te han funcionado en el pasado. Es importante que hablemos de cómo estos pueden combinarse con los medicamentos que te he recetado."

2. Education on Medication Importance:
   - Educate the patient on the benefits of the prescribed medication, including how it complements traditional remedies and helps manage his chronic condition effectively.
   - Discuss potential risks of non-adherence and explain the implications on his health in a gentle and non-confrontational manner.
   - Use clear, simple language: "Los medicamentos ayudan a disminuir el riesgo de complicaciones graves, como ataques al corazón."

3. Involving Family Members:
   - Encourage the patient to involve family members in the discussion, as family support can be influential in his decision-making process.
   - Suggest a family meeting to discuss healthcare goals, emphasizing that family members can help bridge understanding and support adherence.

4. Collaborative Decision Making:
   - Offer to work collaboratively with the patient and his family to create a treatment plan that honors his cultural beliefs while ensuring safety and health.
   - Example proposal: "Podemos encontrar un horario para tus medicamentos que se ajuste a tus preferencias de tratamiento. ¿Podría ser útil tener un recordatorio visual?"
5. Follow-Up:
   - Schedule a follow-up appointment to reassess his health after a trial period of combining both traditional remedies and medications.
   - Reinforce that the healthcare team is there to support him: "Quiero que sepas que estamos aquí para ayudarte en cada paso y que su bienestar es nuestra prioridad."

Chapter III: Simulated Scenarios

La salud es la riqueza real y no piezas de oro y plata

Mahatma Gandhi

Simulated scenarios in medical Spanish provide healthcare professionals with an opportunity to practice vocabulary and communication strategies in realistic settings. This chapter draws from the knowledge gained in previous books, incorporating varied contexts such as pediatrics, oncology, urgent care, and ethical discussions. Each section will feature scenarios that involve patient interaction, ensuring that learners can apply their skills in a practical manner. Additionally, the dialogues provided only in Spanish serve as an added challenge, encouraging readers to enhance their proficiency in medical Spanish.

Scenario 1: Routine Patient Check-Up

Setting: Primary Care Clinic

Participants: Doctor (Dr. Sánchez) and Patient (Mr. García)

Dialogue:

- Dr. Sánchez: "Buenos días, Sr. García. ¿Cómo se siente hoy?"
- Mr. García: "Hola, doctor. Me siento un poco fatigado y he tenido una tos leve desde hace una semana."
- Dr. Sánchez: "Entiendo. Necesito hacerle algunas preguntas para comprender mejor su situación. ¿Ha tenido fiebre?"
- Mr. García: "No, pero he notado que me cuesta respirar a veces."
- Dr. Sánchez: "Voy a escuchar su pecho. Respire profundamente, por favor."

Key Vocabulary:

- Fatiga (fatigue)
- Tos (cough)
- Respirar (to breathe)

This interaction incorporates health assessment questions and basic terminology relevant to patient history and physical examination.

Scenario 2: Pediatric Examination

Setting: Pediatric Office

Participants: Nurse (Nurse Maria), Doctor (Dr. Lopez), and Parent with Child (Mrs. Martinez and her son Carlos)

Dialogue:

- Nurse Maria: "Buenos días, Sra. Martinez. ¿Qué le preocupa hoy sobre Carlos?"
- Mrs. Martinez: "Hola, he notado que tiene fiebre y parece muy cansado. No ha comido bien estos días."
- Dr. Lopez: "Vamos a hacer un examen físico. Carlos, ven aquí y súbete a la cama de examen. ¿Cuántos días ha tenido fiebre?"
- Carlos: "No sé. A veces mucho y luego un poco menos."
- Dr. Lopez: "Lo revisaré ahora. Vamos a tomar su temperatura y hacerle un examen de garganta. Esto puede incomodar un poco, pero es rápido."

Key Vocabulary:

- Examen físico (physical examination)
- Temperatura (temperature)
- Comida (food)

This scenario emphasizes the process of evaluating a child's health while including both the parent and the child in the conversation.

Scenario 3: Discussing Medications and Allergies

Setting: Pharmacy Consultation

Participants: Pharmacist (Pharmacist Catalina) and Patient (Mr. Ramirez)

Dialogue:

- Pharmacist Catalina: "Hola, Sr. Ramirez. Estoy aquí con su receta. Antes de proceder, necesito preguntarle: ¿tiene alguna alergia a medicamentos?"
- Mr. Ramirez: "Soy alérgico a la sulfa. Me gustaría saber si este antibiótico es seguro para mí."
- Pharmacist Catalina: "Este antibiótico no contiene sulfa, así que debería ser seguro. Recuerde tomarlo cada 8 horas y terminar todo el tratamiento. Si experimenta algún efecto secundario, contáctenos de inmediato."
- Mr. Ramirez: "Gracias, haré eso. También, ¿puede decirme si puedo beber alcohol mientras lo tomo?"
- Pharmacist Catalina: "Es mejor evitar el alcohol durante el tratamiento. Puede interferir con el medicamento."

Key Vocabulary:

- Antibiótico (antibiotic)
- Efectos secundarios (side effects)
- Interferir (to interfere)

This dialogue emphasizes the pharmacist's role in patient education about medications and their interactions.

Scenario 4: Emergency Medical Response

Setting: Emergency Room

Participants: Doctor (Dr. Morales), Nurse (Nurse Elena), and EMT (First Responder Carlos)

Dialogue:

- Dr. Morales: "¿Cuál es el estado del paciente que traen?"
- First Responder Carlos: "Este es el Sr. Díaz. Ha tenido un accidente y presenta trauma en el pecho. Está consciente pero tiene dificultad para respirar."
- Nurse Elena: "Voy a preparar las herramientas necesarias para una intubación. Sr. Díaz, ¿puede darme su nombre y qué le ocurrió?"
- Sr. Díaz: "Soy el Sr. Díaz. Chocamos y sentí un dolor fuerte en el pecho."
- Dr. Morales: "Necesitamos una radiografía de inmediato. Vamos a estabilizarlo aquí. Mantenga la calma, estamos aquí para ayudarle."

Key Vocabulary:

- Trauma (trauma)
- Intubación (intubation)
- Calma (calm)

This emergency scenario highlights the need for quick decision-making and effective communication among healthcare professionals. It emphasizes gathering vital information and ensuring patient stability during urgent situations.

Scenario 5: Managing Chronic Illness

Setting: Endocrinology Clinic

Participants: Nurse (Nurse Sofia), Doctor (Dr. Kim), and Patient (Ms. Rodriguez)

Dialogue:

- Nurse Sofia: "Hola, Sra. Rodriguez. Hoy vamos a hablar sobre su diabetes y cómo manejarla. ¿Cómo se ha sentido desde su última visita?"
- Ms. Rodriguez: "He estado tratando de seguir la dieta, pero a veces me resulta difícil resistir los antojos."

- Dr. Kim: "Es normal tener antojos. Pero es crucial seguir un plan. Dediquémonos a revisar su registro de niveles de azúcar. ¿Cuántas veces ha medido su glucosa en la última semana?"
- Ms. Rodriguez: "La he medido tres veces, pero creo que he olvidado dos de ellas."
- Nurse Sofia: "Es importante que trate de medirla diariamente. Podemos trabajar juntos en un calendario que le recuerde hacerlo."

Key Vocabulary:

- Diabetes (diabetes)
- Niveles de azúcar (sugar levels)
- Antojos (cravings)

This dialogue focuses on patient education regarding diabetes management, encouraging adherence to treatment plans through supportive communication.

Scenario 6: Addressing Cultural Practices

Setting: Family Health Clinic

Participants: Nurse (Nurse Gabriela) and Patient (Mr. González)

Dialogue:

- Nurse Gabriela: "Hola, Sr. González. He notado que va a la consulta frecuentemente. ¿Hay algo específico que le gustaría discutir hoy?"
- Mr. González: "Sí, he estado tomando algunas hierbas que me recomendó mi abuela. Tienen un efecto calmante, pero no sé si son seguras."
- Nurse Gabriela: "Hablemos de esas hierbas. A veces pueden interactuar con los medicamentos. ¿Cuáles son las que está usando?"
- Mr. González: "Uso manzanilla y ginseng para relajarme. También me dicen que son buenos para el estómago."
- Nurse Gabriela: "Podemos revisar su efectividad y si hay algún posible conflicto con su tratamiento actual. Siempre es bueno contarme sobre cualquier remedio que esté usando."

Key Vocabulary:

- Hierbas (herbs)
- Efecto calmante (calming effect)
- Interactuar (to interact)

This scenario emphasizes the importance of cultural competence in healthcare, ensuring that patients feel respected and understood while integrating traditional practices into their treatment plans.

Scenario 7: Discussing Patient Rights and Consent

Setting: Hospital Room

Participants: Doctor (Dr. Alvarez), Nurse (Nurse Daniela), and Patient (Ms. Lopez)

Dialogue:

- Dr. Alvarez: "Buenas tardes, Sra. Lopez. Antes de realizar el procedimiento, quiero asegurarme de que comprenda todo. ¿Está lista para hablar sobre el consentimiento informado?"
- Ms. Lopez: "Sí, he leído el formulario. Pero tengo algunas preguntas sobre lo que sucederá durante la cirugía."
- Nurse Daniela: "Correcto, estamos aquí para aclarar cualquier duda. Le realizaremos una cirugía laparoscópica, lo que significa que habrá pequeñas incisiones. ¿Le gustaría que le explique los riesgos asociados?"
- Ms. Lopez: "Sí, por favor. Quiero entender bien para estar más tranquila."
- Dr. Alvarez: "Los riesgos incluyen infección y reacciones a la anestesia, pero son raros. Nuestro equipo está altamente capacitado para manejar cualquier eventualidad."

Key Vocabulary:

- Procedimiento (procedure)
- Consentimiento informado (informed consent)
- Anestesia (anesthesia)

This scenario underscores the significance of informed consent and patient rights, reinforcing the need for transparency and communication in medical practices.

Scenario 8: Follow-Up Appointment for Mental Health

Setting: Mental Health Clinic

Participants: Therapist (Therapist Rosa) and Patient (Mr. Hernández)

Dialogue:

- Therapist Rosa: "Hola, Mr. Hernández. ¿Cómo ha estado desde nuestra última sesión?"
- Mr. Hernández: "Ha sido difícil. Sigo lidiando con la ansiedad y me cuesta mucho dormir."
- Therapist Rosa: "Lo siento mucho. Hablemos sobre lo que ha estado funcionando y lo que no. ¿Ha dado algún paso hacia el manejo de su ansiedad?"
- Mr. Hernández: "He intentado meditar como sugeriste, pero algunas noches es casi imposible."
- Therapist Rosa: "Es un buen comienzo. La meditación puede ser un desafío, especialmente en momentos de agitación emocional. ¿Has considerado implementar técnicas de respiración profunda o mindfulness para complementar tu práctica?"
- Mr. Hernández: "He intentado la respiración profunda, pero a menudo me encuentro perdido en mis pensamientos."

- Therapist Rosa: "Es completamente comprensible. La mente tiende a divagar, especialmente bajo estrés crónico. Enfocarse en la ancla de la respiración puede requerir práctica. Vamos a explorar una serie de ejercicios de regulación emocional que podrían ser beneficiosos."

Key Vocabulary:

- Agitación emocional (emotional agitation)
- Técnicas de respiración profunda (deep breathing techniques)
- Mindfulness (mindfulness)
- Regularización emocional (emotional regulation)

This dialogue encapsulates the complexities of mental health discussions, highlighting the nuances of therapeutic techniques and emotional resilience strategies.

Scenario 9: Multidisciplinary Team Meeting

Setting: Hospital Conference Room

Participants: Doctor (Dr. Villanueva), Pharmacist (Pharmacist Elena), Social Worker (Social Worker Carlos), and Nurse (Nurse Ana)

Dialogue:

- Dr. Villanueva: "Gracias a todos por estar aquí. Hoy vamos a discutir el caso de la Sra. Morales, quien presenta múltiples comorbilidades. ¿Cuál es su evaluación, Ana?"
- Nurse Ana: "La Sra. Morales ha estado lidiando con diabetes tipo 2 e hipertensión. Su adherencia al tratamiento ha sido inconsistente, lo que está exacerbando su condición."
- Pharmacist Elena: "Como consecuencia, debemos evaluar su régimen farmacológico. Lo ideal sería ajustar la dosificación de metformina y considerar alternativas para su hipertensión que no interfieran con su diabetes."
- Social Worker Carlos: "También es imperativo considerar factores sociales. La Sra. Morales enfrenta barreras económicas significativas que dificultan su acceso a medicamentos y atención continua. Necesitamos diseñar un plan para conectarla con recursos comunitarios."
- Dr. Villanueva: "Exactamente. Un enfoque holístico es crucial. Debemos abordar tanto el aspecto médico como los determinantes sociales de su salud para asegurar su bienestar integral."

Key Vocabulary:

- Comorbilidades (comorbidities)
- Adherencia al tratamiento (treatment adherence)
- Régimen farmacológico (pharmacological régimen)
- Determinantes sociales de la salud (social determinants of health)
- Bienestar integral (holistic well-being)

This dialogue emphasizes a collaborative multidisciplinary approach to patient care, highlighting the need for comprehensive strategies that encompass clinical, social, and economic considerations.

Scenario 10: End-of-Life Care Discussion (Continued)

Setting: Palliative Care Unit

Participants: Doctor (Dr. Franco), Nurse (Nurse Isabel), and Patient's Family Member (Ms. Torres)

Dialogue:

- Dr. Franco: "La atención paliativa tiene como objetivo mejorar la calidad de vida durante esta etapa crítica. Estaremos administrando analgésicos opioides para garantizar un control óptimo del dolor y mitigar cualquier sufrimiento."

- Nurse Isabel: "Además, es importante considerar la atención integral, lo que incluye apoyo emocional y psicológico para la familia. Proporcionaremos recursos de asesoramiento y grupos de apoyo durante este proceso difícil."

- Ms. Torres: "Eso sería muy útil. Me preocupa la angustia emocional de todos nosotros, no solo la de mi madre."

- Dr. Franco: "Entiendo completamente. La angustia anticipatoria es una respuesta común en situaciones como esta. Asegurémonos de que todos reciban el apoyo necesario, para que puedan gestionar este proceso de duelo de una manera saludable."

- Nurse Isabel: "Podemos coordinar con un psicólogo especializado en cuidados paliativos para programar sesiones de terapia familiar. La comunicación abierta es fundamental en esta fase. Además, me aseguraré de que su madre reciba un tratamiento sintomático para los posibles efectos secundarios que pueda experimentar, como la disnea."

- Ms. Torres: "Agradezco su enfoque. Solo quiero que mi madre esté tranquila y rodeada de amor."

Key Vocabulary:

- Analgésicos opioides (opioid analgesics)
- Control óptimo del dolor (optimal pain control)
- Atención integral (integrated care)
- Angustia anticipada (anticipatory grief)
- Tratamiento sintomático (symptomatic treatment)
- Disnea (dyspnea)

This scenario exemplifies the complexity of conversations surrounding end-of-life care, emphasizing the significance of addressing not only physical care but also the emotional and psychological needs of both patients and families.

Scenario 11: Multicultural Health Awareness

Setting: Community Health Fair

Participants: Community Health Educator (Educator Clara) and Attendees (Multiple Participants)

Dialogue:

- Educator Clara: "Buenos días a todos. Hoy estaremos abordando temas de salud multicultural y cómo las diferencias culturales pueden influir en la atención médica. Vamos a iniciar con la importancia de los determinantes culturales en la salud."

- Attendee 1: "¿Qué son exactamente los determinantes culturales?"

- Educator Clara: "Los determinantes culturales son factores como creencias, prácticas, y valores que afectan cómo los individuos perciben la salud, el tratamiento médico, y el acceso a los servicios. Por ejemplo, algunas culturas pueden priorizar remedios tradicionales sobre tratamientos farmacológicos."

- Attendee 2: "¿Cómo podemos asegurarnos de que los profesionales de la salud sean sensibles a estas variaciones culturales?"

- Educator Clara: "Es fundamental que los proveedores de salud reciban formación en competencia cultural y aprendan a utilizar un enfoque centrado en el paciente, respetando las preferencias culturales y trabajando en colaboración con los líderes comunitarios."

Key Vocabulary:

- Determinantes culturales (cultural determinants)
- Prácticas de salud (health practices)
- Trato centrado en el paciente (patient-centered care)
- Competencia cultural (cultural competence)

In this dialogue, the conversation emphasizes the significance of understanding cultural contexts in health disparities and the communication skills necessary to provide effective care.

Scenario 12: Interdisciplinary Case Review

Setting: Hospital Interdisciplinary Team Meeting Room

Participants: Chief Physician (Dr. Rodriguez), Clinical Psychologist (Dr. Patel), Nurse Practitioner (Nurse Marta), and Social Worker (Social Worker Elena)

Dialogue:

- Dr. Rodriguez: "Gracias por reunirse hoy. Esta sesión es crucial para abordar el caso de la Sra. Vargas, quien presenta síntomas severos de depresión concomitante con su enfermedad crónica. ¿Puede actualizarme sobre su estado, Dra. Patel?"

- Dr. Patel: "Por supuesto. La Sra. Vargas ha mostrado signos significativos de angustia emocional, que están íntimamente relacionados con su manejo del dolor crónico. He recomendado una iniciativa de terapia cognitivo-conductual para ayudarla a reestructurar su forma de pensar en relación a su enfermedad."

- Nurse Marta: "Además, noté que la Sra. Vargas tiene dificultades con la adherencia a su régimen farmacológico, lo que podría exacerbar sus síntomas. Procederé a revisar su historial de medicación y considerar la consulta con un farmacéutico clínico para optimizar su tratamiento."

- Social Worker Elena: "Es vital que también abordemos los determinantes sociales que pueden estar influyendo en su salud mental. La Sra. Vargas ha mencionado preocupaciones sobre su situación financiera, lo que podría ser un factor que contribuye a su estado de ánimo."

- Dr. Rodriguez: "Exactamente. Esta atención multidimensional es crítica. Necesitamos un plan de acción que incluya el apoyo psicológico y social, además del manejo médico. Coordinaré una reunión con el departamento de servicios sociales para abordar su situación financiera."

Key Vocabulary:

- Angustia emocional (emotional distress)
- Terapia cognitivo-conductual (cognitive-behavioral therapy)
- Adherencia al régimen farmacológico (adherence to pharmacological régimen)
- Determinantes sociales (social determinants)
- Atención multidimensional (multidimensional care)

This scenario illustrates the necessity of interdisciplinary collaboration in managing complex patient cases, encapsulating the importance of addressing both psychological health and medical treatment.

Conclusion

The simulated scenarios presented in this chapter exemplify the multifaceted nature of patient interactions within healthcare settings. They demonstrate the necessity for healthcare professionals to engage proficiently in medical Spanish while navigating complex cultural dynamics and employing advanced medical terminology.

As you practice these conversations and scenarios, remember that effective communication extends beyond mere vocabulary; it encompasses empathy, cultural understanding, and a commitment to delivering holistic and patient-centered care. By mastering these skills, you will not only improve your proficiency in medical Spanish but also enhance the quality of care provided to your Spanish-speaking patients.

Chapter IV: Feedback and Improvement

Sólo el médico y el dramaturgo gozan del raro privilegio de cobrar las desazones que nos dan

Santiago Ramón y Cajal

In this chapter, we will explore how to use feedback and self-assessment to enhance your medical Spanish and cultural competency. Mastering medical Spanish is more than just learning vocabulary and phrases; it's about ongoing self-improvement and developing cultural sensitivity. These tools, which include personal reflection journals, language proficiency checklists, and constructive peer feedback, provide a structured framework for evaluating your progress and identifying opportunities for growth.

Reflection journals offer a personal space for documenting your linguistic journey, capturing both successes and challenges in real-world interactions. They allow you to reflect on patient conversations, understand cultural nuances, and set actionable goals for improvement. Meanwhile, language proficiency checklists provide a clear, structured approach to self-evaluation, helping you pinpoint specific linguistic skills that require further development. These checklists enable you to assess your command over medical vocabulary, pronunciation, and cultural communication skills systematically.

Additionally, incorporating feedback from peers and mentors adds an invaluable external perspective, creating a dynamic learning environment that encourages constructive criticism and realistic practice. Role-playing with peers to simulate clinical scenarios provides insight into your strengths and areas in need of improvement, fostering a collaborative learning experience that enriches your skills and confidence.

Interactive Self-Assessment Tools

1. Personal Reflection Journals

Purpose: A reflection journal is a personal tool to document your journey in learning medical Spanish, capturing both progress and challenges.

- Activity: Start Your Reflection Journal
  - Prompt: Reflect on a recent patient interaction where you used Spanish. What were the highlights of the conversation? Identify any communication barriers.
  - Follow-Up: Continuously update your journal with new vocabulary, insightful experiences, or moments when you successfully navigated cultural nuances.
- Guidelines for Effective Journaling:
  - Write entries consistently, aiming for at least three times a week.

- Use thematic prompts such as "New Vocabulary Learned," "Cultural Insights," or "Communication Barriers Faced" to guide entries and identify trends over time.

2. Language Proficiency Checklists

Using Checklists: Self-assessment checklists are structured tools that help evaluate proficiency in various aspects of language and cultural understanding.

- Interactive Exercise: Develop Your Checklist
  - Task: Create a personalized checklist that includes areas such as medical vocabulary, pronunciation, grammar, and cultural communication skills.
  - Self-Evaluation: Rate each skill on a scale from 1 (beginner) to 5 (advanced). Use this evaluation to pinpoint specific areas for improvement.
- Example Checklist Items:
  - Ability to accurately pronounce common medical terminology in Spanish.
  - Comfort level in explaining symptoms and treatment plans to Spanish-speaking patients.
  - Understanding and application of cultural sensitivities in patient interactions.

3. Peer and Mentor Feedback

Engagement: Feedback from peers and mentors can provide fresh perspectives and insights for improvement.

- Role-Playing Sessions:
  - Group Activity: Pair with a peer or mentor to conduct simulated patient interactions. Focus on scenarios such as pharmacy consultations or explaining test results.
  - Feedback Discussion: Post-role-play, hold a feedback session focusing on strengths and areas to improve. Discuss pronunciation, use of medical terminology, and cultural nuances.
- Leveraging Feedback for Growth:
  - Incorporate feedback by practicing specific scenarios or language constructs that were challenging.
  - Regularly seek opportunities to role-play different scenarios to build confidence and competence.

Setting Goals for Improvement

1. SMART Goals

Framework: SMART goals (Specific, Measurable, Achievable, Relevant, Time-Bound) are essential in systematically advancing your medical Spanish skills.

- Interactive Planning:
  - Workshop Activity: Collaborate with peers to draft SMART goals. Share these with the group, providing and receiving constructive feedback.
  - Examples:
    - "I will learn and use 50 new medical Spanish terms in patient interactions over the next month."
    - "I will practice conducting full patient interviews in Spanish twice a week over the next three months."
- Implementing SMART Goals:
  - Align your goals with your daily work to ensure relevance and immediate applicability.
  - Break goals into smaller tasks with defined timelines to maintain motivation and track progress.

2. Utilizing Technology and Resources

Leveraging Technology: Technology offers various tools and platforms that can enhance language learning through engaging and structured modules.

- Interactive Task: Explore Language Apps and Resources
  - Activity: Use language learning apps like Duolingo or Rosetta Stone, focusing on medical Spanish sections. Engage in interactive exercises designed to enhance vocabulary and pronunciation.
  - Challenge: Participate in a language exchange program or join online forums where you can practice medical scenarios with Spanish speakers.
- Maximizing Online Resources:
  - Utilize healthcare-focused Spanish podcasts or YouTube channels to improve listening comprehension.
  - Join virtual Spanish-speaking communities to immerse yourself in conversational contexts that mirror real-life scenarios.

Strategies for Continuous Improvement

1. Immersion and Practice

Concept: Immersion is a powerful method to enhance language skills by experiencing and interacting with Spanish in multiple contexts.

- Cultural Immersion Day:
  - Activity: Dedicate a day to engage exclusively with Spanish media. Watch a Spanish-language medical drama or read articles on healthcare practices in Hispanic communities.

- Reflection: Note new vocabulary and phrases, summarize plots or articles and discuss these insights with a study group.
- Real-World Application:
  - Volunteer at clinics or community centers that serve Spanish-speaking populations.
  - Engage in Spanish conversation groups or attend cultural events to practice speaking and listening in real-life contexts.

2. Enhancing Cultural Competence

Community Engagement: Understanding cultural nuances enhances communication and builds trust with Spanish-speaking patients.

- Interactive Task: Participate in Cultural Events
  - Attend local or virtual events featuring Hispanic culture or healthcare discussions to gain firsthand experience.
  - Discussion: Post-event, share observations with peers about cultural practices and implications for healthcare delivery.
- Interactive Cultural Learning:
  - Attend workshops focusing on traditional healing practices and their significance in Hispanic cultures.
  - Explore case studies on how cultural beliefs influence medical decisions and patient interactions.

3. Educational Workshops and Seminars

Continuous Learning: Regularly attending workshops and seminars can significantly boost both language skills and cultural understanding.

- Workshop Activity:
  - Task: Participate in seminars on topics such as advanced medical Spanish or cultural competence. Take active notes on new learnings and insights.
  - Role-Play: Following the seminar, enact scenarios where these new skills or cultural insights can be applied, such as discussing treatment options with patients who hold traditional beliefs.

Key Takeaways

By engaging with this chapter's interactive elements, you can transform feedback into actionable insights, set effective objectives, and foster continuous improvement in your medical Spanish proficiency and cultural competence. Remember, the journey of mastering medical Spanish is ongoing and requires dedication. Through self-assessment, active participation in learning activities, and embracing feedback, you can effectively enhance communication, build stronger patient relationships, and improve healthcare outcomes for Spanish-speaking populations.

Book conclusion

Congratulations on completing this monumental series designed to empower healthcare professionals through the mastery of Medical Spanish. Each book, rich with its unique focus and insights, has collectively woven a tapestry that frames the vital importance of linguistic and cultural competence in healthcare.

In **Book 1**: Introduction to Medical Spanish and Basics, you took your first steps into the vibrant world of Spanish. This book was not merely about letters and sounds; it was an invitation to deepen connections with patients by breaking through language barriers. You learned that every "Hola" and "¿Cómo estás?" is an opportunity to show understanding and compassion. Remember your practice exercises? They were the foundation of a skyscraper you are building—a structure of trust and connection.

Moving into **Book 2**: Spanish Medical Communication, you delved into the heart of how the human body communicates its needs and symptoms. Each chapter was like a new color in your palette, enabling you to paint a clearer picture of health and wellness for your patients. You grasped vital vocabulary around anatomy, procedures, and medical emergencies, empowering yourself to navigate sensitive and urgent conversations. Picture the moment you fluidly explain a procedure to a patient in Spanish, easing their anxiety—your words becoming a balm for their fears. That skill not only builds rapport but also promotes patient compliance and satisfaction.

Book 3: Cultural Competence in Healthcare opened your eyes to the rich tapestry of experiences that shape the lives of Spanish-speaking patients. You learned to honor diverse beliefs, practices, and traditions. The lessons on traditional healing and cultural considerations illuminated pathways for deeper relationships. Imagine walking into a patient's home, fully aware of their cultural background, discussing healthcare through their lens. By being culturally competent, you're not just a provider but a partner in their health journey, respecting their beliefs while offering your expertise—a true meeting of minds and hearts.

As you advanced to **Book 4**: Advanced Medical Spanish, the knowledge you gained became even more specialized and nuanced. Whether in pediatrics, oncology, or obstetrics, the language of medicine became your ally in communicating with clarity. Just envision yourself in a pediatric exam room, where a worried parent looks to you for reassurance. Your ability to explain a diagnosis in their preferred language is a powerful moment—a bridge over which trust flows freely. Each term you mastered in this book heightened your confidence, allowing you to speak not just with words but with empathy and understanding.

Book 5: Clinical Conversations challenges you to confront some of the most difficult aspects of healthcare: delivering bad news, managing complex comorbidities, and navigating emotionally charged discussions about end-of-life care. You practiced crucial dialogues that prepared you for these high-stakes moments. When you think about the courage it takes to have these conversations, remember the impact you can have. Your capacity to communicate sensitive information with grace and compassion can significantly ease the burden on patients and their families during some of life's most challenging moments.

In **Book 6**: Patient Care in Spanish, you honed your skills in high-pressure scenarios, concentrating on critical care and mental health interventions. You learned to bridge gaps between patients' needs and the healthcare system, advocating fiercely while providing care that respects their dignity. Picture a patient in a mental health crisis, needing a compassionate ear. Due to your training, you can approach them in their native language, showing that you not only hear their words but feel their pain. This ability to connect in such vulnerable moments can lead to remarkable healing and recovery.

Finally, **Book 7**: Comprehensive Medical Spanish Review served as the capstone of your endeavor, urging you to reflect and integrate all that you've learned. Each simulated scenario forced you to confront real-world challenges with confidence. Whether discussing medications with a patient or navigating a multidisciplinary team meeting, the exercises were crafted to bolster your ability to think critically and respond effectively. This book illustrated that communication is not static; it's a continuously evolving skill vital to patient care.

As you move forward from this journey, carry with you the knowledge that the ability to speak Medical Spanish is not just about vocabulary—it's a profound commitment to serve, empower, and uplift your patients. Each encounter is an opportunity to foster understanding and trust, ensuring every patient feels seen, heard, and cared for.

Your path has been filled with moments of growth, challenge, and inspiration. Let your mastery of Medical Spanish be a beacon of hope in your healthcare practice, a testament to your dedication to inclusivity and empathy.

Remember, as you step into each new day, you are not just a healthcare provider; you are a vital part of your patients' lives, capable of transforming their experience through the warmth of your words and the power of your compassion.

Embrace every opportunity to deepen your connections with Spanish-speaking patients. Think back to all those practice exercises where you learned to navigate various scenarios—from a routine check-up to providing critical care in emergencies. Each scenario is a stepping stone to crafting a more inclusive healthcare environment, one where language barriers dissolve in the face of genuine care.

Visualize the myriad of patients you will meet: the anxious mother holding her child's hand, the elderly gentleman recalling his medication history, or the young adult expressing concerns about their mental health. With the knowledge and skills you've gained from these seven volumes, you are now equipped to address their needs more effectively. Your ability to communicate in Spanish empowers you to advocate for them, ensuring they receive the care they deserve without the restraint of language difficulties.

As you embark on your next steps, continually reflect on the lessons learned. How can you apply them to your daily practice? Consider mentoring others who wish to follow in your footsteps, advocating for language training in your workplace, and fostering an environment where cultural competence is prioritized. By sharing your journey and encouraging others, you help create a ripple effect, inspiring a future generation of healthcare professionals to prioritize not just skill but compassion.

Moreover, remember that this journey doesn't end here. The ongoing nature of language acquisition means that your learning should continue. Engage with your Spanish-speaking communities, participate in workshops, or immerse yourself in Spanish-language media relevant to healthcare. Each interaction is a chance to enhance your fluency, deepen your understanding, and remain attuned to the evolving dynamics of patient care.

In closing, the journey you have embarked upon through mastering Medical Spanish goes beyond professional development; it is a meaningful commitment to the humanity behind healthcare. As you look ahead, let your passion for patient-centered care drive you forward. Strive to create an environment where communication flows freely, empowering your patients to express their concerns and needs without hesitation.

This series has provided you with a powerful toolkit. Now, wield it with confidence and heart. Continue to learn, grow, and adapt, and watch as the lives you touch blossom with the healing impact of effective communication. Together, let us strive for a healthcare landscape where every interaction is not just about words spoken but about lives uplifted, dignity restored, and care delivered with love.

Thank you for embracing this journey. We wish you the best of luck in your language-learning journey and in providing high-quality care to a diverse patient population.

Bibliography

1. Lopez, M. H., & Gonzalez-Barrera, A. (2020, July 27). What is the future of Spanish in the United States? Pew Research Center. https://www.pewresearch.org/fact-tank/2013/09/05/what-is-the-future-of-spanish-in-the-united-states/

2. Diez, M. S. (2022, July 21). By 2050, the U.S. could have more Spanish speakers than any other country. Quartz. https://qz.com/441174/by-2050-united-states-will-have-more-spanish-speakers-than-any-other-country

3. U.S. Census Bureau. (2021, 8 octubre). Hispanic Population to Reach 111 Million by 2060. Census.gov. https://www.census.gov/library/visualizations/2018/comm/hispanic-projected-pop.html

4. Proctor, K., Wilson-Frederick, S. M., & Haffer, S. C. (2017). The Limited English Proficient Population: Describing Medicare, Medicaid, and Dual Beneficiaries. Health Equity, 2(1), 82-89. https://doi.org/10.1089/heq.2017.0036

5. Paredes, A. Z., Idrees, J. J., Beal, E. W., Chen, Q., Cerier, E., Okunrintemi, V., Olsen, G., Sun, S., Cloyd, J. M., & Pawlik, T. M. (2018). Influence of English proficiency on patient-provider communication and shared decision-making. Surgery, 163(6), 1220–1225. https://doi.org/10.1016/j.surg.2018.01.012

6. Kim, G., Worley, C. B., Allen, R. S., Vinson, L., Crowther, M. R., Parmelee, P., & Chiriboga, D. A. (2011). Vulnerability of older Latino and Asian immigrants with limited English proficiency. Journal of the American Geriatrics Society, 59(7), 1246–1252. https://doi.org/10.1111/j.1532-5415.2011.03483.x

7. Shamsi, H. A., Almutairi, A. G., Mashrafi, S. A., & Kalbani, T. A. (2020). Implications of Language Barriers for Healthcare: A Systematic Review. Oman Medical Journal, 35(2), e122. https://doi.org/10.5001/omj.2020.40

8. Breaking Down Language Barriers: The Essential Role of Bilingual Nurses. (2021, 17 diciembre). https://www.stkate.edu/academics/healthcare-degrees/breaking-down-language-barriers-essential-role-bilingual-nurses

9. McCarthy, M., Barry, K., Estrada, C., Veliz, B., Rosales, D., Leonard, M., & De Groot, A. S. (2021). Recruitment, Training, and Roles of the Bilingual, Bicultural Navegantes: Developing a Specialized Workforce of Community Health Workers to Serve a Low-Income, Spanish-Speaking Population in Rhode Island. Frontiers in public health, 9, 666566. https://doi.org/10.3389/fpubh.2021.666566

10. Exclusión de «ch» y «ll» del abecedario. (s. f.). Real Acdemia Española. Retrieved April 11th of 2023, from https://www.rae.es/espanol-al-dia/exclusion-de-ch-y-ll-del-abecedario

11. Real Academia Española. (2005). Representación de sonidos. Diccionario panhispánico de dudas. Retrieved April 11th of 2023, from https://www.rae.es/dpd/ayuda/representacion-de-sonidos

12. REAL ACADEMIA ESPAÑOLA: Diccionario de la lengua española, 23.ª ed., [versión 23.6 en línea]. <https://dle.rae.es> Retrieved April 11th of 2023

13. Karliner, L. S., Napoles-Springer, A. M., Schillinger, D., Bibbins-Domingo, K., & Pérez-Stable, E. J. (2008). Identification of limited English proficient patients in clinical care. Journal of general internal medicine, 23(10), 1555–1560. https://doi.org/10.1007/s11606-008-0693-y

14. Seely, M. D. (2017). An Introduction to Spanish for Health Care Workers: Communication and Culture. Springer Publishing Company.

15. Canfield, J. M., & Weldy, D. L. (2013). Medical Spanish for healthcare professionals: A new approach. Springer Publishing Company.

16. Gwynn, M. (2012). Spanish-English English-Spanish Medical Dictionary. Lippincott Williams & Wilkins.

17. Jacobs, E. A., Lauderdale, D. S., Meltzer, D., Shorey, J. M., Levinson, W., & Thisted, R. A. (2001). Impact of interpreter services on delivery of health care to limited-English-proficient patients. Journal of general internal medicine, 16(7), 468–474. https://doi.org/10.1046/j.1525-1497.2001.016007468.x

18. Canfield, J. M., & Weldy, D. L. (2013). Medical Spanish for healthcare professionals: A new approach. Springer Publishing Company.

19. Harvey, W. C. (2012). Spanish for healthcare professionals. Barron's Educational Series.

20. Aguirre, A. (2010). Spanish for Healthcare Professionals. University of California Press.

21. Barbosa, P. (2015). Spanish for Medical Professionals: Essential Spanish Terms and Phrases for Healthcare Providers. Createspace Independent Publishing Platform.

22. Gómez, J. (2016). Spanish for Health Care Professionals. Routledge.

23. Quiroga, J. (2018). Medical Spanish: A Conversational Approach. Springer Publishing Company.

24. Pérez-López, M. (2022). Essential Spanish vocabulary and phrases for prescription and medication. In J. Doe (Ed.), Medical Spanish (pp. 45-67). Publisher.

25. Yanez, J. (2021). Effective communication with Spanish-speaking patients: essential vocabulary and phrases related to prescription and medication. In R. Smith (Ed.), Multicultural Healthcare: A Handbook for Health Professionals (pp. 123-145). Publisher.

26. Garcia, L. (2020). Spanish for healthcare professionals: essential vocabulary and phrases for prescription and medication. In S. Lee (Ed.), Cultural Competence in Healthcare: A Guide for Health Professionals (pp. 67-89). Publisher.

27. García-Peña, C., & Perdomo, J. (2019). Chapter VII. Medical Emergencies. In P. Rush, S. Hamilton, & K. Foubister (Eds.), Medical Spanish Made Incredibly Easy! (3rd ed., pp. 111-124). Wolters Kluwer.

28. Kaufman, R. (2015). The Spanish Language in the Health Care Industry. Journal of Health Care for the Poor and Underserved, 26(2), 372-380. doi:10.1353/hpu.2015.0066

29. López, L., Grant, R. W., Marceau, L. D., & Espinosa de los Monteros, K. (2016). Understanding the Relationship Between Health Literacy and Health Communication among Spanish-Speaking

Patients with Type 2 Diabetes: A Qualitative Exploratory Study. Journal of Health Communication, 21(sup2), 135-142. doi:10.1080/10810730.2016.1202564

30. Alcalá, R. J., King, T. S., & Henderson, W. G. (2016). Cultural competence in healthcare: a review of the evidence. Journal of Nursing Education and Practice, 6(9), 104-111. https://doi.org/10.5430/jnep.v6n9p104

31. Kuipers, M. A., Volk, M. L., & Patel, N. (2019). Improving care for Hispanic patients. Journal of General Internal Medicine, 34(2), 312-318. https://doi.org/10.1007/s11606-018-4732-8

32. Mackey, L. M., & Elliott, K. S. (2016). Cultural competence in healthcare: What is it? How do we achieve it? Canadian Journal of Dental Hygiene, 50(4), 203-207. https://cjdhs.ca/index.php/cjdhs/article/view/325/264

33. Miglietta, M. A., & Bozzuto, L. (2018). Providing culturally competent care to Hispanic patients. American Nurse Today, 13(11), 22-27. https://www.americannursetoday.com/wp-content/uploads/2018/11/ant11-CE-Cultural-Competence-1118.pdf

34. Rios, E. (2013). Cultural concepts in Hispanic healthcare. In A. Perez & M. Lu (Eds.), Handbook of cultural factors in behavioral health (pp. 335-352). Springer.

35. Galanti, G. (2015). Caring for patients from different cultures. University of Pennsylvania Press.

36. Spector, R. E. (2013). Cultural diversity in health and illness. Pearson Education.

37. Huff, R. M., & Kline, M. V. (Eds.). (2012). Promoting health in multicultural populations: A handbook for practitioners. Sage.

38. Andrews, M. M., & Boyle, J. S. (2016). Transcultural concepts in nursing care. Wolters Kluwer Health/Lippincott Williams & Wilkins.

39. A Rimsza, M. E., Hotaling, A. J., Keown, M. E., Marcin, J. P., Moskowitz, W. B., Sigrest, T. D., & Simon, H. K. (2015). Definition of a Pediatrician. *PEDIATRICS*, *135*(4), 780–781. https://doi.org/10.1542/peds.2015-0056

40. *What is oncology? | What is an oncologist?* (n.d.). American Cancer Society. https://www.cancer.org/cancer/managing-cancer/finding-care/what-is-oncology.html#:~:text=Oncology%20is%20the%20study%20of,diagnosis%2C%20treatment%2C%20and%20survivorship

41. Collection Development Guidelines of the National Library of Medicine [Internet]. Bethesda (MD): National Library of Medicine (US); 2019-. Obstetrics. [Updated 2018 Nov 9]. Available from: https://www.ncbi.nlm.nih.gov/books/NBK518831/

42. Collection Development Guidelines of the National Library of Medicine [Internet]. Bethesda (MD): National Library of Medicine (US); 2019-. Gynecology. [Updated 2018 Nov 9]. Available from: https://www.ncbi.nlm.nih.gov/books/NBK518726/

43. Lopez Vera A. Enhancing Medical Spanish Education and Proficiency to Bridge Healthcare Disparities: A Comprehensive Assessment and Call to Action. Cureus. 2023 Nov 8;15(11):e48512. doi: 10.7759/cureus.48512

44. Al Shamsi H, Almutairi AG, Al Mashrafi S, Al Kalbani T. Implications of Language Barriers for Healthcare: A Systematic Review. Oman Med J. 2020 Apr 30;35(2):e122. doi: 10.5001/omj.2020.40. PMID: 32411417; PMCID: PMC7201401.

45. Bischoff, A., & Hudelson, P. (2009). Communicating with Foreign Language–Speaking patients: Is access to professional interpreters enough? *Journal of Travel Medicine, 17*(1), 15–20. https://doi.org/10.1111/j.1708-8305.2009.00314.x

46. Nair L, Adetayo OA. Cultural Competence and Ethnic Diversity in Healthcare. Plast Reconstr Surg Glob Open. 2019 May 16;7(5):e2219. doi: 10.1097/GOX.0000000000002219. PMID: 31333951; PMCID: PMC6571328.

47. Stubbe DE. Practicing Cultural Competence and Cultural Humility in the Care of Diverse Patients. Focus (Am Psychiatr Publ). 2020 Jan;18(1):49-51. doi: 10.1176/appi.focus.20190041. Epub 2020 Jan 24. PMID: 32047398; PMCID: PMC7011228.

48. Vega WA, Rodriguez MA, Gruskin E. Health disparities in the Latino population. Epidemiol Rev. 2009;31:99-112. doi: 10.1093/epirev/mxp008. Epub 2009 Aug 27. PMID: 19713270; PMCID: PMC5044865.

49. Escarce JJ, Kapur K. Access to and Quality of Health Care. In: National Research Council (US) Panel on Hispanics in the United States; Tienda M, Mitchell F, editors. Hispanics and the Future of America. Washington (DC): National Academies Press (US); 2006. 10. Available from: https://www.ncbi.nlm.nih.gov/books/NBK19910/

50. Escobedo, L. E., Cervantes, L., & Havranek, E. (2023). Barriers in Healthcare for Latinx Patients with Limited English Proficiency-a Narrative Review. *Journal of general internal medicine, 38*(5), 1264–1271. https://doi.org/10.1007/s11606-022-07995-3

51. *FastStats*. (n.d.). Health of Hispanic or Latino Population. https://www.cdc.gov/nchs/fastats/hispanic-health.htm

52. Nadeem, R., & Nadeem, R. (2024, July 19). *2. Hispanic Americans' experiences with health care*. Pew Research Center. https://www.pewresearch.org/science/2022/06/14/hispanic-americans-experiences-with-health-care/

53. *Hispanic/Latino health*. (n.d.). Office of Minority Health. https://minorityhealth.hhs.gov/hispaniclatino-health

54. Dávila, C. (1970). *Intensive care units in Latin America*. https://iris.paho.org/handle/10665.2/12388

55. Velasco, F., Yang, D. M., Zhang, M., Nelson, T., Sheffield, T., Keller, T., Wang, Y., Walker, C., Katterapalli, C., Zimmerman, K., Masica, A., Lehmann, C. U., Xie, Y., & Hollingsworth, J. W. (2021). Association of Healthcare Access With Intensive Care Unit Utilization and Mortality in Patients of Hispanic Ethnicity Hospitalized With COVID-19. *Journal of hospital medicine, 16*(11), 659–666. https://doi.org/10.12788/jhm.3717

56. Rojas, V. (2019). HUMANIZACIÓN DE LOS CUIDADOS INTENSIVOS. *Revista Médica Clínica Las Condes, 30*(2), 120–125. https://doi.org/10.1016/j.rmclc.2019.03.005

57. Office of the Surgeon General (US); Center for Mental Health Services (US); National Institute of Mental Health (US). Mental Health: Culture, Race, and Ethnicity: A Supplement to Mental Health: A Report of the Surgeon General. Rockville (MD): Substance Abuse and Mental Health Services Administration (US); 2001 Aug. Chapter 6 Mental Health Care for Hispanic Americans. Available from: https://www.ncbi.nlm.nih.gov/books/NBK44247/

58. Working with Latino Patients. (n.d.). https://www.psychiatry.org/psychiatrists/diversity/education/best-practice-highlights/working-with-latino-patients

59. Biscioni, D. N., Da Cunha, T. R., & Albuquerque, A. (2023). Bioética y Derechos Humanos en una mirada latinoamericana. *Revista De Bioética Y Derecho*, 227–241. https://doi.org/10.1344/rbd2022.55.37449

60. Ortega, A. N., Rodriguez, H. P., & Bustamante, A. V. (2015). Policy dilemmas in Latino health care and implementation of the Affordable Care Act. Annual Review of Public Health, 36(1), 525–544. https://doi.org/10.1146/annurev-publhealth-031914-122421

61. Lo, L., Ruiz, M., Taira, B., & Carranza, L. (2018). Informed Consent Experience among Spanish-Speaking Patients undergoing Gynecologic Surgery [7I]. *Obstetrics and Gynecology, 131*(1), 99S. https://doi.org/10.1097/01.aog.0000533435.94310.8b

62. Ahmed, L., Constantinidou, A., & Chatzittofis, A. (2023). Patients' perspectives related to ethical issues and risks in precision medicine: a systematic review. *Frontiers in Medicine, 10.* https://doi.org/10.3389/fmed.2023.1215663

Made in United States
Troutdale, OR
12/12/2024